Salvation Outside the Church?

Tracing the History of the Catholic Response

Francis A. Sullivan S.J.

D1606024

PAULIST PRESS
NEW YORK/MAHWAH, N.J.

also by Francis A. Sullivan, S.J.
published by Paulist Press

MAGISTERIUM
THE CHURCH WE BELIEVE IN

Quotations from *The Documents of Vatican II*, edited by Walter Abbott, S.J. (The America Press, 1966), are used with permission.

Library of Congress Cataloging-in-Publication Data

Sullivan, Francis Aloysius.
    Salvation outside the church? : tracing the history of the Catholic
response / Francis A. Sullivan.
        p.   cm.
    Includes bibliographical references and index.
    ISBN 0-8091-3304-0 (pbk.)
    1. Salvation outside the Catholic Church—History of doctrines.
I. Title.
BT755.S85   1992
234—dc20   92-7910
                                                        CIP

Published by Paulist Press
997 Macarthur Boulevard
Mahwah, New Jersey 07430

Printed and bound in the United States of America

Contents

Abbreviations

DOCUMENTS OF THE SECOND VATICAN COUNCIL (1962–65)

AG   *Ad gentes:* Decree on the Church's Missionary Activity

GS   *Gaudium et spes:* Pastoral Constitution on the Church in the Modern World

LG   *Lumen gentium:* Dogmatic Constitution on the Church

NA   *Nostra aetate:* Declaration on the Relationship of the Church to Non-Christian Religions

UR   *Unitatis redintegratio:* Decree on Ecumenism

OTHER SOURCES

AAS   *Acta Apostolicae Sedis*

ACW   *Ancient Christian Writers.* ed. J. Quasten et al., New York, 1946–

AER   *American Ecclesiastical Review*

AS   *Acta Synodalia Concilii Vaticani II*

CCL   *Corpus Christianorum, series latina*

CDF   Congregation for the Doctrine of the Faith

CSEL   *Corpus scriptorum ecclesiasticorum latinorum*

CTS   Catholic Truth Society

DS   Denzinger-Schönmetzer, *Enchiridion symbolorum, definitionum, declarationum*, 34th ed., 1967

FC   *The Fathers of the Church*, Washington, Catholic University of America Press

Mansi   *Sacrorum conciliorum nova collectio*

PG   *Patrologiae cursus completus, series graeca*

PL   *Patrologiae cursus completus, series latina*

RH   *Redemptor hominis*, Encyclical Letter of John Paul II on Christ, the Redeemer of Mankind, March 4, 1979

RM   *Redemptoris missio*, Encyclical Letter of John Paul II on the Permanent Validity of the Church's Missionary Mandate, December 7, 1990

Th Inv   Karl Rahner, *Theological Investigations.* 1961–

Foreword

My interest in the subject of this book was initially aroused during the late 1940s when I was studying theology in preparation for ordination to the priesthood at the Jesuit seminary in Weston, Massachusetts. The tranquillity of those years was dramatically shattered by the news that Fr. Leonard Feeney, S.J., who had taught courses in English literature to many of us at Weston, had publicly denounced the Catholic archbishop of Boston as a heretic for declaring that non-Catholics could be saved. Fr. Feeney's contention was that Archbishop Cushing's view was in direct contradiction to the dogma which states that there is no salvation outside the Catholic Church. He backed up his claim by quoting a number of statements made by medieval popes and councils, which seemed to provide incontrovertible proof that "No salvation outside the church" was indeed a dogma of Catholic faith.

When I was a student at Weston, I presumed that a satisfactory explanation could be given to show how the church was consistent in its faith, even though what it was saying now about the possibility of salvation for non-Catholics was so different from what it had said in the middle ages. But I realized that this would take more research than I was capable of at the time.

The present book is the fruit of a good many years of reflection on this question. I have been stimulated by the experience of teaching courses and seminars on this topic to my students at the Gregorian University. I have profited a great deal from the research done early in this century by Louis Capéran. The fact that his monumental work *Le Salut des Infidèles* has never been published in English was one of my reasons for writing this book. An even more important reason is that developments in Catholic thought in the course of the present century have made possible a substantially new understanding of the necessity of the church for salvation. At the same time it is my conviction that one cannot fully understand what the church is saying on this question today without an appreciation of the reasons why this truth has been expressed so differently in the past. For this reason I have chosen to write "a history of Christian thought on salvation for those outside the church."

I take this opportunity to express my thanks to Teresa Clements, D.M.J., to Gerald O'Collins, S.J., and to Christopher O'Donnell, O.Carm., who have read this book in manuscript, and have given me many helpful suggestions for its improvement.

I dedicate this book to Francis X. Lawlor, S.J., my professor of ecclesiology at Weston, who during 1992 will celebrate his golden jubilee as a priest and his diamond jubilee as a Jesuit.

Francis A. Sullivan, S.J.

1 || "Extra Ecclesiam Nulla Salus"

When we Jesuits of the New England province die, we are buried in a cemetery in the town of Weston, Massachusetts, on the grounds of what was the seminary where most of us studied for the priesthood. However, one of the best-known Jesuits our province has ever had, and one of the most gifted, does not lie with his confreres at Weston. Instead, Fr. Leonard Feeney's grave can be found in the place where he spent the last years of his life, in the rural village of Still River, Massachusetts. The inscription on the gravestone describes him not as a Jesuit, for he was no longer one when he died, but as the founder of the Slaves of the Immaculate Heart of Mary. Fr. Feeney did not leave the Jesuits in order to found a new community, as some founders of religious orders have done. In fact, he did not leave voluntarily, but was dismissed by our father general for what was judged to be a grave offense against his vow of obedience. How this came about is suggested by the inscription in large block letters at the bottom of his gravestone. It reads: EXTRA ECCLESIAM NULLA SALUS.

The command which Fr. Feeney felt he could not in conscience obey required him to leave the archdiocese of Boston. The reason behind this order was the fact that Feeney had publicly accused the archbishop, Richard J. Cushing, of being a heretic for allowing that there was salvation outside the Catholic Church. Feeney refused to leave St. Benedict Center in Cambridge, Massachusetts, where he was the leader and teacher of a group of zealous young Catholics, because he felt that his leaving would be seen as a tacit admission that what the archbishop, and the Jesuits at Boston College, were teaching about salvation for non-Catholics was genu-

3

ine Catholic doctrine, and not the heresy that Feeney was convinced it was. This, of course, is the meaning of the Latin inscription on his gravestone: "No salvation outside the church." For
Feeney, "the church" could mean none other than the Roman Catholic Church, and "no salvation outside it" meant simply and literally
that no one but a Roman Catholic could be saved. Of course he did
not for a moment think that all Roman Catholics were going to be
saved; in fact, he was sure that a great many of them were heretics
for allowing that non-Catholics could be saved, and, needless to say,
there was no salvation for heretics, even if they were Jesuits or
archbishops.

Four years after being dismissed from the Society of Jesus, Fr.
Leonard Feeney was excommunicated by an order of the holy see,
approved by Pope Pius XII. Nineteen years later, when he was
seventy-five years of age, he was reconciled to the Catholic Church
by Bishop Bernard Flanagan, the bishop of the Worcester diocese,
in which Still River is located. Fr. Richard J. Shmaruk, the priest
who acted as Bishop Flanagan's agent in the matter, was quoted in
the press account of the reconciliation as having said that Fr. Feeney
was not required to retract his literal interpretation of the doctrine:
"No salvation outside the church."[1] In any case, this is what his
more intransigent followers chose for his epitaph.[2]

Frank Sheed has written something that perhaps many others
have thought about this strange case:

> In the handling of Father Feeney we hear a troubling echo of the
> handling of the Modernists at the turn of the century. Like them
> he was condemned but not answered. When [Pope] Boniface
> VIII said in the bull *Unam Sanctam* that it was "altogether neces-
> sary for salvation for every human creature to be subject to the
> Roman Pontiff," he seemed to be saying not only what Father
> Feeney was condemned for saying, but what a vast number of
> yesterday's Catholics had grown up believing. Everybody would
> have been helped by a full-length discussion.[3]

My agreement with the opinion expressed by Frank Sheed
about the need for a full-length discussion of the issues raised by Fr.
Feeney is one of my reasons for undertaking the writing of this

book. However, I have no intention of going into the judicial aspects of his case: for instance, to try to determine whether he was justly treated in being dismissed from the Jesuit order and excommunicated by the holy see. What I do intend is to follow, and try to understand, the evolution through which Christian thinking about the salvation of people "outside the church" has gone, from the earliest centuries of the Christian era to our own. This will require, to begin with, a full-length discussion of the teaching of the church fathers, popes and councils on which Leonard Feeney based his conviction that it was heresy to hold that non-Catholics could be saved. Frank Sheed mentioned the bull *Unam Sanctam* of Pope Boniface VIII. This fourteenth century pope was but one of the many popes and councils which had solemnly declared that there was no salvation outside the Catholic Church. In the course of this book it is my intention to examine their statements in detail. However, it seems worthwhile, at the outset, just to quote some of the most significant ones to give the reader an idea of how strong a case Fr. Feeney could make for his position.

Pope Innocent III, in the year 1208, prescribed a profession of faith to be made by Waldensians who wished to be reconciled with the Catholic Church. This profession of faith included the following statement:

> We believe in our hearts and confess with our lips that there is one church, not that of the heretics, but the holy Roman Catholic and apostolic church, outside of which we believe that no one is saved.[4]

The Fourth Lateran Council (1215), under the same Pope Innocent III, issued a definition of Catholic faith against the Albigensian heretics, which included the statement: "There is one universal church of the faithful, outside of which no one at all is saved."[5]

Pope Boniface VIII, in his bull *Unam Sanctam* (1302), declared:

> We are obliged by our faith to believe and to hold that there is one holy catholic and apostolic church; indeed, we firmly believe and sincerely confess this, and that outside of this church there is neither salvation nor the remission of sins.[6]

> Moreover, we declare, state and define that for every human creature it is a matter of strict necessity for salvation to be subject to the Roman Pontiff.[7]

The Council of Florence (1442) in its *Decree for Jacobites* (profession of faith for the reconciliation of various groups of Monophysites) declared:

> [The Holy Roman Church] firmly believes, professes and teaches that none of those who exist outside of the Catholic Church—neither pagans nor Jews nor heretics nor schismatics—can become sharers of eternal life; rather, they will go into the eternal fire "which was prepared for the devil and his angels" (Mt 25:41) unless, before the end of their lives, they are joined to that same church. . . . No one, even if he shed his blood for the name of Christ, can be saved, unless he remain in the bosom and unity of the Catholic Church.[8]

Pope Pius IV, in his bull *Iniunctum nobis*, also known as the Profession of Faith of the Council of Trent (1564), required Catholics to profess and hold "this true Catholic faith, outside of which no one can be saved. . . ."[9]

Pope Pius IX, in his allocution *Singulari quadam* (1854), declared:

> Certainly we must hold it as of faith that no one can be saved outside of the Apostolic Roman Church: that this is the only ark of salvation, that anyone who does not enter this will perish in the flood.[10]

The same pope, in his encyclical *Quanto conficiamur moerore* (1863), declared: "It is a well-known Catholic dogma that no one can be saved outside the Catholic Church."[11]

After reading through this formidable series of papal and conciliar statements, all affirming the necessity of being in the Catholic Church and professing the Catholic faith for salvation, the reader may well be inclined to agree that Leonard Feeney was right after all in claiming that this was a dogma of Catholic faith, and that anyone who taught that non-Catholics could be saved must be a heretic. One can only imagine with what astonishment Feeney and his followers—and perhaps many other Catholics as well—must have read the following statements that were approved by Pope Paul VI and the assembled body of Catholic bishops at the Second Vatican Council. First, referring to Christians who are not members of the Roman Catholic Church, the council declared:

> They lovingly believe in God the Father almighty and in Christ, Son of God and savior. They are consecrated by baptism, through which they are united with Christ. They also recognize and receive other sacraments within their own churches or ecclesial communities. Many of them rejoice in the episcopate, celebrate the holy eucharist, and cultivate devotion toward the Virgin Mother of God. They also share with us in prayer and other spiritual benefits. Likewise we can say that in some real way they are joined with us in the Holy Spirit, for to them also he gives his gifts and graces, and is thereby operative among them with His sanctifying power.[12]

> The brethren divided from us also carry out many of the sacred actions of the Christian religion. Undoubtedly, in ways that vary according to the condition of each church or community, these actions can truly engender a life of grace, and can be rightly described as capable of providing access to the community of salvation. It follows that these separated churches and communities, though we believe they suffer from defects already mentioned, have by no means been deprived of significance and importance in the mystery of salvation. For the Spirit of Christ has not refrained from using them as means of salvation which derive their efficacy from the very fullness of grace and truth entrusted to the Catholic Church.[13]

Then, with regard to those people—two-thirds of the world's population—who do not share Christian faith and baptism, the council had the following to say:

> Those who have not yet received the gospel are related in various ways to the people of God. In the first place there is the people to whom the covenants and the promises were given, and from whom Christ was born according to the flesh. On account of their fathers, this people remains most dear to God, for God

does not repent of the gifts he makes nor of the calls he issues (cf. Rom 11:28–29).

But the plan of salvation also includes those who acknowledge the creator. In the first place among these there are the Moslems who, professing to hold the faith of Abraham, along with us adore the one and merciful God, who on the last day will judge mankind. Nor is God himself far distant from those who in shadows and images seek the unknown God, for it is he who gives to all men life and breath and every other gift, and who as savior wills that all men be saved (cf. 1 Tim 2:4).

Those also can attain to everlasting salvation who through no fault of their own do not know the gospel of Christ or his church, yet sincerely seek God and, moved by grace, strive by their deeds to do his will as it is known to them through the dictates of conscience. Nor does divine providence deny the help necessary for salvation to those who, without blame on their part, have not yet arrived at an explicit knowledge of God, but who strive to live a good life, thanks to his grace. Whatever goodness or truth is found among them is looked upon by the church as a preparation for the gospel. She regards such qualities as given by him who enlightens all men so that they may finally have life.[14]

Pressing upon the Christian, to be sure, are the need and the duty to battle against evil through manifold tribulations and even to suffer death. But, linked with the paschal mystery and patterned on the dying Christ, he will hasten forward to resurrection in the strength which comes from hope. All this holds true not only for Christians, but for all men of good will in whose hearts grace works in an unseen way. For, since Christ died for all men, and since the ultimate vocation of man is one, and divine, we ought to believe that the Holy Spirit, in a manner known only to God, offers to every man the possibility of being associated with this paschal mystery.[15]

Reflecting on the two series of documents that we have cited, the reader has every right to ask: How can the Catholic Church claim to be consistent with its own traditions when, having taught for so many centuries that there was no salvation outside itself, now, in its latest council, it has spoken so optimistically about the possibility of salvation not only for other Christians, but for Jews, Moslems, people of other religions, and people with no religion at all? On the one hand, the attitude toward the salvation of non-Catholics expressed in the earlier documents can only be described as negative and pessimistic. On the other hand, Karl Rahner has described "optimism concerning salvation" as "one of the most noteworthy results of the Second Vatican Council." In his opinion, "these assertions of optimism concerning salvation . . . marked a far more decisive phase in the development of the Church's conscious awareness of her faith than, for instance, the doctrine of collegiality in the Church, the relationship between scripture and tradition, the acceptance of the new exegesis, etc."[16]

I would call attention to two points in what I have quoted from Rahner. The first is his assertion regarding the optimism which characterizes the doctrine of Vatican II about the possibility of salvation for people who do not belong to the Catholic Church. This is surely evident to any impartial reader of the council documents. The second point is his description of this as a "development of the Church's conscious awareness of her faith." This, it seems to me, raises a question that needs to be examined further. The question is whether this radical change from pessimism to optimism, this about-face from the position of "no salvation outside the Catholic Church" to the recognition by Vatican II of the universal possibility of salvation, can really be seen as a genuine development of the church's understanding of her faith. In other words, can this be justified as a legitimate development of doctrine? That there is such a thing as a development of doctrine which the Catholic Church recognizes as legitimate is beyond question. However, in some of its official documents it has described such development in terms that make it questionable whether one can apply this notion to the radical change with which we are dealing here. For instance, the First Vatican Council declared:

> The meaning which our Holy Mother Church has once declared sacred dogmas to have, must always be retained, and there must never be a deviation from that meaning on the specious ground and title of a more profound understanding. "Therefore, let there be growth and abundant progress in understanding, knowledge and wisdom, in each and all, in individuals and in the whole Church, at all times and in the progress of

ages, but only within the proper limits, i.e. within the same dogma, the same meaning, the same judgment."[17]

Likewise, Pope Pius X prescribed an "Oath against Modernism" in which Catholics were required to declare:

> I totally reject the heretical notion of the development of dogmas, by which dogmas would change from one meaning to another, different from the meaning which the Church previously attached to them.[18]

The question, then, can be put this way: despite the obvious difference between the language used by the medieval popes and councils on the question of salvation for those outside the church, and the language used by Vatican II, is there any consistent *meaning* which would justify recognizing this as a genuine development of doctrine? In his opening address to the assembled bishops at Vatican II, Pope John XXIII called their attention to the very important distinction to be made between the faith itself and the way it is expressed, when he said: "The substance of the ancient doctrine of the deposit of faith is one thing, and the way in which it is presented is another."[19] So the question we are asking is whether, on the matter of salvation for those outside the church, there is a substance of the faith here that can be said to have undergone development, rather than to have suffered radical change.

In the Declaration *Mysterium Ecclesiae* of 1973, the Roman Congregation for the Doctrine of the Faith has further elucidated the distinction between the substance of the faith and its historical expression. For the first time, an official document of the Holy See has explicitly recognized the fact that the church's expression of its faith will necessarily be conditioned by a number of historical factors. This is so important for our subject that it seems worthwhile to quote it at length here.

> Difficulties [in the transmission of divine revelation by the church] arise also from the historical condition that affects the expression of revelation. With regard to this historical condition, it must first be observed that the meaning of the pronouncements of faith depends partly upon the expressive power

of the language used at a certain point in time and in particular circumstances. Moreover, it sometimes happens that some dogmatic truth is first expressed incompletely (but not falsely), and at a later date, when considered in a broader context of faith or human knowledge, it receives a fuller and more perfect expression. In addition, when the church makes new pronouncements it intends to confirm or clarify what is in some way contained in sacred scripture or in previous expressions of tradition, but at the same time it usually has the intention of solving certain questions or removing certain errors. All these things have to be taken into account in order that these pronouncements may be properly interpreted. Finally, even though the truths which the church intends to teach through its dogmatic formulas are distinct from the changeable conceptions of a given epoch and can be expressed without them, nevertheless it can sometimes happen that these truths may be enunciated by the sacred magisterium in terms that bear traces of such conceptions. . . . In addition, it has sometimes happened that certain formulas in the habitual usage of the church have given way to new expressions which, proposed and approved by the sacred magisterium, presented more clearly or more completely the same meaning.[20]

In this Declaration of the Roman Congregation, I would particularly note the following points. First, it recognizes the fact that a dogmatic truth that had previously been expressed in a less perfect way can, when subsequently considered in a broader context of faith *or human knowledge*, receive a more perfect expression. Now it seems obvious that the subsequent "more perfect expression" is going to reflect a better understanding of the truth; and it is noteworthy that the church's better understanding of its faith can also be gained through a broader context of human knowledge. In the course of this study we shall see, for instance, how a growth in human knowledge of such sciences as geography, anthropology, and psychology has contributed to a better understanding of the necessity of belonging to the church for salvation.

Second, we are told that the expression of dogmatic truth at a given epoch may reflect conceptions and the mentality proper to that period of history. Thus, if we are going to understand what the medieval popes and councils meant when they denied salvation to those outside the church, we have to try to penetrate their mentality, to grasp their unspoken assumptions, the things which they took for granted, which influenced their way of understanding and thus of expressing their faith.

To give one concrete example: we have seen that the Council of Florence in 1442 declared it to be a matter of Catholic faith that all pagans, Jews, heretics and schismatics would certainly go to hell if they died outside the Catholic Church. But we have every reason to assume that the fathers of the Council of Florence also believed that God is just, and that he does not condemn innocent people to the torments of hell. This unspoken element of their faith must certainly be taken into account if we are going to understand how they could have believed that God was going to condemn all those people to hell for being outside the Catholic Church. The conclusion is inescapable that they must have judged them all guilty in the sight of God and deserving of the punishment awaiting them. How they could have judged them all guilty is a matter we shall have to investigate. For the moment, it is enough to have noted that we cannot understand what the bishops at Florence said about the fate of those outside the church without asking how they could reconcile this with their much more fundamental belief in the goodness and justice of God.

What I intend to do in this book, then, is to seek an understanding of what Christians have believed and taught about the salvation of those outside the church, with a view to determining, if possible, whether there is, after all, a substance of the faith here that underlies the very different ways in which it has been expressed. To anticipate the conclusion to which my study has led me, I will say that it is my conviction that there is such a substance of the faith, namely, the belief that God has assigned to the church a necessary role in the accomplishment of his plan for the salvation of humanity. In the varying conditions in which the church has lived out its history, this belief in its necessity for salvation has led Christians to express their faith in different ways, depending to a great extent on the judgment which Christians were conditioned to make about people who did not share their faith. If I am not mistaken, what has really changed in the course of time is not so much what Christians have believed about the necessity of being in the church for salvation as the judgment which they have made about those who were outside. So we are going to try to understand not only what they said, but what they thought, and why they thought that way, about the possibility of salvation for people who were "outside the church."

At this point, a word is in order about the method we intend to follow in this book. We are going to treat our subject in chronological order, beginning with the earliest fathers of the church, and finishing with the post-Vatican II state of the question. But that does not mean that we are going to try to present the views of every father and every theologian who has had anything to say on our question. Our treatment is necessarily going to be selective, but our purpose is to select the writings of those who we believe have made a significant contribution to the development of Christian thinking about the salvation of those "outside the church." To the extent that it is practical, given the limitations of a book like this, we intend to let those whom we have selected speak for themselves, by quoting the most salient passages of their writings. But of course we shall also provide what would seem to be indispensable background information to put their writings in context, and we shall offer such comments as seem helpful for the interpretation of what we are quoting. We shall begin by seeing what the early church fathers thought about the chances of salvation for Jews and Gentiles during the centuries before the coming of Christ.

2 || The Fathers Prior to St. Augustine

One of the problems put to the early Christians by Jews and Gentiles to whom they proclaimed Christ as the savior of humanity was: "If Christ is the savior of all men, how is it that he came only recently into the world? What about the salvation of all those generations of people who lived and died before he came to save us?" As we shall see, the early Christian writers offered a response to this challenge which manifested a positive attitude toward the possibility of salvation for both Jews and Gentiles during the pre-Christian era.

Salvation for Those Who Lived Before the Coming of Christ

The first such writer whom we shall consider is St. Justin Martyr, the most important second century Greek apologist for the Christian religion. Before his conversion he had been a Platonist philosopher; having recognized in Christianity the truth he had been seeking in philosophy, he became a teacher and defender of his new faith. Three of his works have come down to us: his two *Apologies*, addressed to the Roman authorities who were persecuting the Christians, and his *Dialogue with Trypho the Jew*, in which he answered the objections which Jews were making to the Christian religion. In this latter work he gave the following answer to the question about salvation for Jews who had lived before the coming of Christ.

> Since each person would be saved by his own virtue, I also stated that those who obeyed the Mosaic Law would likewise be

saved. They who are obliged to obey the Law of Moses will find in it not only precepts which were occasioned by the hardness of your people's hearts, but also those which in themselves are good, holy, and just. Since they who did those things which are universally, naturally, and eternally good are pleasing to God, they shall be saved in the resurrection, together with their righteous forefathers, Noe, Henoch, Jacob, and others, together with those who believe in Christ, the Son of God. . . .[1]

It is noteworthy that Justin's argument here would apply not only to Jews who observed the law of Moses, but to all who did what is "universally, naturally and eternally good." In other words, for Justin the philosopher, the law of Moses was salvific because its commandments corresponded to the natural law, prescribing what is "good, holy and just" by its very nature.

As one might expect from this, Justin also gave a positive answer to the question about the possibility of salvation for Gentiles who had kept the natural law. For him, this meant living according to reason, which, as a philosopher, he had known as *logos*. As a Christian, he knew that the *Logos* was incarnate in Christ. This explains his way of answering the question put to him about the Gentiles who had lived before the coming of Christ.

If some should accuse us as if we held that people born before the time of Christ were not accountable to God for their actions, we shall anticipate and answer such a difficulty. We have been taught that Christ is the first-begotten of God, and we have declared him to be the *Logos* of which all mankind partakes. Those, therefore, who lived according to reason (*logos*) were really Christians, even though they were thought to be atheists, such as, among the Greeks, Socrates, Heraclitus and others like them. . . . So also, those who lived before Christ but did not live according to reason were wicked men, and enemies of Christ, and murderers of those who did live according to reason. Whereas those who lived then, or who live now, according to reason are Christians. Such as these can be confident and unafraid.[2]

It is remarkable that we find in the second century this anticipation of Karl Rahner's term "anonymous Christians" to describe those who are justified without Christian faith.

Our next witness from the second century is St. Irenaeus, the bishop of Lyons and, like St. Justin, a martyr for the faith. His major work was directed against the Gnostic heretics, who posed a grave threat to the Christian faith at that period. In the course of this work Irenaeus spoke as follows about the providence of God with regard to those who had lived before the coming of Christ.

> Christ did not come only for those who lived at the time of the Emperor Tiberius, nor does the Father exercise his providence only for those who are living now. Rather, he has provided for all those who from the beginning have lived virtuously in their own generation and feared and loved God, and treated their neighbors with justice and kindness, and have longed to see Christ and to hear his voice. . . .[3]

The last phrase obviously refers to the people of Israel who looked for the coming of the messiah. It can perhaps be taken also to refer to Gentiles who had come to believe in God as savior, and thus could be said to have longed implicitly for the coming of Christ.

We come now to the two great third century teachers of the school of Alexandria, Clement and Origen. Both of them had been trained in Greek philosophy, and applied their learning to the defense and explanation of the Christian faith. Clement had the following to say about the salvation of Gentiles prior to the coming of Christ.

> God has care of all, since he is the Lord of all. And he is the Savior of all; it cannot be said that he is Savior of these, and not of others. As each one was disposed to receive it, God distributed his blessings, both to Greeks and to barbarians; and in their own time those were called who were predestined to be among the faithful elect.[4]

For a cultivated Greek-speaker like Clement, of course, anyone who did not speak Greek was a "barbarian." But God had offered the grace of salvation to them as well.

While Origen was primarily a theologian and exegete, he also applied his talent to the defense of the Christian faith in an important work in which he replied to the objections of a pagan named Celsus. One of these had to do with our question.

Celsus asks: "How is it that after so many centuries it is only now that God has thought to bring men to live righteously, and that previously he had had no concern about that?" I reply that there was never a time when God did not want men to be just; he was always concerned about that. Indeed, he always provided beings endowed with reason with occasions for practising virtue and doing what is right. In every generation the Wisdom of God descended into those souls which he found holy, and made them to be prophets and friends of God.[5]

Of the writers of the fourth century we shall cite only the great preacher of Antioch and Constantinople, St. John Chrysostom. In one of his homilies, he replied to the objection which the pagans of his day were still raising about the "late coming" of Christ.

When the pagans accuse us, saying: "What was Christ doing during all that former time, when he was not yet concerned for the human race? And why has he come at the last minute to provide for our salvation, after neglecting us for so long a time?" we will reply that even before his coming he was already in the world; he was already taking thought of the work he was to accomplish, and he was known to all who proved themselves worthy of such knowledge. You cannot say that at that time he was unknown, because he was not known by all, but only by the upright and the virtuous, any more than you can say that today he is not being adored by men, on the grounds that even now not all have come to adore him.[6]

There is certainly other evidence, in the writings of the fathers prior to St. Augustine, of a positive response to the question concerning the possibility of salvation for people who had lived before the coming of Christ. A fruitful source of speculation about this was also found in the New Testament, in the reference to Christ's "preaching to the dead" during the time between his death and resurrection (1 Pet 3:19 and 4:6). However, what we have seen should suffice to show how general was the view that God had provided the means of salvation to both Jews and Gentiles during the pre-Christian era. It was also commonly held that salvation had always been through Christ, although there were different explanations of this. As we have seen, some went so far as to assert that all the just could be called Christians: a striking anticipation of a modern theory.

We must now see what the fathers prior to Augustine thought about the possibility of salvation for those who lived during the Christian era but were not members of the Christian community. It is in this context that we will begin to find the stern warning that there is no salvation outside the church. We shall look at the principal texts in which this statement is found, with a view to determining, as far as we can, just what the writer meant by it, and against whom it was directed. We shall see that there is an important difference between the way this axiom was used, and the people to whom it was applied, during the first three centuries, when Christians were a persecuted minority in the Roman world, and the way it was used after Christianity had become the official religion of the Roman empire. We begin with the earlier period.

"No Salvation Outside the Church" in the First Three Centuries

On his way to martyrdom in Rome, St. Ignatius, the bishop of Antioch in Syria, wrote letters to the Christian communities of the cities in which he had stopped on his journey. One of the principal themes of these letters was an exhortation to the faithful and their presbyters to remain in close union with their local bishop. Evidently there were instances of disunion in some churches, which led Ignatius to issue the following warning in his letter to the church of Philadelphia, a city in the vicinity of Ephesus.

> Be not deceived, my brethren: if anyone follows a maker of schism, he does not inherit the Kingdom of God; if anyone walks in strange doctrine he has no part in the passion.[7]

It should be noted that here it is not only the "maker of schism," but also those who follow him, who will not inherit the kingdom of God; likewise, it is not only the originator of false doctrine, but also those who walk in it, who will have no part in the passion. When Ignatius warns Christian schismatics and heretics that there is no salvation for them outside the church, he clearly judges them personally guilty for being outside.

We have already quoted a passage of St. Irenaeus, bishop of Lyons, about salvation before the coming of Christ. As we mentioned above, his major work was directed against the Gnostic heretics, who separated themselves from the ordinary Christian communities, claiming to have a higher knowledge of the Christian mysteries than was taught by the bishops in the churches. Against these separatists, Irenaeus declared:

> In the church God has placed apostles, prophets, teachers, and every other working of the Spirit, of whom none of those are sharers who do not hasten to the church, but who defraud themselves of life, by an evil mind and even worse way of acting. For where the church is, there is the Spirit of God, and where the Spirit of God is, there is the church and all grace.[8]

The Gnostics prided themselves on their higher knowledge, but Irenaeus warned them that it is only in the true church that one can have the life and grace of the Spirit, of which heretics and schismatics are defrauding themselves. It is obvious that Irenaeus judged them guilty of their separation from the church, and hence responsible for their own exclusion from the realm of the Spirit.

Origen, the pioneer of Christian allegorical exegesis of the scriptures, introduced the warning that there is no salvation outside the church, in a homily on Joshua, chapter 2, which tells about the two Hebrew spies in Jericho who took refuge in the house of Rahab the prostitute. Origen saw in this house a type of the church, since it was the one place of safety in the city that was about to be destroyed. His application of the Old Testament story to the current life of the church is as follows.

> This command is given to the woman who had been a prostitute before: "All those who are found in your house will be saved. But as regards those who go out of your house, we shall be free of this oath we have made to you." Therefore, if anyone wishes to be saved, let him come into this house of her who once was a prostitute. Even if someone of that people wishes to be saved, let him come into this house, so that he may find salvation. Let him come into this house, in which the blood of Christ is the sign of redemption. . . . So let no one persuade himself, let no

one deceive himself: outside this house, that is, outside the church, no one is saved. For if anyone goes outside, he is responsible for his own death.[9]

Some exegetical remarks may be helpful here. The "woman who had been a prostitute" suggests the image of the Gentile church as the converted sinner; she who had lived in pagan vice is now the chaste bride of Christ. The scarlet cord which Rahab hung out her window was the sign for the invading Hebrew army that her house was to be spared; for Origen it signifies the blood of Christ which is the sign of redemption for the church. Origen's invitation to members of "that people" is clearly directed to the Jews who had not accepted the Christian message of salvation. But the major warning in this passage is directed against those who go out of the house in which alone salvation is to be found. Just as was the case in Jericho, anyone who would go outside now would likewise be responsible for his own death. This clearly refers to Christians who, having once been in the church, would leave it to join a heretical or schismatic sect. There is no salvation outside the church, and those who go outside have only themselves to blame for their loss.

We come now to St. Cyprian, the bishop of Carthage in North Africa, who died as a martyr in 258. Although, as we have seen, others before him had warned that there was no salvation outside the church, Cyprian's name is especially associated with this axiom, which occurs with frequency and urgency in his writings. Despite this frequency, however, there is no instance of his addressing this warning to the non-Christians who were still the majority of the people in the Roman empire of his day. Cyprian directed this warning to Christians who were either in danger of being separated from the church by excommunication, or were already separated by heresy or schism. In every case there is clear evidence that Cyprian judged such people guilty of their separation from the church, and therefore personally responsible for their exclusion from the salvation to be found only in the church. The following are the principal passages in which he warned those "outside the church" that there was no salvation for them where they were. The first is directed to some Christians who were defiantly disobedient to their bishops, and thus in danger of excommunication.

Let them not think that the way of life or salvation exists for them, if they have refused to obey the bishops and priests, since the Lord says in the Book of Deuteronomy: "And any man who has the insolence to refuse to listen to the priest or judge, whoever he may be in those days, that man shall die." (Deut 17:12 f.) And then indeed, they were killed with the sword . . . but now the proud and insolent are killed with the sword of the Spirit, when they are cast out from the church. For they cannot live outside, since there is only one house of God, and there can be no salvation for anyone except in the church.[10]

In a letter dealing with schismatic Christians, Cyprian invokes St. Paul's description of the church as the bride of Christ (Eph 5:32), and asks, "How can a man who is not with the bride of Christ and in his church be with Christ?"[11]

Similarly, in a letter dealing with heretics, Cyprian based his argument on the text where St. Paul says: "And if I deliver my body to be burned and have not love, I gain nothing" (1 Cor 13:3). For St. Cyprian, the unity of the church was essentially a unity of love; and hence anyone who violated this unity by heresy or schism was sinning against the virtue of charity. He drew the logical conclusion: "Neither baptism of public confession [of the faith under torture], nor of blood [shed for the faith], can avail the heretic anything toward salvation, because there is no salvation outside the church."[12]

In his work *On the Unity of the Church*, Cyprian returns to this idea that even martyrdom cannot purge away the guilt of schism.

Nay, even though they should suffer death for the confession of the Name, the guilt of such men is not removed even by their blood; the grievous irremissible sin of schism is not purged even by martyrdom. No martyr can he be who is not in the church; the kingdom shall be closed to him who has deserted her who is destined to be its queen. Peace is what Christ gave us; He bade us be united in heart and mind; He enjoined on us to keep intact and unimpaired the pledges of our love and charity; no one can claim the martyr's name who has broken off his love for the brethren. This is the Apostle Paul's teaching and witness . . . "If I should deliver my body to be burned and have not charity, I profit nothing."[13]

In the same work, Cyprian employs the images of the church as bride, mother, and ark to castigate the schismatic Christian.

> The spouse of Christ cannot be defiled, she is inviolate and chaste. . . . Whoever breaks with the church and enters on an adulterous union, cuts himself off from the promises made to the church; and he who has turned his back on the church of Christ shall not come to the rewards of Christ: he is an alien, a worldling, an enemy. You cannot have God for your Father if you have not the church for your mother. If there was escape for anyone who was outside the ark of Noe, there is escape too for one who is found to be outside the church. . . . Whoever breaks the peace and harmony of Christ acts against Christ; whoever gathers elsewhere than in the church scatters the church of Christ. . . . If a man does not keep this unity, he is not keeping the law of God, he has lost his faith about Father and Son, he has lost his life and his soul.[14]

It would be difficult to express the thesis that there is no salvation outside the church more strongly than St. Cyprian has put it here. No doubt some of his statements, if taken out of context, would exclude from salvation everyone who was outside the church, and not just Christian heretics and schismatics. But in each case, the context shows that he is not directing this warning to pagans and Jews, but to Christians whom he judged guilty of persisting in sins against faith and charity by reason of their allegiance to heretical or schismatic sects.

It is also well known that Cyprian was convinced that baptism administered in such sects not only did not confer the grace of the Holy Spirit, but was simply invalid, on the grounds that if it did not confer the Holy Spirit, it was of no value at all. For this reason he, along with the other bishops of North Africa, insisted that those who came into the Catholic Church from such sects should be baptized again. Cyprian did not see how a sacrament could be valid without being fruitful; it took another century of theological progress, and St. Augustine's explanation, to settle this problem. On this question Cyprian was mistaken, to be sure, but he can hardly be accused of heresy for following what was the tradition of the church of North Africa up to his time.

There is no instance in his writings in which Cyprian explicitly applied his saying "No salvation outside the church" to the majority of people who were still pagans in his day. We know that he judged Christian heretics and schismatics guilty of their separation from the church. Did he also judge all pagans guilty of their failure to accept the Christian gospel and enter the church? We do not know. However, some light on his attitude toward pagans is given by the letter which he wrote to one of them named Demetrianus, who had been involved in persecuting Christians, and was now approaching death. This is what Cyprian wrote to him.

> We implore you to make reparation to God while you still can, while you still have a little time left. We show you the way to salvation. Believe, and you shall live. For a time you have persecuted us; come and rejoice with us forever. It is here below that life is either lost or held onto; don't let your sins or your age make you put off gaining salvation. While still in this world, repentance is never too late. Even at death's door you can beg pardon for your sins, appealing to the one true God in faith. For God's goodness grants acquittal unto salvation to the believer so as to pass from death to immortality. It is Christ who grants this grace. [15]

One gets the impression that Cyprian would not have excluded this man from salvation, even though he was obviously outside the church, provided that even "at death's door" he had made an act of faith in God and repented of his sins. At least there is no mention of the absolute necessity for his salvation that he become a member of the Christian church before he died.

Looking back over the texts that we have cited from Ignatius, Irenaeus, Origen and Cyprian, we see that when these early Christian writers spoke of people being excluded from salvation by reason of their being outside the church, they were consistently directing this as a warning to Christians whom they judged to be guilty of the grave sins of heresy and schism. It is quite possible that, if asked, they would have answered that there was no salvation outside the church for Jews or pagans either. But it is significant for the history of this axiom that we do not find them applying it to others than Christians at this time when Christians were still a persecuted minority. As we shall now see, the case was different when Chris-

tianity had become the official religion of the Roman empire and
most people had accepted the Christian faith.

"No Salvation Outside the Church" in the
Last Decades of the Fourth Century

We have to keep in mind the tremendous change that took
place in the course of the fourth century with respect to the status of
the Christian religion in the Roman empire. During the first decades of this century, Christianity suffered the most cruel and sus-
tained persecution it had ever suffered at the hands of imperial
Rome. However, with the edicts of the emperors Galerius (311) and
Constantine (313), the persecution came to an end, and from the
time of Constantine, Christian emperors began to favor the church
and grant privileges to its clergy. Now that it was no longer danger-
ous to profess the Christian faith, but rather advantageous to do so,
it is not surprising that the fourth century saw a great influx of
people into the church, with the result that toward the end of the
century, the great majority had embraced the Christian faith. Emperor Theodosius I, who ruled from 379 to 395, declared the orthodox Christian religion (that of the bishop of Rome and those in
communion with him) to be the official religion of the empire. He
even forbade the celebration of pagan sacrifices and other pagan
rites; however, he did not change the traditional Roman policy of
toleration toward the Jewish religion.

In this new situation of an officially Christian empire, it is not
surprising that we find a new attitude on the part of Christian writers
with regard to the minority who had not accepted the Christian faith.
It is now that we find the fathers applying the doctrine that "there is
no salvation outside the church" to the situation of pagans and Jews.
As we have seen, the warning addressed to Christian heretics and
schismatics included a judgment about their guilt for being outside
the church. What we find now is a similar judgment of guilt with
regard to everyone who had not accepted the Christian faith. The
reason behind the judgment was the assumption that the message of
the gospel had by now been proclaimed everywhere, and everyone
had had ample opportunity to accept it. The conclusion was that
those who had not accepted it were guilty of refusing God's offer of
salvation, and would be justly condemned.

The most influential Catholic bishop during the reign of Theodosius I was St. Ambrose, bishop of Milan. He had this to say about those who in his day still refused to believe in Christ.

> If someone does not believe in Christ he defrauds himself of this universal benefit, just as if someone were to shut out the rays of the sun by closing his window. For the mercy of the Lord has been spread by the church to all nations; the faith has been spread to all peoples.[16]

An eastern contemporary of Ambrose was St. Gregory of Nyssa, who, in his great *Catechetical Oration*, likewise insisted that all had by now heard the call to faith, and that those lacking faith had only themselves to blame for refusing the gift.

> If, then, faith is a good thing, they say, why has this gift not come to all? Now if what we are saying were taken to mean that faith was distributed to men by the divine will in such a way that some were called, but others receive no call to faith, then with reason one could accuse this mystery of injustice. But if in fact the call has gone out to all, with no difference on account of rank, age or nation . . . how could it be right to blame God for the fact that his word has not achieved its dominion over all? For he who has full power over the universe, for the supreme honor of mankind, left something in our power, of which each one is alone the master, and this is the will, a thing that cannot be enslaved, and has self-determining power, since it is seated in the liberty of thought and mind. Therefore such blame would more justly be attributed to those who have not been drawn to the faith, rather than to him who has called them to believe.[17]

Our third witness to the judgment expressed by bishops of the late fourth century concerning the guilt of those who had not accepted the Christian faith by their day is St. John Chrysostom. It would seem that some members of his flock had objected to his harsh judgment on the pagans, and had wished to excuse them on the grounds of ignorance. Here is his reply.

> One should not think that ignorance excuses the non-believer. . . . When you are ignorant of what can easily be known,

you have to suffer the penalty. . . . When we do all that is in our power, in matters where we lack knowledge, God will give us his hand; but if we do not do what we can, we do not enjoy God's help either. . . . So do not say: "How is it that God has neglected that sincere and honest pagan?" You will find that he has not really been diligent in seeking the truth, since what concerns the truth is now clearer than the sun. How shall they obtain pardon who, when they see the doctrine of truth spread before them, make no effort to come to know it? For now the name of God is proclaimed to all, what the prophets predicted has come true, and the religion of the pagans has been proven false. . . . It is impossible that anyone who is vigilant in seeking the truth should be contemned by God.[18]

Chrysostom returned to this argument in a homily in which he was exhorting his flock to pray for the conversion of pagans.

"Did Christ give himself up for pagans?" you ask. Yes, Christ died for pagans as well; how then can you be unwilling to pray for them? "But how is it," you ask, "that they have not believed?" It is because they did not wish to. And yet Christ did his part on their behalf; his passion bears witness to that.[19]

It was undoubtedly St. John Chrysostom's judgment that there was no salvation for pagans outside the church, and that it was their own fault that they were outside. His judgment on the Jews of his day was even more implacable. The sermons which he delivered at Antioch, warning Christians against participating in Jewish festivals, contain some of the most offensive language about Jews to be found in Christian literature. That he judged the Jews guilty of rejecting Christ, and excluded from salvation as long as they persisted in this rejection, is evident on every page of those sermons. Let it suffice to mention just one remark he made, in the course of an exhortation to some of his flock who were resisting his call to conversion. He warned them: "You have grounds for shame if you do not change for the better, but persist in your untimely contentiousness. That is what destroyed the Jews."[20]

With this we conclude our treatment of the fathers prior to St. Augustine. There are others than the ones we have mentioned who had something to say on our topic; however, their views do not differ substantially from those we have seen.

Three points stand out in the thinking of the writers of this period. The first is their generally positive attitude on the possibility of salvation for both Jews and Gentiles who had lived before the coming of Christ. The second is their uniformly negative attitude about the possibility of salvation for Christians who were separated from the great church by heresy or schism. These they judged guilty of grave personal sin against charity, since they identified the communion of the church with love, and saw everyone who adhered to a schismatic group, and not merely its founders, as guilty of the sin of schism. The third point is that it is only toward the close of the fourth century, when Christianity had become the official religion of the empire, and the majority of its citizens adhered to it, that we find the axiom "No salvation outside the church" being explicitly applied to pagans and Jews. Here the negative judgment was based on the assumption that by now everyone had had the opportunity to accept the Christian message, that its truth was evident to all, and that those who refused to accept it were closing their eyes to the truth by which they could be saved.

It is important to observe that all three of these points are consistent with a belief in God's universal salvific will. Before Christ came, God had not so chosen the people of Israel as to deny the possibility of salvation to the Gentiles. Rather, he had offered the means of salvation to any who proved themselves worthy of receiving it. The exclusion of Christian heretics and schismatics from salvation was seen as the just punishment of their sins against the unity of the body of Christ. Likewise, the exclusion of pagans and Jews was seen as the consequence of their willful rejection of the truth. In no case was the exclusion of people from salvation seen as an arbitrary judgment on the part of God. If people were damned, it was not because God did not will their salvation; it was because they had refused the means of salvation he had provided for them. This does not mean that the judgment of guilt passed by Christian writers against heretics, schismatics, pagans and Jews was necessarily a correct judgment, or one that we can share. They may well have been wrong in their judgment about the guilt of the people who were outside the church. The important thing is that if their judgment was mistaken, it was a mistake about the guilt of people, not about the justice or salvific will of God.

3 ‖ St. Augustine and His Followers

There are several reasons for devoting a chapter of this book to the teaching of St. Augustine. The first is the massive influence that he has had on the history of Christian thought, including that on the possibility of salvation for people who die outside the church. Then there is the complexity of his teaching, especially with regard to the church and its necessity for salvation. As we shall see, one also has to take into account the nature of the controversy in which his statements were made. Augustine's literary career spanned a period of forty years (390–430), equally divided between the first twenty years of controversy with the Donatists, and the latter twenty with the Pelagians. On some issues there is a significant difference between the position he took in the earlier period and what he said in the later.

We shall consider first what St. Augustine said about salvation for those who lived before Christ, then what he said about Christian heretics and schismatics, and finally his views on the possibility of salvation for the non-Christians of his day.

On Salvation for Those Who Lived
Before the Coming of Christ

We have already seen that the early fathers spoke in quite positive terms about the possibility of salvation for both Jews and Gentiles who had lived before the coming of Christ. As is so often the case, St. Augustine followed the traditional view, but he added a new depth with his personal interpretation of it. He expressed his mind on this question most fully in a letter which he wrote to a

28

priest named Deogratias, who had asked him for help in answering objections which some pagans were making to the Christian religion. One of these ran: "Why did he who is called the Savior hide himself for so many ages? What became of the souls of the Romans or Latins who were deprived of the grace of Christ until the time of the Caesars, when he finally came?"[1] Augustine's answer was as follows.

When we say that Christ is the Word of God, through whom all things were made, we say also that he is the Son of God . . . co-eternal with the Father, the unchangeable Wisdom by whom the whole universe was created, and who becomes the happiness of every rational soul. Therefore, from the beginning of the human race, all those who believed in him and knew him and lived a good and devout life according to his commands, whenever and wherever they lived, undoubtedly were saved by him. . . . From the beginning of the human race, sometimes obscurely, sometimes openly, as it seemed to his providence to suit the times, he did not cease to prophesy, and before he appeared in the flesh there were not lacking men to believe in him, from Adam to Moses, among the people of Israel, which by divine ordinance was the prophetic race, and among other peoples. In the sacred books of the Hebrews there is mention of many from the time of Abraham, who were not of his stock, nor of the people of Israel, nor were they joined by any chance alliance to the people of Israel, yet were partakers in his worship; so why should we not believe that sometimes there were other men, here and there among other races, who were worshipers of him, although we do not find mention of them in the same sacred books? The saving grace of this religion, the only true one, through which alone true salvation is truly promised, has never been refused to anyone who was worthy of it, and whoever lacked it was unworthy of it. From the beginning of human history to the end, this is made known for the reward of some and the punishment of others. And that is why it is not made known at all to some, because it was foreknown that they would not believe, yet it is also made known to some who will not believe, as a warning to the former.[2]

In this answer to the question put to him by Deogratias, we find several of Augustine's convictions with regard to the divine economy of salvation. First, salvation has always been through faith in Christ and worship of him; this alone is the true religion. However, this religion has always been available to those who were worthy of it. Even those not of the Hebrew race received some obscure but sufficient revelation of it. If such revelation was not made to some, it was because God foreknew that they would not believe if it were made to them; hence they were responsible for their ignorance of it.

Augustine drew further conclusions from the principles just mentioned. One was that all those who have ever lived justly have been saved by their faith in Christ, have had Christ as their head, and have been members of his body. Thus the body of Christ consists of all the just, beginning with Abel, the first man to die in the friendship of God.

> All together we are members of Christ and are his body; and not we who are in this place only, but throughout the world; and not at this time only, but—what shall I say—from Abel the just man until the end of time, as long as men beget and are begotten, whoever among the just made his passage through this life, whether now, that is, not in this place, but in the present life, or in generations to come, all the just are this one body of Christ, and individually his members.[3]

St. Augustine was not the first to propose the idea of the church as pre-existing the coming of Christ. Origen, among others, had spoken along these lines before him. But Augustine was the first to describe all the just, from the beginning to the end of the world, as constituting the *ecclesia ab Abel*, the "church beginning with Abel."[4] Of primary interest for our topic is the fact that St. Augustine saw Gentiles as well as Jews, before the coming of Christ, as members of that church of the just. Augustine's "City of God" also began with Abel and included all those who had "lived in the world with careful concern not to offend God, and had avoided sin."[5] Here again we see Augustine's recognition of the availability of salvation for all who had lived justly before the coming of Christ. At the same time, we have to keep in mind Augustine's conviction that no one had ever been saved except through faith in Christ, the one mediator of salvation. He does not give a very satisfying explanation of how Gentiles could have arrived at such faith; it would seem that he simply concluded, from the premise that they must have had faith in Christ in order to be saved, that it must have been available to them.

While Augustine recognized that some kind of obscure faith in Christ could have been sufficient during the pre-Christian era, he was absolute in his conviction that once the gospel had been preached and the church had been established, there was no possibility of salvation without orthodox Christian faith and membership in the true church, which for him was the *catholica:* the worldwide church in communion with Rome. This conviction led him to express his full agreement with the principle already laid down by Cyprian and the earlier fathers:

No Salvation for Christian Heretics and Schismatics

The key to understanding Augustine's rigorous exclusion of Christian heretics and schismatics from salvation is his identification of the communion which is the bond of unity in the *catholica*, with the virtue of charity. From this he concluded that anyone who had broken with this communion was guilty of grave sin against charity, and would remain in that state of sin until he was reunited with the Catholic Church. Here are some of the consequences which he drew from these premises.

> Whoever is separated from this Catholic Church, by this single sin of being severed from the unity of Christ, no matter how estimable a life he may imagine he is living, shall not have life, but the wrath of God rests upon him.[6]

> The love of which the Apostle says: "The love of God is poured out in our hearts by the Holy Spirit who is given to us" (Rom 5:5), is a love which those do not have who are cut off from the communion of the Catholic Church. And for this reason even though they should "speak with the tongues of men and angels" . . . (1 Cor 13:1–3) it profits them nothing. For that person does not have the love of God who does not love the unity of the church, and from this one rightly understands that the Holy Spirit is not received anywhere but in the Catholic Church.[7]

Elsewhere Augustine puts this more succinctly, saying: "The enemy of unity has no share in divine love. Consequently, those who are outside the church do not have the Holy Spirit."[8]

Augustine did not agree with Cyprian's view that baptism and other sacraments administered in a heretical or schismatic sect would be simply invalid. On the other hand, he agreed with Cyprian that they would not confer the Holy Spirit or his gifts of grace, for the reason that those receiving them were blocking the reception of grace by their persistence in schism, which he saw as grave sin against charity. Thus he insisted: "When a person is baptized in some heretical or schismatic group, outside the communion of the church, his baptism is of no profit to him, inasmuch as he gives his consent to the perversity of those heretics or schismatics."[9]

An even more emphatic statement of this position is the following passage of one of Augustine's sermons in which, referring to a Donatist bishop, he said:

> Outside the church he can have everything except salvation. He can have honor, he can have sacraments, he can sing alleluia, he can respond with Amen, he can have the gospel, he can hold and preach the faith in the name of the Father and the Son and the Holy Spirit: but nowhere else than in the Catholic Church can he find salvation.[10]

Finally, Augustine insists that even if a member of a heretical sect were to suffer martyrdom, this would not save him:

> Nor will his baptism be of any benefit to the heretic if, while outside the church, he were put to death for confessing Christ. This is altogether true. The fact of dying outside the church proves that he did not have charity.[11]

In our modern ecumenical age we no doubt are inclined to think St. Augustine unreasonably harsh in judging everyone who belonged to a separated Christian group as sharing in the guilt of schism, and thus as living in a state of grave sin against charity. One might well ask whether he did not recognize the difference between the people who caused the rupture of ecclesial communion in the first place, and those who, perhaps without personal fault, belonged to the separated group in subsequent generations. As a matter of fact, Augustine did recognize a difference between them; but in his eyes, while the latter group sinned less grievously than the former, they were still guilty of grave sin. Here is his judgment on the case:

> Those who out of ignorance are baptized there [in a schismatic group], thinking it to be the church of Christ, commit a less grievous sin in comparison with those [guilty of initiating the schism]; and yet, they also are wounded by the sacrilege of schism. One cannot say that they are not gravely hurt by it, on the grounds that others are more gravely hurt.[12]

The question remains whether Augustine admitted the possibility that some Christians belonging to separated groups might be in such good faith that they could be saved outside the Catholic Church. A passage that seems to favor this view is found in a letter which he wrote to several Donatists. There he said:

> The Apostle Paul said: "As for a man that is a heretic, after admonishing him once or twice, have nothing more to do with him" (Tit 3:10). But those who maintain their own opinion, however false and perverted, without obstinate ill will, especially those who have not originated the error by bold presumption, but have received it from parents who had been led astray and had lapsed . . . those who seek the truth with careful industry and are ready to be corrected when they have found it, are not to be rated among heretics.[13]

Does Augustine mean that such people can be saved outside the Catholic Church? The context of the letter shows that what he had in mind was to defend himself against the accusation that in writing this letter, he was disobeying the scriptural injunction to have nothing to do with heretics. In other words, he was saying that the men to whom he was writing this letter were not the kind of heretics with whom a Christian must have nothing to do. On the other hand, later passages of the same letter show that he was far from optimistic about their chances of salvation if they remained in their sect. On the contrary, that he saw them in danger of losing their souls is clear from his warning: "It is not a question of danger to your gold or silver, your land or your farms or even your bodily health; we are calling on your souls to grasp eternal life and avoid everlasting death."[14] His final words to them are even stronger:

> God sees that nothing forces you to remain in that pestilential and sacrilegious state of schism; you can be free of it if, for the sake of gaining a spiritual kingdom, you would overcome a worldly attraction and if, for the sake of avoiding eternal punishments, you would not fear to offend the friendship of men which will profit you nothing in the judgment of God.[15]

St. Augustine's way of speaking of some people as being apparently "inside" but really "outside," and of others as being apparently "outside" but really "inside" the church has led some to conclude that he admitted the possibility that some people who were separated from the Catholic Church might nevertheless be enjoying the friendship of God and on the way to salvation. However, for Augustine, this distinction is based on the foreknowledge of God, as is clear from the following passage:

> There are some of that number [of those who will be saved] who at present are living sinful lives, or are even wallowing in heresies or in pagan superstitions, and yet even there "the Lord knows who are his own," for, in that ineffable foreknowledge of God, many who seem to be outside are really inside, and many who seem to be inside are outside.[16]

Furthermore, Augustine was convinced that if anyone who was now "outside" by reason of heresy or schism was "inside" by reason of God's foreknowledge, that person would inevitably be joined to the Catholic Church before he or she died.

> But if it be the case that some of those people [presently separated] belong to us in the hidden foreknowledge of God, it is necessary that they should return to us. How many who do not belong to us still seem to be within, and how many who do belong to us still seem to be outside. "The Lord knows who are his own." And those who are within but do not belong to us, when the occasion presents itself, will go out; and those who

belong to us, but are now outside, when they find the occasion, will return.[17]

While it goes against our ecumenical sensibilities, we have to recognize the fact that St. Augustine held out little hope for the salvation of any Christian who died in a state of separation from the Catholic Church. As we shall now see, he held out even less hope for the salvation of those who in his day had still not accepted Christian faith and baptism.

No Salvation for Jews and Pagans

As we have seen, St. Augustine was convinced that even during the pre-Christian era there had been no salvation except through faith in Christ. Needless to say, he was all the more convinced that this was true now that the gospel had been preached and the church established. Augustine applied with total rigor the text of Mark 16:15–16: "Go into the whole world and proclaim the gospel to every creature. Whoever believes and is baptized will be saved; whoever does not believe will be condemned." Augustine was convinced that those who had heard the message of the gospel and had not become Christians must be guilty of sinful rejection of the faith, and of the church in which alone salvation could be found. Their damnation would be the result of their misuse of their free will, as we see in the following passage.

> "God wants all to be saved and come to the knowledge of the truth" (1 Tim 2:4), but not in such a way that he takes away their free will, whose good or bad use brings upon them a just judgment. Hence, unbelievers act against the will of God, when they do not believe in the gospel message. They do not triumph over it, but rather they defraud themselves of a great, indeed, of the greatest good, and involve themselves in great evils. They have to experience in suffering the power of him whose mercy and gifts they have contemned.[18]

As one might expect, Augustine numbered unconverted Jews among those guilty of contemning the mercy and gifts of God by their refusal to accept Christian faith. While exhorting his flock to show great love for the Jews, he left no doubt as to his judgment about the guilt of Jews who continued to reject Christ.

> Dearly beloved, whether the Jews receive these divine testimonies with joy or with indignation, nevertheless, when we can, let us proclaim them with great love for the Jews. Let us not proudly glory against the broken branches; let us rather reflect by whose grace it is, and by much mercy, and on what root, we have been ingrafted. Then, not savoring of pride, but with a deep sense of humility, not insulting with presumption, but rejoicing with trembling, let us say: "Come ye and let us walk in the light of the Lord," because "his name is great among the Gentiles." If they hear and obey, they will be among them to whom the Scripture says: "Come ye to him and be enlightened, and your faces shall not be confounded." If, however, they hear and do not obey, if they see and are jealous, they are among them of whom the psalm says: "The wicked shall see and shall be angry, he shall gnash his teeth and pine away."[19]

"No Salvation for Unbelievers"—Even for Those Who Had No Chance To Hear the Gospel Preached

We have seen in the previous chapter that toward the end of the fourth century there was a rather general belief among Christians that by now everyone had had a chance to hear the gospel, so that no unbeliever could escape condemnation on the grounds of inculpable ignorance of the Christian faith. It would seem that in his earlier period, Augustine may have shared this view. However, at a certain point in his career he became aware of the fact that there were still tribes in Africa, beyond the limits of the Roman empire, to whom the gospel had not yet been preached. In other words, he had become aware of the existence of large numbers of people who had still had no opportunity to come to Christian faith. He spoke of this in a letter which he wrote to assure a bishop that the end of the world was not imminent, since the gospel had not yet been preached in the whole world. He wrote:

> Here in our own land, that is, in Africa, there are countless barbarian tribes among whom the gospel has not been preached. We have daily evidence of this from the captives who are

brought from there and are now subjected to slave labor by the Romans.[20]

In another letter to the same bishop, Augustine spoke of areas of the world that had not been explored, so that it was impossible to say how many nations there might be to whom the gospel had not yet been preached.[21]

Much earlier than this, in his letter to Deogratias, referring to Gentiles who might have had no chance to come to saving faith, Augustine insisted that no one lacked this opportunity who was worthy of it, and that if God refused it to anyone, it was because he foresaw that if it were offered the person would refuse it. In other words, Augustine's earlier solution was to lay the blame on the individual for the fact that the opportunity to come to faith was not given to him.

In his later, anti-Pelagian period, Augustine proposed a new solution to this problem: namely, that the universally contracted guilt of original sin was sufficient to justify God in condemning not only infants who died without baptism, but also adults who died in ignorance of the Christian faith. There is good reason to believe that it was his effort to reconcile the exclusion of these two categories of people from salvation with the justice of God that led St. Augustine to his theory about the consequences of original sin for the whole human race.

St. Augustine was firmly convinced that those who were outside the church through lack of faith and baptism could not be saved, and he knew of no alternative between salvation and condemnation to hell. It was only centuries later that the idea of "limbo" for infants dying unbaptized would gain currency. In Augustine's view, such infants, excluded from salvation for lack of baptism, must be in hell, to suffer, as he put it, "the mildest punishment of all."[22] Reflecting on what he understood to be the certainty that infants dying without baptism and adults dying in ignorance of the Christian faith must certainly be damned, Augustine came to the conclusion that if God is just in condemning such as these, it must follow that he would be just if he were to condemn the whole human race to hell. The guilt that would justify God if he chose to do this could only be the guilt of original sin. And thus Augustine arrived at his idea that all the descendants of Adam constitute a *massa damnata*, deserving to be condemned to hell, so that if some are spared, it is by the sheer mercy of God. Here are two examples of Augustine's thinking on this matter.

> Now this grace of Christ, without which neither infants nor adults can be saved, is not given in return for merits, but is a free gift; for this reason it is called "grace." Wherefore, all those who are not set free by that grace, whether because they could not hear [the message of the Gospel], or because they refused to obey it, or, being unable to hear it because of their infancy, they did not receive the baptismal bath by which they could have been saved—all these, I say, are justly damned, because they are not without sin—either the original sin that they contracted, or the sins that they added by their own wicked deeds. . . . The entire mass, therefore, incurs the penalty, and if the deserved punishment of condemnation were meted out to all, it would without doubt be justly meted out. . . . Anyone who judged rightly could not possibly blame the justice of God in wholly condemning all mankind.[23]

> If, as truth itself tells us, no one is delivered from the condemnation that we incurred through Adam except through faith in Jesus Christ, and yet, those people will not be able to deliver themselves from that condemnation who will be able to say that they have not heard the Gospel of Christ, since faith comes through hearing. . . . Therefore neither those who have never heard the Gospel nor those who by reason of their infancy were unable to believe . . . are separated from that mass which will certainly be damned.[24]

Augustine's Interpretation of the Salvific Will of God

A further consequence of Augustine's reasoning about the certain damnation of infants dying without baptism and adults dying in ignorance of the Christian faith was that he did not see how it could be true that God wills that all be saved. His concept of the will of God was that it must always be efficacious; that is, whatever God truly wills must necessarily happen as he wills it. Since Augustine was sure that these infants and adults would not be saved, he did not see how God could be said to will their salvation. This led him to interpret 1 Timothy 2:4, "Who wishes all to be saved and to come to the knowledge of the truth," in such a way as to deny that God willed the salvation of those who Augustine was certain would not be saved. Here is one of his explanations of that text.

> In the words: "Who wishes all to be saved and come to the knowledge of the truth," the "all" means the many whom He wishes to come to grace. It is much better to take it this way, because no one comes but those whom He wishes to come. "No one can come to me," the Son says, "unless the Father who sent me draw him," and "No one can come to me unless it be given him by my Father." Therefore all are saved and come to the knowledge of the truth at His willing it, and all come at His willing it. For those such as infants who do not as yet have the use of free will are regenerated by the will of Him through whose creative power they are generated, and those who have the actual use of free will cannot exercise it except through the will and assistance of Him by whom the will is prepared. If you ask me why He does not change the wills of all who are unwilling, I shall answer: Why does He not adopt through the bath of regeneration all infants who will die, whose wills are quiescent, and therefore not contrary? If you found this too profound for you to investigate, it is profound for both of us, in both aspects: namely, why, both in adults and in infants, God wishes to help one and does not help another. Nevertheless, we hold it to be certain and everlastingly firm, that there is no injustice with God, so that He should condemn anyone who had done no wrong, and there is goodness with God by which He delivers many without personal merit. In those He condemns we see what is due to all, so that those He delivers may thence learn what due penalty was relaxed in their regard and what undue grace was given them.[25]

Followers of Augustine

Reactions against the more extreme elements of Augustine's anti-Pelagian theology led some Catholics, especially leaders of the monastic movement in southern France, to what has become known as "semi-Pelagianism." While these people insisted that God's salvific will was truly universal, and rejected the idea that God predestines some people to eternal damnation, they also agreed with St. Augustine on the absolute necessity of grace for salvation. However, they also insisted that the divine distribution of grace must correspond not simply to God's inscrutable choice, but also to the prior dispositions of the person, so that one could dispose oneself to receive grace, and thus merit the beginning of faith and salvation. (This doctrine was rejected by the Council of Orange in 529.)[26]

A faithful follower of Augustine, St. Prosper of Aquitaine in France, brought this to Augustine's attention toward the end of the latter's life, and then wrote against it himself. But Prosper showed himself capable of discerning between the essential doctrine of Augustine on the absolute primacy of grace, without which no human effort is capable of accomplishing any step toward salvation, and some of the consequences which Augustine thought must be drawn from this principle. For instance, Augustine thought that the principle of the absolute gratuitousness of grace meant that God must be free to deny the grace necessary for salvation to anyone he chooses, without any consideration of the personal merits of the person. He held that this denial of grace, having the inevitable consequence of eternal damnation, would be justified by the guilt of original sin which all mankind has inherited from Adam. It must be admitted that the idea of God's choice to deny the grace necessary for salvation, without any consideration of the personal merits of the person, with the consequence of eternal damnation for that person so denied grace, comes awfully close to the idea of predestination to eternal damnation.

Prosper's instincts were against such a concept, and to his credit he departed from his master on this point. While defending God's freedom to distribute his grace as he chose, Prosper insisted that God made a universal offer of "general" grace, while reserving "special" graces to those whom he chose to favor with such gifts. In this way, Prosper could defend the universal salvific will of God, expressed in the offer of "general" grace to all without exception. A work of this period, now generally attributed to Prosper of Aquitaine, is entitled *The Call of All Nations.*[27] In this work Prosper again and again insists that God sincerely wills that all should be saved, while admitting that the fate of infants dying without baptism remains an insoluble mystery which we can only leave to the wisdom and mercy of God.[28] On the other hand, he clearly departs from

Augustine's later solution to the problem of those who die as unbelievers because they have never had a chance to hear the gospel. On this question, Prosper's first principle is that Christ died not only for believers, but for unbelievers and sinners.

> There can be no reason to doubt that Jesus Christ our Lord died for the unbelievers and the sinners. If there had been any one who did not belong to these, then Christ would not have died for all. But he did die for all men without exception. . . . No one of the ungodly, who differed only in their degree of unbelief, could be saved without Christ's redemption. This redemption spread throughout the world to become the good news for all men without exception.[29]

However, Prosper was aware that in his own day there were still nations which had not yet had the opportunity to hear the good news of Christ's redemption. His solution to this problem is vastly different from that of Augustine.

> It may be true that, just as we know that in former times some peoples were not admitted to the fellowship of the sons of God, so also today there are in the remotest parts of the world some nations who have not yet seen the light of the grace of the Saviour. But we have no doubt that in God's hidden judgment, for them also a time of calling has been appointed, when they will hear and accept the Gospel which now remains unknown to them. Even now they receive that measure of general help which heaven has always bestowed on all men. Human nature, it is true, has been wounded by such a severe wound that natural speculation cannot lead a person to the full knowledge of God if the true light does not dispel all darkness from his heart. In his inscrutable designs the good and just God did not shed this light as abundantly in the past ages as he does in our own day.[30]

For Prosper, the "abundant light" which provides the "full knowledge" of God, is an instance of the "special grace" which God freely bestows when and on whom he chooses. It is only since Christ came that this special grace has been granted to the Gentiles.

The Scriptures prove beyond doubt that the great wealth, power and beneficence of grace which in these last times calls all the Gentiles into the kingdom of Christ, was in former centuries hidden in the secret counsel of God. No knowledge can comprehend, no understanding can penetrate the reason why this abundance of grace which has now come to the knowledge of all nations, was not revealed to them before. Yet we believe with complete trust in God's goodness that "he wills all to be saved and to come to the knowledge of the truth." This we must hold as his changeless will from eternity, which manifests itself in the different measures in which he in his wisdom chose to augment his general gifts with special favours. Thus those who did not share in his grace plead guilty of malice, and those who were resplendent with its light cannot glory in their own merit but only in the Lord.[31]

The last sentence here suggests that for Prosper, the general grace which the Gentiles received before the special grace of the light of the gospel was given to them was sufficient for their salvation, and that if they were condemned by God, it was due to their own malice, and not, as Augustine would say in his later works, to the inherited guilt of original sin.

However, other followers of St. Augustine were not so discerning as Prosper of Aquitaine. One who followed Augustine to the last iota of his anti-Pelagian teaching, and even expressed it in its most radical form, was a North African bishop like Augustine: Fulgentius of Ruspe (468–533). Here is a passage of a work of Fulgentius entitled *On the Truth of Predestination*, which will show how faithfully he followed the lead of St. Augustine.

If it were true that God universally willed that all should be saved and come to the knowledge of the truth, how is it that Truth itself has hidden from some men the mystery of his knowledge? Surely, to those whom he denied such knowledge, he also denies salvation. . . . Therefore, he willed to save those to whom he gave knowledge of the mystery of salvation, and he did not wish to save those to whom he denied the knowledge of the saving mystery. If he had intended the salvation of both, he would have given the knowledge of the truth to both.[32]

The following statement by Fulgentius was destined to enter into the history of our question in an extraordinary way, as it was incorporated into a decree of the Council of Florence in 1442.

> Most firmly hold and by no means doubt, that not only all pagans, but also all Jews, and all heretics and schismatics who die outside the Catholic Church, will go to the eternal fire that was prepared for the devil and his angels.[33]

We conclude this chapter devoted to St. Augustine and his followers with the observation that, despite his enormous influence on the future of Christian thought, some of Augustine's views did not so prevail as to become part of the mainstream Christian tradition. One was his idea that God would condemn unbaptized infants to hell for the inherited guilt of original sin. Another was that, likewise for the guilt of original sin, God would justly condemn adults who had never had a chance to hear the gospel and thus to make an act of saving faith. And a third was Augustine's conclusion that there were some people whom God simply did not wish to be saved. As we shall find in the next chapter, the mainstream Christian tradition found a better, if not an ideal, solution to the problem of infants dying without baptism; it insisted that God would come to the aid of a person who was inculpably ignorant of the faith; and it took seriously the biblical assurance that "God desires all to be saved and to come to the knowledge of the truth" (1 Tim 2:4).

4 ‖ Medieval Councils, Popes and Theologians

A ninth century Saxon monk named Gottschalk, who was an avid reader of the anti-Pelagian works of St. Augustine and those of Fulgentius of Ruspe, published a work whose thesis was that since God predestined some people to eternal damnation, it could not be said that God willed the salvation of all, or that Christ had suffered for the redemption of all. Hincmar, archbishop of Reims, in whose diocese Gottschalk's monastery was located, summoned a local council at Quiercy-sur-Oise in the year 849, at which Gottschalk's doctrine was condemned. However, to some of Hincmar's contemporaries it seemed that to condemn Gottschalk was to question the authority of St. Augustine himself. To justify the sentence against Gottschalk, Hincmar wrote his *Treatise on predestination and free will*,[1] in defense of the universality of God's salvific will, and summoned a second council to decide the matter. This council, held at Quiercy in 853, declared the following propositions to express the true Catholic doctrine.

> Almighty God wills the salvation of all without exception, even though not all are saved. The fact that some are saved is the gift of the saviour; the fact that some perish is their own just deserts.

> Just as there is, has been, and will be no man whose nature was not assumed by Christ Jesus Our Lord, so also there is, has been and will be no man for whom He did not suffer, even though not all are redeemed by the mystery of his passion.

> The fact that not all are redeemed by the mystery of his passion does not have to do with the greatness or abundance of the price

44

paid, but with the part of the unbelievers, and those who do not believe with that faith "which works through love" (Gal 5:6).[2]

There is little doubt that the decrees of this council reflect the doctrine of Hincmar, which he showed, in his writings on predestination and free will, to be well founded in the teaching of the fathers, and especially in that of the bishops of Rome.

If he had been aware of it, Hincmar could also have appealed to the doctrine of the last of the doctors of the eastern church, St. John of Damascus, who lived in the century before Hincmar. It was John Damascene, as he is usually called, whose distinction between the antecedent and the consequent will became the generally accepted way of reconciling the universality of God's salvific will with the fact that not all are saved. Here is how he explained the distinction.

> One must know that with his antecedent will, God wills that all should be saved and share his kingdom. For he did not create us in order to punish us, but, being good, in order that we might partake of his goodness. However, being just, he wills that sinners be punished. The first will of God is called "antecedent"; this is God's good pleasure, and proceeds from God himself. The second, however, called the "consequent" will, proceeds from our cause. This is God's will to punish us for sin, either with salutary punishment for our emendation, or with reprobation to final punishment. But God does not will our sins at all, either antecedently or consequently; he only permits them to our free will.[3]

The fact that in the eastern church there had never been any doubt about the universality of God's salvific will, and that the controversy raised by Gottschalk in the west had been settled in favor of the doctrine of Hincmar of Reims, meant that for the medieval theologians there was no question of returning to St. Augustine's later exegesis of 1 Timothy 2:4. His theory of a less-than-universal salvific will did not prevail to become part of the main-line Christian tradition. There was a clear consensus among medieval theologians that God's "antecedent" salvific will is truly universal.

Another of Augustine's views which did not survive was that infants who died unbaptized would suffer (mitigated) punishment in hell for the guilt of original sin. It was St. Anselm (1033–1109) who provided the key to the solution of this problem, with his insight that original sin consists in the privation of the original justice of our first parents. From this premise, Peter Abelard (1079–1142) drew the conclusion that the consequence of original sin, for infants dying unbaptized, would be simply the privation of the beatific vision, and not the positive punishment due to personal sin. Abelard's conclusion was confirmed by Peter Lombard, whose *Book of Sentences,* completed in 1158, became the standard textbook of theology for the middle ages and beyond.

Lombard's influence was such that his doctrine on the fate of unbaptized infants was taken up and confirmed by Pope Innocent III in a letter which he wrote to the bishop of Arles in 1201. The pope wrote: "The punishment of original sin is the lack of the vision of God; that of actual sin is the torment of everlasting hell."[4] After this papal approval of the medieval theologians' solution to the problem of the fate of unbaptized infants (subsequently known as the "limbo" solution), the rigorous doctrine of St. Augustine on this question was generally abandoned. The Catholic Church has never definitively declared the "limbo" solution to be the true one, but it has defended it against the Jansenists who claimed that it involved something of the heresy of Pelagianism.[5]

It is not my intention in this book to follow the further discussion, among Catholic theologians, of the question concerning the fate of unbaptized infants. There has been, and still is, a lively discussion of this problem, but an adequate treatment of it would unduly extend the limits of the present work. I intend to limit myself to the development of thinking about the salvation of adults who die "outside the church." For this development, the significance of the rejection of St. Augustine's view that unbaptized infants would suffer the pains of hell lies in the fact that it involved a consensus, among medieval theologians, that God does not inflict the pains of hell for any other cause than the guilt of personal sin. As can easily be seen, this consensus also involved the rejection of St. Augustine's idea that God would condemn, possibly for original sin alone, adults who had never had the opportunity to hear the gospel and make an act of Christian faith. The common view of medieval theologians was that the only unbelief that would warrant the pains of hell was the personal sin of infidelity.

So far in this chapter we have seen how the development of

Christian thinking, despite the massive influence of St. Augustine, involved the elimination of some elements of his theology which constituted grave obstacles to a more positive approach to the problem of salvation for those outside the church. Of primary importance, in this respect, was the achievement of a consensus among medieval theologians that God's salvific will is truly universal, and that he does not condemn anyone to the pains of hell who is not guilty of grave personal sin.

It is time now to discuss the teaching of these medieval theologians in detail. My intention here is to limit myself to a discussion of the teaching of St. Thomas Aquinas. I do not think any apology is needed for making this choice. I shall treat the thought of St. Thomas in much the same way as I treated that of St. Augustine: dividing the material into several parts, according to the various aspects of the question. We shall begin by seeing how he applied the traditional axiom: "No salvation outside the church."[6]

"No Salvation Outside the Church" in the Writings of St. Thomas

In our first chapter we saw that one of the papal and conciliar affirmations of the axiom "No salvation outside the church" was made in the decree *Firmiter* of Pope Innocent III at the Fourth Lateran Council in the year 1215. St. Thomas wrote a commentary on that decree, in which he had the following to say:

> Next, he [Pope Innocent] comes to the article about the effect of grace. First, he speaks of the effect of grace with regard to the unity of the church, saying: "There is one universal church of the faithful, outside of which no one at all is saved." Now the unity of the church primarily depends on its unity of faith, for the church is nothing other than the congregation of the faithful. Since it is impossible to please God without faith, there can be no place of salvation other than in the church. Furthermore, the salvation of the faithful is consummated through the sacraments of the church, in which the power of Christ's passion is operative.[7]

A point to note in Thomas' commentary here is that he gives reasons why there is no salvation outside the church: it is because it is only in the church that one finds the faith and the sacraments which are the necessary means for achieving salvation.

In his commentary on the *Book of Sentences* of Peter Lombard, Thomas observes, concerning the sacrament of the eucharist:

> The *res* of this sacrament is the unity of the church, outside of which there is neither salvation nor life.[8]

In medieval terminology, the *res* (reality) of a sacrament is the grace which it signifies and effects; here again a reason is given for the necessity of being in the church: to participate in the grace of the eucharist.

Again, the eucharist provides the context for the application of the axiom, in his commentary on the gospel of John:

> He eats the body of Christ and drinks his blood spiritually who participates in the unity of the church, which is a unity of love. . . . He who does not eat in this way is outside the church, and, consequently, outside of love, for this reason he has no life in him.[9]

In his commentary on the Apostles' Creed, explaining the article on the "one church," Thomas says:

> No one ought to despise the church, or allow himself to be cast out and expelled from her, because there is only one church in which men are saved, just as no one could be saved who was outside the ark of Noah.[10]

As we have seen, the analogy between the church and the ark of Noah, as the sole place where salvation could be found, was an ancient one, and it is not surprising that St. Thomas made use of it. It occurs again in Thomas' last work, his *Summa theologiae*, where he is speaking of the eucharist:

> The *res* of this sacrament is the unity of the church, without which there can be no salvation; for no one can find salvation outside the church, just as there was none apart from the ark of Noah, which signifies the church.[11]

It is noteworthy that almost every time that St. Thomas spoke of the necessity of being in the church for salvation, he explained this as based on the necessity of sharing in the means of salvation, such as faith and sacraments. This suggests that to understand his teaching on the necessity of the church, we should begin by seeing how he explained the necessity of Christian faith and baptism for salvation. We shall begin with his treatment of the necessity of faith in Christ.

St. Thomas on the Necessity of Faith in Christ

St. Thomas followed St. Augustine in holding that salutary faith had always, in some sense, been faith not only in God, but also in Christ as the one mediator of salvation. However, an important development in Thomas' understanding of this was his recognition that faith in the one mediator could be implicitly contained in that faith in God which is described in Hebrews 11:6, "Whoever would draw near to God must believe that he exists and that he is the rewarder of those who seek him." In fact, Thomas held that all the articles of faith are implicitly contained in this verse of scripture, which speaks of God's existence and his providence for the salvation of humanity. As he explained it, the truth that God exists implicitly includes everything pertaining to the divine being, and that he is the rewarder of those who seek him includes everything that pertains to the economy of salvation. Since the economy of salvation includes Christ as mediator of salvation for mankind, St. Thomas understood faith in God as "rewarder" (faith in divine providence) implicitly to include faith in Christ.[12]

As we shall see, Thomas admitted that in some cases a faith in Christ that was only implicit could suffice; however, referring to faith in the existence and providence of God as described in Hebrews 11:6, he declared:

> It must be said that in every age and for everyone, it has always been necessary to believe explicitly in these two things.[13]

It was an absolute principle with St. Thomas that no one has ever been saved without faith in the existence and providence of God. It was likewise an absolute principle with him that "no one has ever had the grace of the Holy Spirit except through faith in Christ, either explicit or implicit."[14]

The question, then, is: For whom, and under what conditions, would merely implicit faith in Christ suffice? First, St. Thomas admitted the sufficiency of such implicit faith in Christ for Gentiles before the Christian era: if not for all of them, at least for the ordinary folk to whom no revelation of the future messiah had come. Thomas believed that "many of the Gentiles had received revelations about Christ"; however, he added:

> If some Gentiles were saved, without receiving any revelation [about Christ], they were not saved without faith in the Mediator. Because even though they did not have explicit faith, they did have a faith that was implicit in their faith in divine providence, believing that God is the liberator of mankind in ways that He himself chooses.[15]

In other words, for most Gentiles who were saved before the coming of Christ, implicit faith in Christ had sufficed. St. Thomas admits the sufficiency of such faith also in the case of the centurion Cornelius, who, before he had heard the gospel from St. Peter, was already pleasing to God. Thomas explains:

> At that time, Cornelius was not an unbeliever, else his works would not have been acceptable to God, whom none can please without faith. However, he then had implicit faith [in Christ], when the truth of the Gospel had not yet been manifested to him. Hence Peter was sent to him, to give him full instruction in the faith.[16]

Thus, for St. Thomas, implicit faith in Christ sufficed not only for Gentiles who lived before the coming of Christ, but also for Cornelius who lived after the coming of Christ, but had not yet heard the gospel preached. This raises an interesting question: How long did such a possibility last, for people who had not yet heard the gospel? Cornelius was in a unique position, being the first Gentile to whom the gospel was announced. Did St. Thomas believe that in his own day, there were still people to whom the gospel had not yet been announced? And if so, did he believe that for them, too, implicit faith in Christ would suffice for justification? There are several elements in his writings that have to be taken into consideration with regard to this question.

St. Thomas on the Necessity of Explicit Christian Faith

While St. Thomas allowed for the sufficiency of implicit faith in Christ before the gospel had been promulgated, he was categorical in asserting the necessity of explicit Christian faith in his own day.

> After grace had been revealed, all, both the learned and the simple, are bound to have explicit faith in the mysteries of Christ, especially with regard to those mysteries which are publicly and solemnly celebrated in the church, such as those which refer to the mystery of the incarnation.[17]

How absolute his conviction was on that score is illustrated by the response which he gave to the problem raised by the possibility that even in his own day there might be someone who had had no chance to hear the message about Christ. His response, that God would provide the means by which such a person could arrive at explicit faith in Christ, shows how exceptionless he believed the necessity of that faith to be. On the other hand, his response also involved his conviction about the universality of God's salvific will. We shall first see how he expressed his conviction about this, and then see how he applied this principle to the problem posed by those who had no opportunity to believe in Christ since the gospel had never been preached to them.

St. Thomas on the Universal Salvific Will of God

With medieval theologians generally, St. Thomas took seriously the universality of God's salvific will, understanding this to mean that God offers the grace necessary for salvation to everyone who does not personally put an obstacle in the way. Here are some texts of St. Thomas on this point.

In those things which are necessary for salvation, God is never wanting and has never been wanting to a person who was seeking his salvation, unless this was due to the person's own fault.[18]

It belongs to divine providence to provide for each person what is necessary for salvation, unless the obstacle comes from the person himself.[19]

Since the ability to impede or not to impede the reception of divine grace is within the scope of free choice, not undeservedly is responsibility for the fault imputed to him who offers an impediment to the reception of grace. In fact, as far as He is concerned, God is ready to give grace to all, indeed "He wills all men to be saved, and to come to the knowledge of the truth" as is said in 1 Timothy. But those alone are deprived of grace who offer an obstacle within themselves to grace, just as, while the sun is shining on the world, the man who keeps his eyes closed is held responsible for his fault, if, as a result, some harm follows, even though he would not be able to see unless he were provided in advance with light from the sun.[20]

It belongs to the mercy of Him who *wills that all should be saved* (1 Tim 2:4) that in those things that are necessary for salvation, a person should easily find the remedy.[21]

In the above texts, we see that the universality of God's salvific will means concretely that God offers the grace necessary for salvation to everyone who does not put an obstacle in the way through personal fault. The same idea is put more succinctly by Aquinas and the other medieval theologians, with their axiom: *Facienti quod in se est, Deus non denegat gratiam* (To one who does what lies in his power, God does not deny grace). We must now see how Aquinas applied it to the case of a person who had no opportunity to hear the Christian message and arrive at the explicit faith in Christ, without which he held that no one in his own day could be justified and saved.

The Problem of People Who Had Not Heard the Gospel

Along with other medieval theologians, St. Thomas, at least in his earlier writings, presumed that practically everyone had had an adequate opportunity to hear the Christian message, so that a case of truly invincible ignorance of the basic elements of Christian faith would be very rare indeed. Needless to say, we have to try to grasp the mentality of medieval Christians, whose vision was circumscribed by the limits of the world known to them. In this world they knew that, besides Christians, there were also Jews and Moslems; but they believed that both Jews and Moslems had heard enough about Christ so that they could not claim the excuse of invincible ignorance for their lack of faith in him. Medieval Christians could hardly conceive of anyone being completely ignorant about Christ, unless it were a person totally isolated from the civilized world. And so the problem about the salvation of a person who had heard nothing about Christ was presented by medieval theologians as the case of a child who had been brought up in the wilderness, or among brute beasts. St. Thomas' conviction that, on the one hand, explicit faith in Christ was necessary, and on the other that God would not leave a sincere person without the means necessary for his salvation, led him to offer the following solution to this case.

> The exposition of what must be believed for salvation would be provided to that person by God, either by a preacher of the faith, as in the case of Cornelius, or by a revelation, so that it would then be within the power of the free will to make an act of faith.[22]

> If anyone were brought up in the wilderness or among brute animals, provided that he followed his natural reason in seeking the good and avoiding evil, we must most certainly hold that God would either reveal to him, by an inner inspiration, what must be believed, or would send a preacher to him, as he sent Peter to Cornelius.[23]

In his *Commentary on Romans*, St. Thomas brought up the same case, but did not mention the possibility that God would provide by way of revelation or inspiration; here he said only that God would send someone to preach the gospel to such a person brought up in the wilderness, provided that he were doing what he could with the grace he received from God.[24]

Finally, in the *Summa theologiae* we find a different treatment of the problem. Here there is no mention of the "child brought up in the wilderness," but, in general terms, of those who have heard nothing about the faith. What is more important, in the *Summa*, which is the most mature work of St. Thomas, there is no mention of the idea that if such people were doing what lay in their power, God would surely provide the means whereby they would be given the opportunity to come to explicit faith in Christ. Here the solution seems to be a more Augustinian one; in fact, a work of St. Augustine is cited as the authority for it. To the objection that people who have not had a chance to hear the gospel cannot be obliged to have explicit faith, Thomas replies:

> Man is obliged to do many things that he cannot do without healing grace, such as to love God and his neighbor, and likewise to believe articles of faith. Now, to whom the divine help is given, it is given out of God's mercy, and to whom it is denied, it is denied out of his justice, as a punishment for previous sin, at least original sin, as Augustine says, in his book *De correptione et gratia*.[25]

The idea that God could justly deny necessary grace as a punishment for personal sin is merely the reverse of the axiom that God does not deny grace to one who does what is in his power to do. But that God could justly deny necessary grace as a punishment for original sin alone is quite a different idea, which St. Thomas derived from one of St. Augustine's anti-Pelagian works, with which he became more acquainted in the course of his career.

This has led to speculation whether Thomas, when writing the *Summa*, may no longer have been confident that God would send a preacher, to provide that a person who was "doing what lay in his power" would not lack the possibility of coming to explicit faith in Christ. J. de Guibert suggested that in the course of his life, Thomas may have come to realize that not only the rare "child brought up in the wilderness" but whole nations still had never heard the gospel preached, and that to solve the problem he resorted to the Augustinian solution, that their ignorance of the gospel could be understood as a punishment for sin, at least original sin.[26] However, other Thomistic scholars have rejected de Guibert's theory, noting that in his *Commentary on Romans*, from the same period as the *Summa*, St. Thomas still proposed the more positive solution, which shows that he continued to maintain his conviction about the universality of God's salvific will. We have also quoted a text from the *Summa*, which asserts that because it is God's will that all be saved, it belongs to his mercy to provide that in those things that are necessary for salvation, a person will easily find the remedy.[27] At the same time, de Guibert has raised an interesting question, as to whether St. Thomas, during his career, came to realize that there were nations to whom the gospel had still not been preached.

St. Thomas on the Knowledge of the Gospel in His Day

The common assumption of medieval theologians seems to have been that the gospel had been preached everywhere, and that it would be only the rare exception (the child brought up in the wilderness) if someone had not heard about Christ. But there are some reasons to think that Aquinas may have come to know that this was not so rare. First of all, in the thirteenth century, Franciscan and Dominican missionaries had penetrated quite far into Asia, and Marco Polo came back from China. However, St. Thomas makes no reference to this in his writings. On the other hand, in his commentary on Psalm 48, he says:

> Faith in Christ flourishes principally among the people of the west, because in the northern regions there are still many Gentiles, and in the eastern lands there are many schismatics and infidels.[28]

The word "still" (*adhuc*) in reference to the Gentiles of "the northern regions" suggests that these people are still pagans, while the infidels "in the eastern lands" are more likely to be the Moslems. Now our question is: Did Thomas think of those Gentiles of "the northern regions" as people to whom the gospel had not yet been preached? A contemporary Dominican, named Humbert of the Romans, also spoke of pagans to be found in the northern regions, referring to them as idol-worshipers called *Phiteni*, whose conversion was hoped for.[29]

To the question whether, by his own day, the Gospel had been preached everywhere in the world, St. Thomas gave a nuanced answer, distinguishing between the "renown" (*notitia* or *fama*) of Christ which had penetrated every region of the world, and the preaching of the gospel "with full effect," which involved the establishment of the church.[30] St. Thomas held that the latter had not yet been accomplished everywhere, and that its accomplishment was a condition to be fulfilled before the final coming of the kingdom of God. St. Thomas further nuanced his opinion by saying that while the "renown" of the gospel had reached all nations, that did not mean that it had reached every individual; there might be some who, like the "child brought up in the wilderness," had heard nothing at all about Christ. In his *Commentary on Romans*, as we have seen, he added that to such individuals, if they were doing what lay in their power, God would send a preacher.

It seems clear that when St. Thomas spoke of people who had heard nothing about Christ, he was thinking of isolated individuals, rather than of whole nations, since he held that the "renown" of the gospel had actually penetrated to all nations by his day. Presumably, then, he thought that it had also reached those Gentiles of "the northern regions" of whom he spoke in his commentary on Psalm 48. Did he think that most of them, with perhaps a few isolated exceptions, had heard enough about Christ so that their unbelief in him was culpable? It must be admitted that we do not find a clear answer to this question in the writings of St. Thomas. But perhaps some light can be thrown on it by a consideration of his teaching about the various kinds of unbelief.

St. Thomas' Treatment of Unbelief (Infidelitas)

It would seem that for Aquinas, the only kind of unbelief that would not be culpable would be that of a person who had heard nothing about the faith. He explains:

> Unbelief may be taken in two ways: first, by way of pure negation, so that a man be called an unbeliever, merely because he does not have faith. Secondly, unbelief may be taken by way of opposition to the faith, in which sense a person refuses to hear the faith, or despises it, according to Isa. 53:1, "Who hath

believed our report?" It is this that completes the notion of unbelief, and it is in this sense that unbelief is a sin. If, however, we take it by way of pure negation, as we find it in those who have heard nothing about the faith, it bears the character not of sin, but of punishment, because such ignorance of divine things is a result of the sin of our first parent. Such unbelievers are damned on account of their other sins, which cannot be taken away without faith, but not on account of the sin of unbelief.[31]

From this it would seem that for St. Thomas, it is only a person who has heard nothing about Christ whose lack of Christian faith would be inculpable. Such a person would not be damned for lack of faith, but for personal sins, which "cannot be taken away without faith." Does this mean that everyone lacking faith would inevitably be damned for personal sins? Or would St. Thomas still admit that an individual whose lack of faith was inculpable might "do what lay in his power," and that to such an individual God would provide the means by which he could arrive at an act of saving faith? Again, we note the failure of the text of the *Summa* to mention this more optimistic solution, of which he had spoken elsewhere.

In any case, the lack of Christian faith on the part of anyone who had heard about Christ would involve the sin of unbelief, of which Thomas distinguishes three kinds.

> Since the sin of unbelief consists in rejection of the faith, it can take place in two ways: either one rejects the faith that has never been accepted, and this is the unbelief of pagans or Gentiles, or one rejects Christian faith that was once accepted. Either it was accepted in its prefiguration (*in figura*), and this is the unbelief of the Jews; or it was accepted in the very manifestation of the truth, and this is the unbelief of heretics.[32]

There can be no doubt about the fact that St. Thomas judged all Jews and heretics to be guilty of sinful unbelief, along with "Gentiles," such as the Moslems, who were thought to have heard enough about the Christian religion to be guilty of rejecting it. He went on to distinguish degrees of gravity of this sin, arguing that the sin of Christian heretics was the gravest of all.[33] On the other hand, he recognized that ignorance diminishes the gravity of the sin of unbelief, as we see in the following remark.

> Unbelief includes both ignorance, as an accessory thereto, and resistance to matters of faith, and in the latter respect it is a most grave sin. In respect, however, of this ignorance, it has a certain reason for excuse, especially when a man sins not from malice. . . .[34]

As we have already seen, St. Thomas recognized the possibility that someone might be so totally ignorant of the faith that his unbelief would be simply inculpable. At the same time, it seems clear that he shared, with his contemporaries, the view that no Jews or Moslems would have such an excuse, or would escape the just condemnation for their rejection of the Christian faith.

It will be recalled that at the beginning of our treatment of St. Thomas, we noted that he based the necessity of being in the church on the necessity of faith and sacraments. Having at some length considered his doctrine regarding the necessity of faith for salvation, we can be more brief in our treatment of his teaching about the necessity of the sacraments. We begin with the sacrament of baptism.

St. Thomas on the Necessity of Baptism for Salvation

St. Thomas bases this necessity on the nature of baptism as the sacrament of incorporation into Christ. To the question whether all are bound to receive baptism, he replies:

> I answer that men are bound to that without which they cannot obtain salvation. Now it is manifest that no one can obtain salvation except through Christ. . . . The purpose for which baptism is conferred on a man, is that being regenerated thereby, he may be incorporated in Christ, being made one of his members. . . . Consequently it is manifest that all are bound to be baptized, and that without baptism there is no salvation for anyone.[35]

However, the next article shows that it is possible to attain salvation without having actually received the sacrament of baptism. To the question whether a person can be saved without baptism, he replies:

> The sacrament of baptism may be wanting to someone in two ways. First, both in reality and in desire (*et re et voto*), as is the case with those who neither are baptized, nor wish to be baptized: which clearly indicates contempt of the sacrament, in regard to those who have the use of free will. Consequently those to whom baptism is wanting thus, cannot obtain salvation: since neither sacramentally nor mentally are they incorporated in Christ, through whom alone can salvation be obtained. Secondly, the sacrament of baptism may be wanting to someone in reality but not in desire: for instance, when someone wishes to be baptized, but by some ill-chance is overtaken by death before receiving baptism. Such a person can obtain salvation without being actually baptized, on account of the person's desire for baptism, which desire is the outcome of faith that works through charity, whereby God, whose power is not tied to visible sacraments, sanctifies a person inwardly.[36]

From this we see that while incorporation into Christ is necessary for salvation, this incorporation may take place "mentally," through a desire for baptism that is based in faith and charity. Furthermore, St. Thomas teaches that the desire for baptism which can suffice for the forgiveness of sins can be either explicit or implicit. To the objection that baptism is not necessary, since one can already have obtained the forgiveness of sins before being actually baptized, St. Thomas replies:

> A person receives the forgiveness of sins before baptism in so far as he has baptism of desire, explicitly or implicitly; and yet when he actually receives baptism, he receives a fuller remission, for the remission of the entire punishment. So also Cornelius and others like him receive grace and virtues through their faith in Christ and their desire for baptism, implicit or explicit; but afterwards when baptized, they receive a yet greater fullness of grace and virtues.[37]

We can presume that when St. Thomas speaks of an implicit desire for baptism, what he has in mind is that the dispositions of faith and charity which a person possesses conform his will to the will of God in his regard. Thus, even though he does not know that the will of God includes his baptism, his disposition of soul implicitly embraces that object also. We shall now see that Thomas takes a similar approach to the question of the necessity of receiving the eucharist for salvation.

St. Thomas on the Necessity of the Eucharist for Salvation

To the question whether the eucharist is necessary for salvation, he replies:

> Two things have to be considered in this sacrament, namely, the sacrament itself, and what is contained in it. Now . . . the *res* of the sacrament [= the grace signified and effected by it] is the unity of the mystical body, without which there can be no salvation; for there is no entering into salvation outside the church, just as in the time of the deluge there was none outside the ark of Noah, which denotes the church. . . . As it has been said above, prior to the reception of a sacrament, its *res* can be had by the very desire (*ex ipso voto*) of receiving the sacrament. Hence, before actual reception of this sacrament, a person can obtain salvation through the desire of receiving it, just as one can before baptism, through the desire of baptism.[38]

An interesting point of St. Thomas' teaching on the desire for the eucharist is that he attributes such a desire to children by reason of their having been baptized.

> Because by baptism one is ordered toward the Eucharist, it follows that children, by the fact of being baptized, are ordered by the church toward the Eucharist. Therefore, just as they believe through the church's faith, so they desire the Eucharist through the church's desire, and as a result, receive its grace.[39]

Having seen how St. Thomas understood Christian faith and sacraments as necessary means for salvation, we shall now consider the element of his teaching that seems most favorable to modern theories of salvation for those who lack these means.

St. Thomas on Justification Through One's First Moral Decision

St. Thomas proposes this idea when giving his answer to the question whether it would be possible for a person to commit a venial sin while still in the state of original sin. He replies that this cannot happen. First, because one cannot sin even venially before reaching the use of reason. Secondly:

> When a person reaches the age of reason, he is not at all excused from the guilt of venial or mortal sin. But the first thing that occurs to him to think about, is to make a decision about himself. If he orders himself toward the proper end, through grace he will obtain the remission of original sin. But if he does not order himself toward the proper end, to the extent that at his age he is capable of this decision, he will sin mortally, through failing to do what lies in his power to do.[40]

Several points are worth noting on this. The person envisioned in this article is someone who reaches the age of reason still unbaptized, since if he had been baptized he would not be in the state of original sin. But in medieval times, children of Christian parents were baptized as infants. Was this child then brought up by infidels? Would he have been capable of making an act of faith in Christ? And how could he have attained justification (the remission of original sin) without faith in Christ? Is this person like the well-known "child brought up in the wilderness," who would have to be enlightened before he could make an act of saving faith? As we know, Thomas held that this had to be explicit faith in Christ. It is puzzling that with regard to this person who arrives at justification through his first moral decision (aided, of course, by grace) there is no mention of the necessity of an act of faith. Are we to presume that Thomas takes this for granted, and does not bother mentioning it? It would certainly be a singular lack of consistency in the thought of St. Thomas if he allowed the possibility of justification without the explicit Christian faith which he so emphatically declared to be absolutely necessary for all in his day. Perhaps he implied it in the reference to the grace through which the person would obtain the remission of original sin. It would seem that in the act whereby the person ordered himself toward God, one should also recognize an implicit desire of baptism, which would be necessary for the attainment of justification in one who is not baptized.

While it does leave a number of questions unanswered, this answer which St. Thomas gave to the question whether a person could commit a venial sin while still in the state of original sin has become the foundation of several modern theories about the possibility of salvation for those "outside the church." We shall discuss such theories later on in this book.

We can conclude this chapter by noting three points in the teaching of St. Thomas which would eventually prove helpful to Catholic theologians in their efforts to solve the new problems they had to face when it became known that there were vast continents whose inhabitants had never before heard the gospel preached. The first of these ideas is Thomas' notion of a faith in Christ that is implicitly contained in the faith in God that is described in Hebrews 11:6. The second is his recognition of the sufficiency of an implicit desire (*votum*) for baptism and the eucharist when these sacraments cannot be received in reality (*in re*). And the third is his teaching on justification through a person's first moral decision. In the following chapters we shall see how the Dominicans of Salamanca and the Jesuits of the Roman College made good use of these ideas that they found in the writings of St. Thomas Aquinas.

5 ‖ Before and After the Discovery of the New World

In the preceding chapter, we have seen how the conviction of medieval theologians that no one lacking Christian faith and baptism could be saved was conditioned by the fact that their world was practically co-extensive with Christian Europe. Given the limits of their horizon, it is understandable that they could have presumed that anyone who was not a Christian had heard enough about the faith to be guilty of having rejected it. In their world, it was only the "child brought up in the wilderness" who would not have heard about Christ.

In this chapter we are going to see how the medieval worldview was drastically altered with the discoveries of the fifteenth and sixteenth centuries, and how Christian thinkers began to revise their understanding of the possibility of salvation for people "outside the church" in the light of this newly acquired knowledge.

However, before we study this new development of Christian thinking, we shall look briefly at two documents of the Catholic Church, dating from the two centuries prior to the discovery of America, which continued to express the medieval point of view. The first of these was the bull *Unam sanctam* of Pope Boniface VIII, of the year 1302; the other was the *Decree for the Jacobites* of the Council of Florence, of the year 1442.

The Bull "Unam sanctam" of Pope Boniface VIII

A bull is a papal letter that is sealed with a *bulla*, which is a special kind of seal attached to documents of particular importance. The bull *Unam sanctam* begins with a profession of faith in the

63

oneness of the church, outside of which there is no salvation. It stresses, more than previous papal and conciliar statements of this doctrine had done, the role of the pope as head, under Christ, of this one church.

> We are obliged by our faith to believe and to hold that there is one holy, catholic and apostolic church; indeed, we firmly believe and sincerely confess this, and that outside of this church there is neither salvation nor the remission of sin. . . . This church represents one mystical body; the head of this body is Christ, and the head of Christ is God. In it there is "one Lord, one faith and one baptism" (Eph 4:5). For in the time of the flood there was one ark of Noah . . . having one ruler and governor, namely Noah, outside of which we read that everything existing on the earth was destroyed.[1]

> This one and unique church, therefore, has not two heads, like a monster, but one body and one head, namely, Christ and his vicar, Peter's successor, for the Lord said to Peter personally, "Feed my sheep" (Jo 21:17). He said "my sheep," universally, not singly of these or those; hence it is understood that he entrusted all his sheep to him. If therefore the Greeks or others say that they were not entrusted to Peter and his successors, they must necessarily confess that they are not among Christ's sheep, for the Lord said in John, "There shall be one fold and only one shepherd" (Jo 10:16).[2]

It is to be noted that in enunciating the traditional doctrine about the necessity of being in the church for salvation, Boniface VIII puts particular emphasis on the role of the pope as head of the church, with the consequence that those cannot be members of Christ's flock who are not under its visible shepherd.

In the following section of the bull, Pope Boniface develops a medieval theory about the supremacy of the spiritual power over the temporal power, giving the pope as head of Christendom the authority to "institute and to judge" temporal rulers. This theory is obviously dependent on the actual situation of Europe at the time, when kings and emperors were crowned by the popes, and as Christians were subject to his spiritual authority. The pope developed this theory in terms of the "two swords," declaring that both the spiritual sword and the temporal sword are in the power of the church. The latter is used on behalf of the church; the former is used by the church.

> It is fitting, however, that sword be subject to sword, and that the temporal authority be subject to the spiritual. . . . For Truth itself bears witness, that the spiritual power has the right to establish the earthly, and to judge it if it's not good.[3]

After this assertion of the supremacy of the spiritual over the temporal power, which in the contemporary situation meant the supremacy of the pope over the king of France, with whom Boniface was in bitter conflict at the time, the final sentence of the bull reads as follows:

> Moreover, we declare, state and define that for every human creature it is a matter of necessity for salvation to be subject to the Roman Pontiff.[4]

In the historical note which Adolf Schönmetzer, the learned editor of the recent editions of Denzinger, provided for this bull, he asserts that only this final sentence is a dogmatic definition. He interprets it in the light of the first paragraphs of the bull, which affirm the necessity of belonging to the Catholic Church for salvation, rather than as defining Boniface's theory of the supremacy of the spiritual over the temporal power. In support of this interpretation, Schönmetzer notes that the final sentence is taken from a work of St. Thomas, where the necessity of being subject to the Roman Pontiff is simply another way of expressing the necessity of being in the communion of the Catholic Church in order to be saved.[5]

Schönmetzer's historical note reflects what has been the more common interpretation of the bull among Catholic theologians, namely, that while Pope Boniface undoubtedly held and taught the medieval theory of the supremacy of the spiritual over the temporal power, what he solemnly defined in the final sentence is nothing more than the classical doctrine that there is no salvation outside the Catholic Church.[6] However, one recent study of the issue, by George Tavard, offers a different approach. Tavard insists that the final sentence must be understood in the light of the main theme of the bull, which is papal supremacy over temporal rulers. On the other hand, Tavard believes that this lacks an essential condition required for a dogmatic definition, since even in Boniface's time there was no consensus on this doctrine in the church, and it has not survived as part of the church's patrimony of faith.[7]

Without attempting to decide which of these two interpretations is preferable, we can conclude by noting that no Catholic theologian now holds that Boniface's theory about the supremacy of the spiritual over the temporal power is a dogma of Catholic faith. It is safe to say that if his bull defined anything, it was simply the traditional doctrine that there is no salvation outside the Catholic Church.

The Decree for the Jacobites of the Council of Florence

The council which is commonly called that of Florence began in Basel in 1431, was translated to Ferrara in 1438, to Florence in 1439, and finally to Rome, where it concluded in 1445. The principal effort of this council was to bring about reunion with the separated eastern churches. A number of decrees of reunion were enacted, but subsequent events proved most of them ineffectual for lasting reunion. Among these decrees was the one for the reunion of several Coptic Churches, whose members were also called Jacobites. The decree was in the form of a profession of Catholic faith, to which the Jacobites were obliged to declare their adherence. Among other articles was the following:

> [The holy Roman Church] . . . firmly believes, professes and preaches that no one outside the Catholic Church, neither pagans nor Jews nor heretics nor schismatics, can become partakers of eternal life; but they will go to the eternal fire prepared for the devil and his angels, unless before the end of their life they are joined to it. For union with the body of the church is of so great importance that the sacraments of the church are of use toward salvation only for those remaining in it, and fasts, almsgiving, other works of piety and the exercises of a militant Christian life bear eternal rewards for them alone. And no one can be saved, no matter how much he has given in alms, even if he sheds his blood for the name of Christ, unless he remains in the bosom and unity of the Catholic Church.[8]

The alert reader will no doubt recognize the first sentence of this conciliar decree as one which we have quoted previously from a work of St. Augustine's sixth century disciple, Fulgentius of Ruspe.[9] The final sentence is likewise a quotation from the same work by Fulgentius.[10] As we have seen above, Fulgentius followed Augustine even in his more extreme theories concerning the consequences of original sin. However, there is no reason to think that the bishops at the Council of Florence who cited this text of Fulgentius would have agreed with him that people who lacked Christian faith because they had never heard the message of the gospel could be condemned to the torments of hell for the guilt of original sin alone. This would be contrary to the new understanding of the nature and consequences of original sin which had been officially sanctioned by Pope Innocent III.

On the other hand, we have good reason to understand this decree in the light of what was then the common belief that all pagans, Jews, heretics and schismatics were guilty of the sin of infidelity, on the grounds that they had culpably refused either to accept the true faith or to remain faithful to it. We have seen how St. Thomas distinguished three kinds of sinful unbelief: that of pagans, that of Jews, and that of Christian heretics and schismatics. The bishops at Florence were merely drawing the logical conclusion from St. Thomas' teaching about these sins of infidelity. Their decree cannot be understood except in the light of their judgment concerning the grave culpability of all those who they declared would be condemned to hell.

We have to try to grasp the fact that it simply did not occur to the medieval mind that people like the Jews, living in the midst of Christendom, could persist in their Jewish belief and their rejection of Christian faith, and not be guilty of sin thereby. Still less could medieval Christians believe in the inculpability of the Moslems, who were the enemies of Christendom against whom the crusades had been waged, and who even at the time of the Council of Florence were threatening to conquer the city of Constantinople, the last stronghold of Christianity in the east.

On the other hand, the bishops at the Council of Florence certainly believed that God is good, that being good he is just, and that a just God does not condemn innocent people to the fires of hell. The conclusion is inescapable that they must have believed all pagans, Jews, heretics and schismatics to be guilty, and deserving of eternal punishment. We can agree with them that unrepented grave sin against faith would exclude people from eternal salvation; however, we cannot agree with their judgment that all those people were undoubtedly guilty of such sin.

At the same time we have to admit that this judgment, passed by the Council of Florence in 1442, represents what had been the common thinking of Christians all through the middle ages about the sinful state of those who were outside the church. We might take a moment here to reflect on the practical consequences of passing such a judgment on the various categories of people whom Christians judged guilty of the sin of infidelity. For St. Thomas, as we have seen, heresy is the most grievous kind of infidelity, and in fact it was considered not only a sin but a crime, punishable by both church and state, even with capital punishment. Since unity in Christian faith was an essential bond of the unity of Christian society, heresy and schism were seen as crimes against society as well as against religion.

Jews also were judged guilty of sinful unbelief. The medieval mind could not conceive how they could be innocent in their rejection of Christ, since Christianity seemed to have been so abundantly proved to be the true religion, even by the fact that the great mass of society had accepted it. The Jews were seen as a people accursed by God, doomed to wander the world without a homeland of their own as a punishment for the crime of deicide. Since Christians judged them to be a people under God's condemnation, destined for the eternal fires of hell unless they accepted the Christian faith and were baptized, it is not surprising that their treatment of the Jews reflected this kind of judgment. It is true that the holding and practice of the Jewish faith were not considered crimes punishable by law, as was the heresy of Christians. It was only Jews who had accepted Christian baptism, and subsequently returned to Jewish practices, who were liable to be punished for the crime of apostasy. But the various forms of civil disability imposed on the Jews in medieval Europe, and the massacres which they suffered from time to time, especially at the hands of the crusaders as they marched through Europe on their way to the east, were surely not uninfluenced by the commonly shared judgment that the Jews were accursed by God and destined for eternal punishment for their sinful rejection of the true faith.

While, for St. Thomas and medieval Christians generally, the unbelief of those who, like the Moslems, were neither Christian heretics nor Jews was a less grievous sin, still it involved their being destined to eternal punishment by God, since it was taken for granted that they knew enough about the Christian faith to be guilty for having rejected it. Indeed, they were the sworn enemies of the Christian religion, against whom, from the year 1095, successive crusades were fought. The justice of waging war against the "infidels" was obvious to the medieval mind, both for their occupation of the holy land, and for their sinful rejection of Christ and the Christian religion.

The New Questions After the Discovery of the New World

The Decree for the Jacobites, which declared that all pagans were destined for the fires of hell, was enacted in the year 1442. Just fifty years later, Columbus discovered America, shattering what had been the assumption of the medieval mind that the world was practically co-extensive with Christendom. Now Christian thinkers had to ask themselves: How can we continue to judge all pagans guilty of sinful unbelief, when we know that countless people have been living without the knowledge of the gospel, through no fault of their own? And how can we reconcile our belief in the universality of God's salvific will with the fact that he apparently has left all those people without any possibility of becoming members of the church, outside of which they could not be saved?

Since Spain was the first European nation to establish colonies in America, it is not surprising that the Spanish Dominicans teaching in the faculty of theology at the University of Salamanca were among the first theologians to wrestle with this problem. We shall now see what progress three of them made toward its solution.

The Dominican Theologians of the University of Salamanca

The three whose contribution to our topic we shall consider are Francisco de Vitoria (1493–1546), Melchior Cano (1505–1560), and Domingo Soto (1524–1560). These men were teaching in the University of Salamanca during the first half-century of the Spanish colonization of Latin America. They were aware of the fact that there were vast numbers of people in America who had never heard the Christian message before the arrival of the missionaries. Yet, being faithful followers of St. Thomas, as all Dominicans would be, they had to deal with his teaching that there was no salvation without explicit faith in Christ, and without at least the desire of being baptized and entering the church. At the same time, with St. Thomas, they believed in the universal salvific will of God, which meant that God did not leave people without the means by which they could be saved if they cooperated with God's grace. We shall see how they sought to reconcile the traditional Thomist doctrine with the situation that had been created by the discovery of the new world.

Francisco de Vitoria, O.P.

The first of these Dominican theologians did not actually offer a new solution to the problem as to how God would have provided for the salvation of the natives of America before the missionaries arrived to preach the gospel to them. He continued to maintain, with St. Thomas, that in the New Testament era there was no salvation without explicit faith in Christ. On the question of God's salvific will in regard to people who had no chance to hear the gospel, he followed the solution which St. Thomas had given. Here is how de Vitoria put it:

> When we postulate invincible ignorance on the subject of baptism or of the Christian faith, it does not follow that a person can be saved without baptism or the Christian faith. For the aborigines to whom no preaching of the faith or Christian religion has come will be damned for mortal sins or for idolatry, but not for the sin of unbelief. As St. Thomas says, however, if they do what in them lies, accompanied by a good life according to the law of nature, it is consistent with God's providence that he will illuminate them regarding the name of Christ.[11]

De Vitoria did not seem to realize that the discovery of whole continents whose inhabitants had not previously heard the Christian message, made it very difficult to maintain the medieval solution that God would have provided the means by which those who had been doing what lay in their power could have arrived at explicit Christian faith. On that score, he made no contribution to the solution of the new problem.

However, this was actually not his immediate concern. What troubled him was the injustice that the Spanish colonizers were inflicting on the natives of America, by making war on them, and enslaving them when they had been conquered. The *conquistadores* were justifying their actions by applying the theory that for centuries had justified making war against the Moslems: namely that infidels could rightly be conquered and enslaved for their crimes against the Christian religion. In the year 1539, de Vitoria gave a series of lectures in which he argued that the unbelief of the Indians gave the Spanish colonizers no just cause for making war on them and enslaving them. His first argument was based on St. Thomas:

> Before the barbarians heard anything about Christianity, they did not commit the sin of unbelief by not believing in Christ. This proposition is precisely that of St. Thomas in II-II qu. 10, art. 1, where he says that in those who have not heard of Christ, unbelief does not wear the guise of sin, but rather of punishment, such ignorance of things divine being a consequence of the sin of our first parent.[12]

In other words, one could not rightly judge the natives of America guilty of sinful unbelief, and on that score justly to be conquered and enslaved, as medieval Christendom had considered the Moslems to be.

However, de Vitoria had to reply to the further reason that was being given to justify the waging of war on the natives: namely, that the Christian message had been declared to them, and that they had refused to accept it. It is here that his reply made an important contribution to the development of Christian thinking about the salvation of "unbelievers." As we have seen above, it would seem to have been the view of St. Thomas and his contemporaries that it was only those who had heard nothing about the faith whose unbelief would be inculpable. De Vitoria insisted that the unbelief of the natives did not become culpable by reason of their having heard the

Christian message, if it had been declared to them only in the way that this was being done by the *conquistadores*. He insisted that the message of the Gospel had to be presented in a convincing way, for the hearers to be put under an obligation to accept it.

> The Indians in question are not bound, directly the Christian faith is announced to them, to believe it, in such a way that they commit mortal sin by not believing it, merely because it has been declared and announced to them that Christianity is the true religion and that Christ is the Saviour and Redeemer of the world, without miracle or any other proof or persuasion. . . . For if before hearing anything of the Christian religion they were excused, they are put under no fresh obligation by a simple declaration and announcement of this kind, for such announcement is no proof or incentive to belief.[13]

> From this proposition it follows that, if the faith be presented to the Indians in the way named only, and they do not receive it, the Spaniards can not make this a reason for waging war on them or for proceeding against them under the law of war. This is manifest, because they are innocent in this respect and have done no wrong to the Spaniards.[14]

Finally, de Vitoria adds another reason why the natives are not blameworthy for their lack of belief: the scandalous behavior of the Spanish colonizers is a hindrance to their being convinced of the truth of the Christian message. He continues his indictment:

> It is not sufficiently clear to me that the Christian faith has yet been so put before the aborigines and announced to them that they are bound to believe it or commit fresh sin. I say this because (as appears from my second proposition) they are not bound to believe unless the faith be put before them with persuasive demonstration. Now, I hear of no miracles or signs or religious patterns of life; nay, on the contrary, I hear of many scandals and cruel crimes and acts of impiety. Hence, it does not appear that the Christian religion has been preached to them with such sufficient propriety and piety that they are bound to acquiesce in it, even though many religious and other ecclesias-

tics seem both by their lives and example and their diligent preaching to have bestowed sufficient pains and industry in this business, had they not been hindered therein by men who were intent on other things.[15]

This is an important advance over the medieval way of thinking about non-believers. During the middle ages, it does not seem to have occurred to Christians to ask whether the Christian message had been proclaimed to the Jews in a convincing way, or whether the evil actions of Christians might have proved an obstacle to their being persuaded of the truth of Christianity. It is possible that de Vitoria may not have thought of applying this idea to the unbelief of Jews, but at least he introduced the idea that people who had heard the Christian message might not be guilty of the sin of infidelity for not accepting it. It was perhaps an even more important advance to recognize that the scandalous behavior of Christians might make their message so unconvincing as to absolve from guilt those who heard it but remained unconvinced of its truth. It would take a long time before Christians saw the application of this to the unbelief of the Jewish people, but at least the idea had been launched.

As we have seen, Francisco de Vitoria did not seem to realize that the discovery of whole continents whose inhabitants had never heard the gospel preached made it necessary to rethink the medieval idea that in the Christian era no one could be saved without explicit faith in Christ. The absence of any evidence that anyone in the new world had been enlightened about the Christian faith before the missionaries came made it necessary to conclude either that no one there had ever done what he could to keep the natural law, or that the medieval theory that God would provide a preacher to such a person was not really valid. While de Vitoria did not seem aware of the problem, two of his Dominican confreres at Salamanca did recognize it. Melchior Cano and Domingo Soto found help for the solution of this problem in the teaching of St. Thomas about the sufficiency, for Gentiles before the coming of Christ, of a faith in Christ that was implicit in their faith in God as "rewarder of those who seek him" (Heb 11:6). As we shall see, Cano developed this into what can be described as a halfway solution, and Soto took it further to its logical conclusion.

Melchior Cano, O.P.

In 1547 Cano taught a course *On the Sacraments in General,* in which he included a dissertation *On the Necessity of Christian Faith for Salvation.*[16] As a faithful follower of St. Thomas, Cano taught that while, before the coming of Christ, implicit faith in Christ had sufficed for Gentiles who had no knowledge of the messiah to come, in the Christian era there was no salvation without explicit Christian faith. Furthermore, Cano understood this necessity of faith in Christ to be not merely a matter of a divine precept, but rather an intrinsic necessity following from the role of Christ as the one mediator of salvation for all mankind. It was for this reason that even for those Gentiles who had known nothing of Christ, an implicit faith in the coming mediator was necessary.

Cano also followed St. Thomas' teaching about the first moral decision, holding that one who in that act ordered himself to the right end would obtain the remission of original sin and through grace would be justified. On the other hand, no one could be justified without faith. Hence, Cano concluded that the supernatural aid which that person received to make the right moral decision must also include an illumination of the mind such as to make it possible to make an act of faith. But since the person in question would have reached the age of moral decision unbaptized, he would not have been instructed in the Christian faith, and therefore could not have made an act of explicit faith in Christ unless the illumination had enlightened him explicitly about Christ. Cano thought that such explicit enlightenment about Christ without a preacher being sent would be highly unlikely, and he knew that there was no evidence of any such a preacher having been sent to the inhabitants of America before the recent discovery of that continent. He concluded that it would be more reasonable to believe that such persons would have been given the illumination sufficient to make an act of faith in God, as described in Hebrews 11:6, which, as St. Thomas had taught, implicitly contained faith in Christ as mediator of salvation. From this line of reasoning he concluded that a merely implicit faith in Christ should have sufficed for the justification of those people in America who had "done what lay in their power" to keep the natural law.

However, Cano could not bring himself to depart from the

traditional doctrine about the necessity of explicit faith in Christ for ultimate salvation. His solution was to distinguish between what would suffice for justification (the remission of original sin) and what would suffice for eternal salvation. Thus, a person could reach the state of grace without explicit faith in Christ, but, somehow, before his death, he would have to arrive at explicit Christian faith in order to be worthy to share the beatific vision. As can easily be seen, this was a halfway solution that could hardly satisfy Cano's colleagues in the faculty of theology at Salamanca. One of them, Domingo Soto, offered a more satisfying answer to the problem.

Domingo Soto, O.P.

In the first edition of his work *De natura et gratia* (1547), Domingo Soto had proposed that a person who was inculpably ignorant of the faith could be justified by responding to God on the basis of the knowledge about God that he could arrive at by the use of his natural faculty of reasoning. However, in the second edition of this work, two years later, Soto said frankly that, having thought over the matter more carefully, he rejected that earlier opinion and returned to the traditional doctrine that there is no justification or salvation without a faith that is based on divine revelation.

This led him to pose the problem: What about the salvation of the people who had lived in America during the centuries prior to the arrival of the Spanish missionaries? Some held that their lack of Christian faith was culpable, on the grounds that if they had been keeping the natural law, God would have enlightened them with the light of the true faith. But Soto held it more reasonable to say that before those people ever heard the gospel preached, their lack of Christian faith had been inculpable. If they had been keeping the natural law, with God's help, they would have received the light by which they could have made an act of faith, without which no one could be justified. Then Soto observed that it was not easy to believe that this divine light would have been such as to bring them to explicit faith in Christ, without anyone being sent to preach the gospel to them. He noted that in the case of Cornelius, Peter had to be sent to preach the gospel to him before he could make an act of explicit Christian faith. Soto concluded, as Melchior Cano had done before him, that it would seem more credible that God would provide the light necessary for the implicit faith in Christ (Soto uses the term *fides confusa*) which had sufficed for people who lived before the coming of Christ.

However, Soto rejected Cano's halfway solution that such faith would have sufficed for justification but not for final salvation. He could see no sound basis for making such a distinction, which would involve the unreasonable hypothesis that once a person had reached justification, God would have to provide the means by which that person could come to explicit faith in Christ before he died. Soto concluded that the implicit faith in Christ which St. Thomas had recognized as sufficient for the salvation of Gentiles who lived before Christ should also be recognized as having sufficed for the salvation of the people of the new world during the centuries before the gospel had been preached to them.[17]

Two important advances, therefore, were made by the Dominicans of Salamanca: de Vitoria's recognition of the fact that people who had heard about Christ could still be guiltless of their unbelief if the gospel had been presented to them in an unconvincing way, and Soto's admission that implicit faith in Christ would have sufficed for the salvation of people whose lack of explicit Christian faith was inculpable. Common to these Dominican theologians was an unshaken belief in God's universal salvific will, which would leave no one who was doing what lay in his power without the means necessary for salvation.

Not all contemporary Christian thinkers, however, shared this view. We must now see how one of the most influential of the reformers, John Calvin, understood the purposes of God with regard to the people of the new world who had for so many centuries been deprived of the light of the Christian message.

John Calvin (1509–1564)

Calvin's doctrine on predestination includes the idea that if some people have not been given the opportunity to hear the gospel message, this is rightly seen as a sign that God has predestined them to eternal damnation. Here are some representative passages of his *Institutes of the Christian Religion* that spell out his notion of divine predestination.

By predestination we mean the eternal decree of God, by which he determined with himself whatever he wished to happen with regard to every man. All are not created on equal terms, but some are preordained to eternal life, others to eternal damnation; and, accordingly, as each has been created for one or other of these ends, we say that he has been predestined to life or to death.[18]

We say, then, that Scripture clearly proves this much, that God by his eternal and immutable counsel predetermined once for all those whom it was his pleasure one day to admit to salvation, and those whom, on the other hand, it was his pleasure to doom to destruction. We maintain that his counsel, as regards the elect, is founded on his free mercy, without any respect to human worth, while those whom he dooms to destruction are excluded from access to life by a just and blameless, but at the same time, incomprehensible judgment. In regard to the elect, we regard calling as the evidence of election, and justification as another symbol of its manifestation, until it is fully accomplished by the attainment of glory. But as the Lord seals his elect by calling and justification, so by excluding the reprobate either from the knowledge of his name or the sanctification of the Spirit, he, by these marks, in a manner discloses the judgment which awaits them.[19]

As the Lord by the efficacy of his calling accomplishes towards his elect the salvation to which he had by his eternal counsel destined them, so he has judgments against the reprobate, by which he executes his counsel concerning them. Those, therefore, whom he has created for dishonour during life and destruction at death, that they may be vessels of wrath and examples of severity, in bringing to their doom, he at one time deprives of the means of hearing his word, at another by the preaching of it blinds and stupifies them the more. The examples of the former case are innumerable, but let us select one of the most remarkable of all. Before the advent of Christ, about four thousand years passed away, during which he hid the light of saving doctrine from all nations. . . . The Supreme Disposer then makes way for his own predestination, when depriving those whom he has reprobated of the communication of his light, he leaves them in blindness. Every day furnishes instances of the latter case, and many of them are set before us in Scripture.[20]

From the above passages it is clear that for Calvin the mere fact that the newly discovered peoples had not, until now, had a chance to hear the gospel preached is a manifest sign that all their ancestors were among the reprobate, for if God had willed their salvation, he would have made it possible for them to come to the knowledge of the truth, and thus to faith in Christ, without which there was no possibility of their salvation. Even now, when they have a chance to hear the gospel, it is God's intention, with regard to those whom he has predestined to damnation, that it should blind them and make them all the more guilty.

It is obvious how great a contrast there is between this doctrine of Calvin, and what we have already seen was the effort of the Dominicans of the University of Salamanca to solve the problem posed by the discovery of the people of America who had for so long been deprived of the light of the gospel. We shall now look at the teaching of another contemporary Catholic theologian; one who was an outstanding controversialist precisely against the doctrine of John Calvin.

Albert Pigge (1490–1542)

Six years after the appearance of the first edition of Calvin's *Institutes of the Christian Religion*, the Flemish theologian Albert Pigge (also spelled Pighi) published his work *The Free Will of Man and Divine Grace*.[21] Arguing against Calvin's teaching that God had predestined to eternal damnation those people who were deprived of the knowledge of the gospel message, Pigge appealed to the story of the Gentile Cornelius, who was already pleasing to God at the time when the gospel was still being preached only to Jews. From this case, Pigge argued that as divine providence fixes different times for the promulgation of the gospel to different groups of people, it also provides the necessary means for their salvation according to the situation in which people find themselves. Here are his words:

> This is altogether certain: that it is impossible to establish the same time by which it can be said, or could ever be said, that the Gospel was sufficiently promulgated to everyone. For God has not determined the same time for the calling of all nations. For

even now, in many regions of the world, there are many nations on whom the light of the Savior has not shone, and a greatly increasing number to whom this light is only now beginning to shine through our missionaries. There can be no doubt that such peoples are in the same condition that Cornelius was in before he was instructed in the faith by Peter.[22]

The Apostle says, "Whoever would draw near to God must believe that he exists and that he rewards those who seek him." There are many who believe these things about God, even though they are totally ignorant of the Christian faith; thus did Cornelius believe, and was pleasing to God for his faith, before he was taught about Christ.[23]

It will be recalled that for St. Thomas, the faith which made Cornelius pleasing to God before he heard the message of the gospel from Peter was not merely faith in God, but was implicit faith in Christ. This was the solution, as we have seen, of the Dominicans of Salamanca, who followed Thomas in requiring at least implicit faith in Christ for salvation. As far as I can see, Pigge did not insist on this requirement. For him, the faith that was necessary and sufficient for those who were inculpably ignorant of the gospel was simply the faith described in Hebrews 11:6: to believe that God exists and is the rewarder of those who seek him. He evidently was convinced that God would have made such faith possible for the people who had lived in the new world before the gospel had been promulgated in those regions. For otherwise God would not have been providing the means necessary for their salvation, and that was contrary to the truth of the universal salvific will of God, which he strenuously defended against Calvin's doctrine of predestination.

What is most interesting in Pigge's treatment of this question is that his reflection on the possibility that people who were invincibly ignorant of the Christian message could be justified by their faith in God, without faith in Christ, led him to reflect on the possibility of salvation for Moslems who were inculpably ignorant about the truth of the Christian religion.

In entering on this question, he says that he realizes he is setting out on an uncharted sea, full of great problems and obscurities. He does not refer to anyone who had explored this territory before him. As far as I have been able to ascertain, he was the first Christian thinker to suggest that a Moslem's lack of Christian faith might actually be inculpable, and that he could be saved by his faith in God. Here is how he put his idea.

> One cannot doubt that in so great a multitude of those who follow the doctrine of Mohammed, being imbued with this by their parents from infancy, there are some who know and revere God, as the cause of all things, and the rewarder of the good and the wicked, and who commend to him their salvation, which they hope from him, and they keep the law of nature written in their hearts, and they submit their wills to the divine will. What is to be thought about such people? Are they to be seen in the same situation that Cornelius was in before he was instructed in the Christian faith? If you say that by now the Gospel of Christ has been sufficiently promulgated in the whole world, so that ignorance can no longer excuse anyone—reality itself refutes you, because every day now numberless nations are being discovered among whom, or among their forefathers, no trace is found of the Gospel ever having been preached, so that to all those people up to our time Christ was simply unheard of. . . . Now if the ignorance of the Christian faith did not prevent Cornelius, even without baptism, from being pleasing to God in Christ, how much less will the much more invincible ignorance of these people prevent them from being able to please God in Christ.

> I grant that the Moslems have heard the name of Christians. But they have been so educated that they think that our faith is false and mistaken, while the faith in which they have been educated is the true faith, and they believe that God commands them to hold that faith. For it is thus that they have been instructed by their parents and elders, to whom natural reason prescribes that the young and simple be submissive, unless or until divine illumination teaches them otherwise. And so they feel it would be wrong, indeed, that they would be damned if they doubted, for they believe as they were taught in order to please God and to avoid damnation. They do not know anything about divine revelation; they have not seen signs or miracles that would prove their religion false, nor have they heard of them in such a way that they would be truly obliged to believe those who told

them of such things. . . . Therefore, erroneous faith does not condemn, provided the error has a reasonable excuse and that they are invincibly ignorant of the true faith.[24]

It seems clear that it was the stimulus of having to reflect on the state of inculpable ignorance of the newly discovered people of America and the Indies, and his conclusion that for them faith in God, without faith in Christ, must have sufficed for salvation, that led Albert Pigge to draw a conclusion that, as far as I know, no Christian had drawn before him: that Moslems, too, could be inculpably ignorant of the truth of the Christian religion, and could find salvation through their sincere faith in God. It is a striking coincidence that this work of the Catholic theologian, Albert Pigge, was published exactly one hundred years after the Council of Florence had declared that Catholics must believe that anyone who died outside the Catholic Church would inevitably be damned to the eternal fires of hell.

In our next chapter, we shall see how the Jesuits of the sixteenth and seventeenth centuries continued the rethinking of traditional Catholic theology about the salvation of people who lived and died "outside the church."

6 || The Jesuits and the Jansenists

Before we begin our treatment of the Jesuits of the sixteenth and seventeenth centuries, and of their adversaries, the Jansenists, we shall look briefly at the documents of the Council of Trent, to see what contribution that important council may have made to the question whether people "outside the church" could be saved. The first point to note is that the traditional axiom does not appear in the decrees of the council, perhaps because the reformers were as insistent as the Catholic tradition had been that there was no salvation to be had outside the church. Martin Luther, for example, declared, in his *Large Catechism:*

> For where Christ is not preached, there is no Holy Spirit to create, call and gather the Christian Church, and outside it no one can come to the Lord Christ. . . . But outside the Christian Church (that is, where the Gospel is not) there is no forgiveness, and hence no holiness. [1]

Since the Council of Trent was concerned with points of controversy with the reformers, it is understandable that it did not take up doctrines that were not disputed. On the other hand, speculation by Catholic theologians about the salvation of those who had lived in America before the missionaries arrived was evidently too recent a development for conciliar decision.

At the same time, there are two points in the decrees of Trent that have a bearing on our question. One has to do with the necessity of faith for justification, the other with the necessity of baptism. On the necessity of faith, the council made the following statements:

The instrumental cause [of justification] is the sacrament of baptism which is the sacrament of faith, without which [faith] no one has ever been justified.[2]

When the Apostle says that man is justified "through faith" and "gratuitously" (Rom 3:22,24), those words are to be understood in the sense in which the Catholic Church has held and declared them with uninterrupted unanimity, namely, that we are said to be justified through faith because "faith is the beginning of man's salvation," the foundation and root of all justification, "without which it is impossible to please God" (Heb 11:6), and to come into the fellowship of his sons.[3]

The decree on the necessity of baptism is as follows:

After the promulgation of the Gospel, this transition [from the state in which man is born a son of the first Adam, to the state of adoption as sons of God] cannot take place without the bath of regeneration or the desire of it (eius voto), as it is written: "Unless one is born of water and the Spirit, he cannot enter the kingdom of God (Jn 3:5)."[4]

It is obvious that any solution which Catholic theologians working after Trent could offer to the problem of the salvation of those "outside the church" would have to take into account these decrees about the necessity of faith and baptism for justification. I would call attention to two points in these decrees that allowed them some leeway in seeking a solution. One was the fact that in speaking of the necessity of faith, the council had based its doctrine on Hebrews 11:6, which mentions only the necessity of believing "that God exists and that he is the rewarder of those who seek him." The fact that the council did not say that explicit faith in Christ was always necessary for justification left open the avenue which Cano and Soto had explored, and on which Pigge had gone further, namely, that for people who were invincibly ignorant about Christ, faith in God could suffice for their justification.

The second helpful point was the recognition by the council that baptism of desire (voto) could suffice for justification. This could then be coupled with the suggestion of St. Thomas, to the effect that the desire for baptism need not in every case be explicit.[5]

These ideas would obviously be useful to Catholic theologians when they sought to explain how people who knew nothing about baptism could be said to have satisfied the necessity of this sacrament for their salvation.

Having taken a look at the decrees of the Council of Trent, we move on to the contribution which members of the Society of Jesus made to the development of Catholic thinking about the salvation of people "outside the church." Since we have considered the ideas of three Dominican theologians of the University of Salamanca, it is fitting that we consider those of three Jesuit theologians of the Roman College. This college, which is now known as the Gregorian University, was founded by St. Ignatius in 1551. I shall step back a few years, however, and begin the discussion of the Jesuit contribution to our question by examining the thought of a Jesuit who died in 1552, the year after the Roman College was founded. He was not a professor of theology, but a missionary, and one of the most famous the church has ever known.

St. Francis Xavier, S.J. (1506–1552)

Francis Xavier, Ignatius Loyola and the other companions who founded the Society of Jesus were qualified for ordination to the priesthood by the studies in theology which they completed at the University of Paris. In 1535, while Xavier was a student there, several of the Dominican professors reported with obvious satisfaction to King John of Portugal: "Here at this university, as in all others, the teaching of St. Thomas, our Angelic Doctor, is held by all in the highest regard."[6] Thus we have good reason to presume that Xavier was well acquainted with the teaching of St. Thomas to the effect that God does not deny his grace to anyone who is doing what he can to seek God. We have no reason to think that Xavier would have questioned the truth of a principle that had been universally accepted by Catholic theologians since the middle ages: "To one who does what lies in his power, God does not deny grace." This consideration gives us an *a priori* reason for questioning a statement that has often been made about Xavier, namely that his missionary zeal was motivated by his conviction that all the "heathen" who had died without Christian faith and baptism must certainly be in hell.[7]

It would seem that this idea about Xavier's motivation for his missionary zeal is based on a misunderstanding of the answer which he gave to a question that had been put to him by his Christian converts in Yamaguchi, Japan. Xavier's biographer, Georg Schurhammer, reports this exchange on the basis of a letter which Xavier wrote after his departure from Japan.

> His Christians had only one concern. They felt sorry for their deceased parents, wives, children, relatives and friends; and they asked the priest if those in hell could not be freed from it through prayers and alms, as the bonzes universally taught, and if God could not free them, and why they had to remain there forever. Master Francis gave them a satisfying answer for everything, but as far as hell was concerned, he had to tell them that no one could be redeemed from it, grieved as he was when he saw his beloved Christians weeping for their dead. On the other hand, he hoped that the thought of the eternity of hell would be an incentive for them not to be negligent about their own salvation, and that they would thus escape the everlasting punishments of their ancestors.[8]

It is understandable that this account has been interpreted to mean that Xavier was convinced that everyone who had died without Christian faith and baptism must be in hell. It would seem from this account that his converts believed that their ancestors were in hell, and we are not told that Xavier tried to console them by the thought that perhaps some of them had escaped that fate. However, the question put to Xavier was not whether there was any hope that their ancestors might not be in hell; the question was whether they could be freed from hell by the prayers which Christians would offer for them. This question was prompted by the teaching of the Buddhist monks that people could be freed from hell by prayers and almsgiving. To the question that was put to him, Xavier had to answer that there was no hope that anyone in hell could ever be delivered from it.

The reply which Xavier gave to his converts in Yamaguchi does not really prove that he thought there was no hope for the salvation of anyone who had died without Christian faith and baptism. Nor is this proved by the prayer which he was accustomed to say during mass just before receiving communion. This prayer began as follows:

> Everlasting God, Creator of all things, remember that you alone have created the souls of infidels, whom you have made to your image and likeness. Behold, O Lord, how hell is being filled with them to your dishonor.[9]

The pathos of this prayer can well be explained by the fact that Xavier believed, with St. Paul (cf. Rom 1:18–32), that people would be justly condemned for sins of idolatry and vice. He had seen enough of these in his missionary work to be pessimistic about the chances that many pagans had escaped condemnation to hell. His urgency about preaching the gospel was heightened by his experience that only through the acceptance of Christian faith and the grace of the sacraments were people cured of their tendencies to idolatry and vice.

On the other hand, there is documentary evidence that Xavier did not exclude the possibility that people who had lived in those regions before the missionaries arrived could have known and kept the natural law. Evidence for this is found in the accounts of the "disputations" which Xavier and his fellow Jesuit Cosme de Torres conducted with the Buddhist monks in Japan. In the answer which Xavier gave to questions put to him by the "bonzes," we see that he had not forgotten the theology he had learned at Paris, which assured him that God does not deny his grace to anyone who is doing what he can to obey the law of God that is "written in his heart."[10] Here is Schurhammer's summary of one of those disputations. The monks asked:

> If God was merciful, why had he not revealed himself to the Japanese before the priests came from Tenjiku? And if it was true, as they taught, that those who do not worship God go to hell, God had had no mercy on their ancestors, since he had let them go to hell without granting them a knowledge of himself.

> Xavier answered this last objection by stating that the law of God was the first of all. Before the laws of China came to Japan, the Japanese had known that killing, stealing, bearing false witness and acting against the other Ten Commandments were

evil, and they had experienced remorse as an indication that
they had done ill. For it was written in the hearts of men that
they must avoid evil and do good. The pagans thus knew the
Commandments of God without their being taught to them by
any other than the Creator of all men. And if they had any
doubt about this, they should make the following experiment:
they should take a man who had grown up on a mountain
without knowledge of the laws which came from China and
who could neither read nor write. And they should ask this man
who had grown up in the forest, if killing, stealing, and acting
against the Ten Commandments were sins or not, and if their
observance was good or evil. From the answer given by this
man, who was still such a barbarian, and who had not been
instructed by any other man, they would be able to see clearly
that this man knew the law of God. But who had taught this
man good and evil if it were not the God who had created him?
And if such knowledge was found among barbarians, how
much more was it found among men of intelligence. Before
there was any written law, the law of God had been written in
men's hearts. This explanation proved to be very satisfying to
all his hearers, and they showed how pleased they were with
it.[11]

One can hardly doubt that this argument from the case of a
man who had grown up on a mountain, or in the forest, without
contact with other men, was suggested to Xavier by the teaching of
St. Thomas about the "child brought up in the wilderness," to
whom, if he were doing what he could to keep the natural law, God
would provide the means by which he could make an act of saving
faith and be justified. This is not to say that Xavier was inclined to
be optimistic that there were many who, without the help of Christian faith and sacraments, had rejected idolatry and vice, and thus
received the grace through which they were saved. However, his
answer to the question whether God had shown his mercy to those
who had lived in Japan before the missionaries arrived suggests that
he had not forgotten the axiom: "To one who does what lies in his
power, God does not deny grace."

Having seen how a Jesuit missionary in far-off Japan made use
of the theology he had learned in Paris, we shall now see how three
Jesuit theologians teaching in Rome handled the question about

salvation for people "outside the church." The first of these theologians is a canonized saint and doctor of the church.

St. Robert Bellarmine, S.J. (1542–1621)

Bellarmine began teaching at the Roman College in 1576, and was named its rector in 1592. During his tenure at the Roman College, such famous missionaries as Matteo Ricci and Roberto de Nobili had been students there, and we know that Bellarmine was well acquainted with the work that Jesuits were doing in the Indies, both East and West. However, his major concern was not with the problems of the new world, but with the controversies going on in Europe between Catholics and Protestants. One of these controversies had to do with the nature of the church. Against the reformers who held that the true church consists only of the elect, or of the predestined, or of those justified by faith, Bellarmine argued that such a church would be invisible, since God alone would know who belonged to it. Bellarmine insisted that there is only one church, that it is visible, and that everyone can know who belongs to it. This led him to the conclusion that all the conditions required for membership in the church must also be visible. For this reason he described the true church as the community of people joined together by the visible bonds of the profession of the same faith, the reception of the same sacraments, and communion with the lawful pastors under the Roman pontiff. Preoccupied as he was with maintaining the visibility of the church, he proposed a "definition" of the church which named only the external elements by which one can know who belongs to the church and who does not.[12]

It is a common mistake to take Bellarmine's definition to mean that he thought that the church consisted exclusively of visible elements. The truth of the matter is that he saw the visible elements as constituting the "body" of the church, but he also insisted that the church has a "soul," which he identified with the inner gifts of the Holy Spirit, such as faith, hope, and charity. Obviously, the soul is the higher and more noble part of the church; and yet, for Bellarmine, only the visible elements constituting its "body" are required for membership in it. As he saw it, to require any interior qualifications for membership in the church would conflict with its visibility.

This led him to the conclusion that one could still be a member of the church if one partook of its "body" without any participation in its "soul," that is, without interior grace or virtue. (Obviously he did not mean that this would suffice for salvation.) On the other hand, he recognized the possibility that a person might partake of the "soul" of the church, by having faith and charity, without being actually a member of the church. He mentioned two examples: that of a catechumen who has made a perfect act of charity, and that of a person under sentence of excommunication who has regained the state of grace through perfect contrition.

Bellarmine held that neither of these persons would be in the church as one of its members, since the catechumen lacked the sacrament of baptism, and the excommunicated person lacked communion with the pastors until he was officially reconciled. Since Bellarmine held that such persons could be in the state of grace, and thus on the way to salvation, he had to reply to the objection based on the axiom: "No salvation outside the church." With regard to the justified catechumen, his reply was as follows:

> I reply that the saying: "Outside the Church no one is saved," should be understood of those who belong to the Church neither in reality nor in desire, just as theologians commonly speak about baptism. Because catechumens, even though not in the church *re* (in reality), are in the church *voto* (by desire), and in that way they can be saved.[13]

Then, with regard to the excommunicated person who has regained the state of grace before being officially reconciled with the church, he replied:

> Such a one is in the church *animo sive desiderio* (with his mind or by desire), which is sufficient for his salvation; however, he is not in the church bodily, that is, by external communion, and it is the latter which makes one in the strict sense a member of the church on earth.[14]

In these passages of Bellarmine's treatise *On the Church Militant*, we have, for the first time, an interpretation of the axiom: "No salvation outside the church," which explicitly recognizes that a person who is not actually a member of the church can be saved by the desire of belonging to it. As Bellarmine himself points out, this is really a further application of the doctrine which had been officially confirmed by the Council of Trent, to the effect that the lack of actual baptism might be supplied by the desire of receiving it. Since baptism is the sacrament of incorporation in the church, there is a logical connection between a desire for baptism and a desire of membership in the church.

St. Robert Bellarmine also treated the question of the possibility of salvation for people who had never heard the gospel preached. In his work *On Grace and Free Will*, Bellarmine explained that the doctrine of the universal salvific will of God means that God provides sufficient help for salvation to everyone, at least at some time and place, either immediately or mediately. His explanation is as follows:

> We say "at some time and place," because here we do not determine whether such help is available at every moment of a person's life. . . . We are saying that there is no one who does not, at some time, receive such help. Then we say "either mediately or immediately," because we believe that those who have the use of reason receive holy inspirations from God, and thus, without other mediation, they have enabling grace, and if they cooperate with this, they can be disposed for justification, and eventually arrive at salvation.[15]

Against his own position, he proposed the following objection:

> The beginning of salvation is faith. . . . But many do not have sufficient help from God to come to faith, since the gospel has not yet been preached to them, and a great many more in the past did not have such help, since the preaching of the gospel had not yet reached them.

His reply is as follows:

> This argument proves only that not all receive the help by which they can immediately be converted and believe; but it does not prove that some people simply lack sufficient help for

salvation. People to whom the gospel has not yet been preached, can know through creatures that God exists, and then they can be moved by God's prevenient grace to believe that God exists and rewards those who seek him, and from such faith they can be further led by God directing them and helping them, to prayer and works of charity, and in this way they can obtain, through prayer, a greater light of faith, which God will easily communicate to them, either by himself, or through the mediation of angels or men.[16]

We are not told whether this "greater light of faith" would mean that they would arrive at explicit faith in Christ, nor is it certain whether Bellarmine held, with St. Thomas, that explicit faith in Christ was necessary for everyone in the New Testament era. However, the fact that Bellarmine used the expression "a greater light of faith," without specifying that this would have to be explicit Christian faith, suggests that he may have recognized implicit faith in Christ as sufficing for the countless generations of people who, by his day, were known to have lived without ever hearing the gospel preached.

In any case, it is clear that for Bellarmine, such people could not have been saved without at least a desire of baptism and membership in the church. If they had only implicit Christian faith, they could have had only an implicit desire for baptism and membership in the church. So the question whether Bellarmine believed that implicit Christian faith and an implicit desire for membership in the church could suffice for salvation depends on what he meant by the "greater light of faith" which he was confident all those would receive who were corresponding with the gifts of grace that they received from God.

The next Jesuit theologian whose contribution to our question we shall consider, is Francisco Suarez, who spent most of his teaching career in Spain, but also taught at the Roman College from 1580 to 1585.

Francisco Suarez, S.J. (1548–1619)

As we have seen, it was the doctrine of St. Thomas and the other medieval theologians that, since the coming of Christ, explicit

Christian faith was so necessary for salvation that if someone were brought up in the wilderness with no knowledge of Christ, God would send a messenger to preach the gospel to him. By the year 1580, when Suarez began teaching in Rome, it was obvious that vast multitudes of people in the newly discovered regions of the world had lived and died in complete ignorance of the Christian faith. The missionaries found no evidence that any of those people had ever been enlightened about the Christian religion, as the medieval theologians thought they would be if they were doing "what lay in their power to do." On the other hand, God would certainly have provided such people with the means that were necessary for their salvation. Suarez drew the conclusion that the necessity of explicit Christian faith for salvation must be comparable to the necessity of baptism and membership in the church. This meant that explicit faith in Christ was required not by intrinsic necessity, but by virtue of a positive disposition of God. Just as the lack of actual baptism could be supplied by the desire of receiving it, so also the lack of actual faith in Christ could be supplied by the desire of having it. Here is his explanation of the matter.

> Belief in God is *per se*, and as it were from the nature of the matter, intrinsically necessary for justification, because without it one cannot be converted toward God as one must in order to be justified. On the other hand, explicit faith in Christ, if it is necessary, is so only by reason of the disposition of God and a positive divine law. And therefore, if a person is doing what he can with some kind of help of grace, or at least is not putting an obstacle in the way, it is much more certain that he will be illumined by God so as to arrive at a supernatural knowledge of God himself, than that he would be illumined so as to have explicit knowledge about Christ. The reason is that, with regard to those things that are necessary only by virtue of divine institution and positive law, God does not usually, even in a case of necessity, exercise extraordinary providence so that such means can be actually had and applied. Rather, it is normal for the desire or wish to use such means to suffice, as is clearly the case with regard to baptism and confession.[17]

The objection is raised that this would mean that some people could be saved outside the church. Suarez responds:

With regard to the objection based on the dictum: "No salvation outside the church," some say (cf. Cano, *De locis*, cap. 3), that this proposition should be understood of the universal church that has always existed,[18] and not of the one church specially instituted by Christ. But that reply does not satisfy, because there is always only one church, and the councils really speak of the church of Christ, and of this church it must in some sense be true, that outside of it there is no salvation. It is better, then, to respond with the distinction between necessity *in re* and *in voto;* thus, no one can be saved who does not enter this church of Christ either in reality or at least in wish and desire. That is how Bellarmine responds. Now it is obvious that no one is actually in this church without being baptized, and yet he can be saved, because just as the desire of baptism can suffice, so also the desire of entering the church. Now we are saying the same thing with regard to anyone who has faith in God, and sincere repentance for sin, but who is not baptized, whether he has arrived at explicit or only implicit faith in Christ. For, with implicit faith in Christ he can have an implicit desire for baptism, which St. Thomas teaches can suffice.[19]

From the terms he uses here, it is clear that Suarez saw as equivalent having implicit faith in Christ and having the desire of faith in Christ. This implicit faith or desire would have to be rooted in the person's faith in God, which Suarez believed God would always make possible for those who were doing what they could to please him. This, of course, was a corollary of his belief that God provides to everyone the help necessary for salvation, unless the person puts an obstacle in the way. To this the objection was raised that people who never hear the gospel do not receive from God the help that they need for their salvation. Suarez replied that even in this case, God still provides sufficient help, and explains how this is so.

Another way of explaining this sufficiency is indicated in these words of the first chapter of John: "He was the true light that enlightens every man who comes into this world." (Jn 1:9) The Fathers understand these words to refer to an internal and supernatural illumination, which they held is communicated to all adult persons, universally, as far as it depends on God. According to this interpretation, even to those unbelievers to whom the gospel or Christian faith has never been preached by men, God provides a way by which they are enlightened and moved sufficiently for an act of faith, provided that they put no obstacle in the way. And God does this either by arranging in an extraordinary way that a preacher be sent to them, or by teaching them by the ministry of angels, or by God himself interiorly enlightening and calling them, with the result that this saying will be true for all: "Behold, I stand at the door and knock." (Rev. 3:20)[20]

From the way that Suarez begins his response by appealing to the interpretation of John 1:9 in terms of an interior illumination, it is clear that he preferred this explanation to that which required God to send a preacher or an angel to those who had never heard the gospel preached. His advance over St. Robert Bellarmine consists in his clear recognition that implicit faith in Christ, or the desire of such faith, would suffice for those who had never heard the gospel preached, and that such faith or the desire of it would also be the basis for an implicit desire for baptism and membership in the church. In other words, for Suarez, these requirements for salvation were reduced to the necessity of faith in God, the light for which God himself would provide to those who put no obstacle in the way.

The third of the Jesuit theologians of the Roman College whom we shall now consider agreed with the solution proposed by Suarez, but went on to apply it in a way that went much further toward modern Catholic thinking than anyone before him had done.

Juan De Lugo, S.J. (1583–1660)

Juan De Lugo taught at the Roman College from 1621 to 1643, and subsequently was named a cardinal, as Robert Bellarmine had been before him. On the question of the possibility of salvation for people who had never had a chance to hear the message of the gospel, he gave the same response that Suarez had given: that they would receive the grace with which they could observe the natural law; and if they kept this, they would be enlightened so that they could arrive at faith in God, and with this they could have the implicit desire for Christian faith, baptism and membership in the church that would suffice for their salvation.

However, De Lugo went beyond Suarez and Bellarmine in applying this solution not only to those who had never heard the gospel preached, but also to people who knew about Christ, but either did not believe in him, or had a faith that was not orthodox. De Lugo dared to suggest that heretics, Jews and Moslems might not be damned, as the Council of Florence had said they would, but, on the contrary, might be saved through their sincere faith in God. Here is how he put it.

Those who do not believe with the Catholic Church can be divided into several categories. There are some who, while they do not believe all the dogmas of the Catholic religion, do acknowledge the one true God; such are the Turks and all Moslems, as well as the Jews. Others acknowledge the triune God and Christ, as most heretics do. . . . Now if these people are excused from the sin of infidelity by reason of invincible ignorance, they can be saved. For those who are in invincible ignorance about some articles of faith but believe others, are not formally heretics, but they have supernatural faith, by which they believe true articles, and on this basis there can follow acts of perfect contrition, by which they can be justified and saved. The same must be said about the Jews, if there are any who are invincibly mistaken about the Christian religion; for they can still have a true supernatural faith in God, and about other articles, based on Sacred Scripture, which they accept, and so, with this faith, they can have contrition, by which they can be justified and saved, provided that explicit faith in Christ is not required with a necessity of means, as will be explained later on. Finally, if any Turks and Moslems were invincibly in error about Christ and his divinity, there is no reason why they could not have a true supernatural faith about God as the supernatural rewarder, since their belief about God is not based on arguments drawn from natural creation, but they have this belief from tradition, and this tradition derives from the church of the faithful, and has come down to them, even though it is mixed up with errors in their sect. Since they have relatively sufficient motives for belief with regard to the true doctrines, one does not see why they could not have a supernatural faith about them, provided that in other respects they are not guilty of sinning against the faith. Consequently, with the faith that they have, they can arrive at an act of perfect contrition.[21]

Against the position which De Lugo has espoused here, he proposes and answers the following objection:

> It would follow that a Jew or other non-Christian could be saved; for he could have a supernatural faith in the one God, and be invincibly ignorant about Christ. But such a person would not be a Christian, because one is called a Christian by reason of his knowledge of Christ. But that conclusion seems inacceptable, and contrary to the teaching of Pope Boniface in the Bull *Unam sanctam*, and the Decree *Firmiter* of Pope Innocent III, where it is said that there is no salvation outside the church.

De Lugo gives the following reply:

> The possibility of salvation for such a person is not ruled out by the nature of the case; moreover, such a person should not be called a non-Christian, because, even though he has not been visibly joined to the church, still, interiorly he has the virtue of habitual and actual faith in common with the church, and in the sight of God he will be reckoned with the Christians.[22]

I believe that what I have just quoted justifies my claim that De Lugo went further toward the modern Catholic position on the salvation of those "outside the church" than any of his predecessors had done. Obviously, his position depends on his recognition that heretics, Jews and Moslems might not be guilty of sinful unbelief, as St. Thomas and the medieval theologians had judged them to be. As medieval Christians saw it, it was only those who had heard nothing about Christ whose lack of Christian faith could be guiltless. It seemed obvious to them that the Jews were guilty of rejecting Christ, that the Moslems were the enemies of the Christian faith, and that heretics were guilty of sinning against the true faith.

How did De Lugo come to his opinion that at least some among these three classes of people might not actually be guilty of sinful unbelief? It would seem to be the result of his giving his attention, in a way that the medieval theologians had not done, to the process by which people come to faith. This led him to realize that it was not enough to have heard about Christ to make the unbeliever guilty. People like the Jews and the Moslems could have heard about Christ, and still not be obliged in conscience to accept the Christian religion. Here is how he explained his position.

> One should note, with Suarez, that there is a certain intermediate state of those people to whom the faith has not been proposed sufficiently so that they are obliged to embrace it, but who have heard enough about it to be obliged to inquire further and to examine the motives for belief in the teaching of the faith. Thus, while a first preaching of the faith might not suffice to impose a proximate obligation of believing, it could suffice for a remote obligation. People in this situation, of whom there are a great many nowadays, among the heretics, the pagans, and especially among the Turks and other Moslems, if they do not exercise the required diligence [in inquiring further], will no longer have an ignorance that is invincible and inculpable. However, if they do exercise the required diligence, but still are not able to find sufficient knowledge for a prudent decision to embrace the Christian faith, their ignorance will still remain invincible.[23]

De Lugo applied this kind of analysis also to the case of the person baptized as an infant in a heretical sect; the question here is: When does such a person become guilty of the sin of heresy? He replied:

> One who is baptized as an infant by heretics, and is brought up by them in false doctrine, when he reaches adulthood, could for some time not be guilty of sin against the Catholic faith, as long as this had not been proposed to him in a way sufficient to oblige him to embrace it. However, if the Catholic faith were subsequently proposed to him in a way sufficient to oblige him to embrace it and to abandon errors contrary to it, and he still persisted in his errors, then he would be a heretic.[24]

At this point it is important for us to try to realize how revolutionary these ideas of De Lugo must have seemed to his contemporaries. After all, the Council of Florence had declared it to be a matter of faith to hold that all pagans, Jews, heretics and schismatics who died outside the Catholic Church would inevitably be damned to hell. St. Thomas and the whole medieval tradition had

taught that there was no salvation for anyone in the Christian era
without explicit faith in Christ. They were convinced that anyone
who had heard about Christ and did not believe in him must be
guilty of the sin of unbelief, for which he would be justly damned.
Medieval popes and councils had declared again and again that
there was no salvation outside the church. And yet here we have a
Catholic theologian, teaching in Rome, who dared to suggest not
only that people who had never heard of Christ might be saved, but
that some Jews, Moslems and heretics might not be guilty of the sin
of unbelief, and in that case might find salvation through their
sincere faith in God and contrition for their sins. The medieval
presumption had been that everyone who sincerely sought the truth
would inevitably be led to embrace the orthodox Christian faith.
De Lugo dared to suggest that some who sincerely sought the truth
might not recognize it in the Christian religion, and might still be
saved by the faith in God which they found in their own religion.

How did De Lugo arrive at these revolutionary ideas? It was
through reflection on the data of faith in the light of newly acquired
human knowledge. In the first place, there was the newly acquired
knowledge of the existence of vast continents whose inhabitants had
lived for centuries without Christian faith. This led both Dominicans and Jesuits to conclude that salvation must be possible, even in
the Christian era, through faith in God without explicit faith in
Christ. The other newly acquired knowledge lay in the field of
human psychology: namely, the recognition that a sincere inquiry
into the claims of the Christian religion might leave some people
unconvinced of its truth, and that, until they were convinced of its
truth, they were not guilty of sin in rejecting it.

What we find in these Catholic theologians of the sixteenth and
seventeenth centuries is an openness to truth from whatever source
it came to them, and a readiness to reexamine traditional ideas and
assumptions in the light of newly acquired human knowledge. One
has to admire not only their honesty in facing the problems which
the discoveries of their age presented to them, but also their courage
in proposing solutions that not only ran counter to the previous
theological tradition, but seemed also to contradict the teaching of
medieval councils and popes that there was no salvation outside the
church. Their attitude was perhaps best expressed by Suarez, when

he said, referring to those decrees, that *in some sense* it must be true that there is no salvation outside the church. They saw it as their task to determine *in what sense* this could still be true, when one examined it in the light of knowledge which medieval Christians had not possessed.

It should come as no surprise to learn that such ideas as these encountered opposition within the Catholic Church, on the part of those who held fast to more traditional views. As is often the case, the reaction of the "traditionalists" led them to express their views in an extreme fashion, with the result that some of their propositions met with official censure by Rome.

Among those who were most critical of the doctrine that was being taught by the Jesuits at the Roman College was a Catholic theologian at the University of Louvain, Michael de Bay (Latinized as Baius: 1513–1580). While he claimed to be a faithful follower of St. Augustine, his teaching on questions concerning human nature and grace was first censured by the faculty of theology at Paris, and then by Rome. Among seventy-nine of his propositions that were condemned by Pope Pius V in 1567 were the following:

> 25. All the works of infidels are sins, and the virtues of the [pagan] philosophers are vices.[25]

> 68. The purely negative infidelity of those to whom Christ has not been preached, is a sin.[26]

From the general tenor of the seventy-nine propositions that were censured by Rome, it is obvious that de Bay was propagating a rigid form of Augustinianism which did not represent the mainstream of Catholic thought. Events proved, however, that rigid Augustinianism exercised a strong attraction for many Catholics in the seventeenth and eighteenth centuries. Against the optimistic position being taught by the Jesuits regarding the possibility of salvation without explicit Christian faith, a reaction set in which accounts for the fact that it took so long for the optimistic view to prevail in the Catholic Church. The most prominent and influential reactionary movement within Catholicism during that period is known as Jansenism.

Jansenism

Cornelius Jansen (1585–1638) died in the communion of the Catholic Church as the bishop of Ypres. It was only two years after his death, with the publication of his work entitled *Augustinus*, that controversy erupted concerning his teaching. Drawing from St. Augustine his arguments against what he judged to be the Pelagian and semi-Pelagian errors of his own day, Jansen denounced certain doctrines being taught by the Jesuits as a revival of semi-Pelagianism. However, it was the doctrine of Jansen, not that of the Jesuits, that met with censure by Rome. In 1653 Pope Innocent X condemned five propositions that were either verbally or substantially contained in his work *Augustinus*. The fifth of these propositions is as follows:

> It is Semipelagian to say that Christ died, or shed his blood, for absolutely all men.[27]

The pope declared that if this proposition is understood to mean that Christ died only for those who were predestined to be saved, then it is heretical.[28]

Needless to say, the position of the Jesuits had been based on the universality and sincerity of the divine salvific will, which meant that God offered to everyone the grace sufficient for their salvation. To claim that Christ had died only for those who were predestined to be saved would amount to a denial that God offered sufficient grace for salvation to those who would not actually be saved.

Despite the condemnation of the five propositions by Rome, the doctrine of the *Augustinus* gained a wide following among Catholics, including many of the clergy and religious, especially in Belgium and France, during the latter half of the seventeenth century. In 1690 Pope Alexander VIII authorized the publication of a decree of the Holy Office, in which thirty-one propositions found in the writings of Jansenist theologians were condemned. Among these, the following are especially pertinent to our theme.

> 4. Christ gave himself as an oblation to God for our sake: not for the elect only, but for all and only the faithful.[29]

5. Pagans, Jews, heretics and others of that kind receive no influence at all from Jesus Christ; hence one rightly concludes that their wills are naked and defenseless, totally lacking sufficient grace.[30]

8. An infidel necessarily sins in every work.[31]

11. Everything that does not proceed from supernatural Christian faith, working through love, is sinful.[32]

30. Anyone who finds a point of doctrine clearly based in St. Augustine can absolutely hold and teach that doctrine, paying no attention to any papal bull.[33]

A leading figure in the Jansenist movement during the seventeenth century was Antoine Arnauld (1612–1694), one of whose many works is entitled *On the Necessity of Faith in Jesus Christ for Salvation*.[34] Here Arnauld argued strenuously against the idea that those to whom the gospel had not been preached could be saved by faith in God, without Christian faith. On the contrary, he insisted that anyone lacking explicit faith in Christ would necessarily be damned. This led him to declare that only a follower of the Pelagian heresy would doubt that, before they were enlightened by the gospel, all the inhabitants of America had been damned.[35] It will be recalled that John Calvin had issued an equally harsh verdict on the fate of the natives of the new world who, for no fault of their own, had lacked explicit Christian faith.

After the death of Arnauld, the leading proponent of Jansenism was Paschasius Quesnel (1634–1719). Among his propositions that were condemned by Pope Clement XI in 1713 was the following: "No grace is granted outside the church."[36] With the condemnation of this Jansenist proposition, Catholic theologians were assured that it was the doctrine of their church that grace is granted to people who are "outside" it. However, during the eighteenth century there was far from unanimity among Catholic theologians about the possibility of salvation for those "outside." The strength of Jansenism had made many theologians wary of embracing any of the more optimistic solutions that had been proposed by such earlier theologians as Pigge, Soto, Suarez and De Lugo. Many felt obliged to uphold the teaching of St. Thomas and the medieval theologians about the necessity of explicit Christian faith for salvation. In any case, there was no doubt about the fact that "No salvation outside the Church" was still the official doctrine. The decrees of the medieval popes and councils to that effect had never been repealed.

7 | The Nineteenth Century

During the seventeenth and eighteenth centuries, the Jesuits had been the most formidable adversaries of the Jansenists, and the most vigorous defenders of the principle of the universal salvific will of God in its application to the question of the possibility of salvation for people who had either never heard the Christian message, or were inculpably ignorant of their obligation to embrace it. However, when the nineteenth century began, the Jesuits were no longer on the scene, having been suppressed by Pope Clement XIV in 1773. Needless to say, the Jansenists saw the suppression of the Society of Jesus as implying a censure of the doctrines which Jesuits had championed, and as a vindication of their own rigorous positions, even though, in fact, doctrine had had practically nothing to do with the pope's decision to suppress the order.

Inevitably, however, the disgrace into which the Society of Jesus had fallen made Catholics hesitant to embrace doctrines with which Jesuits had been identified. One such doctrine was that for those who were inculpably ignorant of the Christian message, or of its truth, explicit Christian faith was not strictly necessary for salvation. Jesuits had taught that such people could be saved, as those who lived before the coming of Christ could be, by a faith in Christ, or a desire of such faith, that would be implicit in their faith in God.[1] As we have seen, this was a departure from the teaching of St. Thomas and the whole medieval tradition, which had required explicit Christian faith for the salvation of everyone in the Christian era. After the suppression of the Jesuit order, hardly any Catholic theologians dared to question the traditional teaching on this point.

While their explanations differed, Catholics and Protestants in the last quarter of the eighteenth century were in substantial agreement on the absolute necessity of explicit Christian faith for salvation, with the inevitable conclusion that anyone lacking such faith, for whatever reason, was doomed to eternal damnation. Only Christians could be saved; the whole of the non-Christian world was damned. For medieval Christians, this had not seemed an unreasonable conclusion, since for them the non-Christian world consisted almost exclusively of Jews and Moslems, whom they judged guilty of having rejected Christ. But by the eighteenth century, it had become known how immense was the non-Christian world, most of whose inhabitants could not be accused of having heard and rejected the Christian message. How could a just God have allowed so many to have lived and died without the opportunity of professing the faith without which they would surely be damned? Can a person who uses his reason believe in a God who would be so unjust?

It is not surprising that such a question would be put to Christians in the age of enlightenment, the age which claimed the triumph of reason over revelation as the only reliable witness to truth. One man who raised this question in a particularly cogent way was Jean-Jacques Rousseau.

Jean-Jacques Rousseau (1712–1778)

In his famous work *Émile* (1762), Rousseau presented what no doubt were his own religious convictions in the section of his book which he entitled *The Creed of a Priest of Savoy*.[2] Rejecting both the dogmas of the Christians and the atheism of the "philosophers" of the age of enlightenment, Rousseau professed his belief in God as known by reason alone. He argued that while it was certain that we have the power to know God by the proper use of our reason, there is no way of being certain that what people claim to have received by way of divine revelation had actually been revealed by God. Indeed, the unreasonableness of certain doctrines that Christians held as part of revealed truth cast doubt on the reliability of revelation as a source of true knowledge of God.

Among the doctrines commonly believed by Christians was that only those professing Christian faith could be saved, with the consequence that the whole non-Christian world must inevitably be doomed to hell. As we see in the following passages of his work, Rousseau found in this doctrine one of his principal arguments against the truth of revealed religion, on the grounds that it proved that the God of Christian revelation would be an unjust God. Here is a sample of his argument.

> If there were one religion on earth outside of which there would be only eternal torment, and if in some part of the globe a single mortal of good faith would not have been impressed by its obvious truth, the God of that religion would be the most unfair and the most cruel of tyrants.[3]

> It is claimed that our missionaries go everywhere. . . . Even if it were true that the gospel is announced throughout the world, what would be gained by that? The day before the arrival of the first missionary in a country, there surely died there someone who couldn't hear him. Now, tell me what we shall do with that someone? Were there only in the whole universe a single man to whom Jesus Christ had never been preached, the objection would be as strong for that single man as for a quarter of mankind.[4]

At this point Rousseau dramatically takes on the character of a person who has just heard the message of the gospel for the first time.

> You announce to me a God who was born and who died two thousand years ago on the far side of the world in I know not what small town, and you tell me that all those who will not have believed in this mystery will be damned. Are those not very strange things to be believed so quickly on the mere authority of a man whom I do not know? Why did your God bring about so far away from me events which he willed that I must know? Is it a crime not to know what happens in the Antipodes? Can I guess that there was in another hemisphere a Hebrew people and a city of Jerusalem? You might as well hold me responsible for knowing what goes on on the moon. You have come, you tell me, to teach me of it; but why did you not come to teach my father? or why do you damn that good old man for never having known anything about it? Must he be punished throughout eternity for your idleness, he who was so kind, so charitable, and who sought only the truth? Be of good faith and

put yourself in my place; see if I must, merely on your word, believe all the unbelievable things that you tell me and reconcile so many injustices with the concept of the just God whom you announce to me.[5]

Rousseau was aware of the difference between the way Calvinists and the way Catholics would answer the question he was putting to them. He found neither answer satisfactory, as we see in the following passage of his "Creed."

Unable to escape these considerations, some prefer to make God unjust, and to punish the innocent for their fathers' sins, rather than to renounce their barbarous doctrine. Others get out of the difficulty by kindly sending an angel to instruct whoever, in an invincible ignorance, may have led a morally good life. What a fine invention that angel is! Not satisfied with enslaving us to their artificial devices, they place God himself in the necessity of using them. . . . See, my son, to what absurdity pride and intolerance lead when each seeks to cling completely to his ideas and to claim that he alone is right among all mankind.[6]

Needless to say, Rousseau's attack on the Christian religion did not go unanswered. In fact it received an almost immediate censure from the most prestigious Catholic theological faculty of the day, the Sorbonne of Paris.[7] M. Legrand, a Sulpician, was commissioned to write the official response to Rousseau's *Émile* in the name of the faculty. It is instructive to see that he did not invoke the idea that for those who were inculpably ignorant of the Christian religion, an implicit faith in Christ could suffice for their salvation. As Louis Capéran remarks: "In France, in the 18th century, in an official document engaging the responsibility of the Sorbonne, it was not possible to speak of implicit faith in Jesus Christ."[8] In other words, at that period it was thought necessary, at all costs, to maintain the doctrine that no one could be saved without explicit faith in Christ. How then did the spokesman of the Sorbonne answer Rousseau's argument that the God of Christian revelation must be unjust?

He went back to St. Thomas for his answer. First of all, unbelief on the part of those who have heard nothing about the faith is not a sin. As St. Thomas put it, such unbelievers are damned on account of their other sins, which cannot be taken away without faith, but not on account of the sin of unbelief.[9] Furthermore, if people who had heard nothing about Christ were "doing what lay in their power" to keep the natural law, God would take even exceptional measures to enlighten them about the Christian faith. On the other hand, if some people were not so enlightened, it must be on account of their sinful lives, for which God could justly deprive them of salvation. Hence, their failure to achieve eternal salvation was their own fault, and God could not be charged with any injustice in depriving them of it.[10] This was indeed the solution offered by the medieval theologians. But the theologian of the Sorbonne did not seem concerned about the difference between St. Thomas' knowledge of the non-Christian world and his own. For St. Thomas, a person who had heard nothing about Christ must be a rare and exceptional case, like the "child brought up in the wilderness," for whom God would provide in even extraordinary ways. But by the late eighteenth century, it was well known that millions of people had lived and died without any knowledge of the Christian religion. It was also well known that there was no evidence that any of those people had been enlightened by God so as to arrive at explicit Christian faith before the missionaries arrived to preach the gospel to them. The argument used by the Sorbonne to vindicate the justice of God would make it necessary to conclude that among all those millions of people, none had "done what lay in their power" to keep the natural law, since otherwise God would have enlightened them with explicit Christian faith.

In short, to continue to hold that all those who lacked explicit Christian faith were damned, while defending the justice of God in condemning them, meant judging all non-Christians guilty either of culpable rejection of the faith, or of grave sins which made them unworthy of being enlightened about the faith. It must be admitted that while this argument might conceivably vindicate the justice of God, it required one to hold a terribly pessimistic view about the proportion of humanity that would be saved, and thus of the largesse with which God distributed his saving grace.

Such pessimism was typical of most Catholic theology in the last decades of the eighteenth century and the first of the nineteenth. It is surely no mere coincidence that this was also the period during which the Society of Jesus remained under the papal decree of suppression. Nor is it surprising that after the restoration of the Society by Pope Pius VII in 1814, and the return of the Roman College to the Jesuits in 1824, a more optimistic approach began to be taken by Catholic theologians to the question of the salvation of people lacking Christian faith.

Of the professors who were assigned to the Roman College at its reopening under Jesuit auspices, one was destined to serve on its faculty of theology for half a century, and to become the most noted and influential Catholic theologian of his day. We must now see what contribution Giovanni Perrone made to the development of Catholic thinking about salvation for those "outside the church."

Giovanni Perrone, S.J. (1794–1876)

The key to Perrone's thinking on this question is his notion of the *lex evangelica*, the "gospel law," which prescribed those requirements for salvation which became obligatory only when the gospel had been promulgated. Among such requirements were explicit Christian faith, baptism, and membership in the church. Obviously, none of these had been necessary for salvation in the pre-Christian era. Perrone argued that even during the Christian era, these things became obligatory for people only when the "gospel law" had been sufficiently promulgated to them. One could not specify some point in time and say that since then the "gospel law" had been promulgated in such a way that everyone was obliged by it. He observed that in the sixteenth century one could hardly say that the gospel had been sufficiently promulgated to the inhabitants of America. Even less could one say that by then it had been promulgated to the peoples of Australia and Oceania, who had only more recently been discovered. Following the logic of his argument, Perrone insisted that it was not enough for the "gospel law" to have been promulgated in a region; it became obligatory for individuals only when they personally became aware of their obligation to observe it.[11]

From this it is clear how Perrone solved the problem of the salvation of people lacking explicit Christian faith, baptism and membership in the church. Until they became conscious of the law which prescribed these things, they were simply not bound by that law. To put it in more technical terms, Perrone held that explicit

Christian faith, baptism and membership in the church were necessary by a "necessity of precept." He knew that there were theologians who held that they were necessary also with a "necessity of means," but he presented this as a question disputed among theologians, and left it at that.[12] His own solution to the problem of the salvation of non-Christians clearly was based on the view that as long as people were inculpably ignorant of their obligation to believe in Christ and be baptized, they could be saved without Christian faith and baptism. This, of course, also meant that they could be saved without being members of the church. We must now see how Perrone interpreted the traditional axiom: "No salvation outside the church."

His interpretation is based on what we have seen was his basic principle: the obligation to belong to the church is part of the "gospel law," which simply does not bind those who are inculpably ignorant of it. Hence the axiom applies only to those to whom this law has been promulgated, and are personally guilty of not observing it. He enunciates his proposition in the following way.

> For those who die in a culpable state of heresy, schism or unbelief, there can be no salvation; in other words, no salvation is had outside the Catholic Church. Now, as is clear from the way the proposition is enunciated, we are speaking only of those who are in a culpable state of heresy, schism or unbelief. In other words, we speak only of formal, not merely material sectaries. The latter are such as have been brought up from infancy in errors and prejudices, and have no suspicion that they are really in heresy or schism, or if such suspicion does arise in their minds, they seek the truth with all their heart and with a sincere mind. Such people we leave to the judgment of God, for it is his to see into and examine the thoughts and ways of the heart. For the goodness and mercy of God does not permit anyone to suffer the eternal torments of hell who is not guilty of willful fault. To affirm the contrary would be against the explicit teaching of the church.[13]

In this explanation of *Extra ecclesiam nulla salus*, we see clear echoes of the teaching of Perrone's predecessors at the Roman College, Suarez and De Lugo. And yet there is a difference between his theology and theirs. They had not reduced the necessity of belonging to the church to a mere necessity of precept. Following Bellarmine, they had insisted that membership in the church was a necessary means for attaining salvation, as baptism was, and that when membership could not be had in actual fact, it must be supplied for by the desire for it, even an implicit desire. In other words, belonging to the church was not a mere law to be observed, but a means that had to contribute in some real way to the attaining of salvation. The Council of Trent had decreed, with regard to baptism, that no one could attain justification without at least a desire of this sacrament. If its necessity had been merely a question of a law to be obeyed, there would have been no point in requiring such a desire on the part of those inculpably ignorant of the law. The requirement of the desire makes sense only in the hypothesis that by reason of its being the object of desire, the means itself is still involved in the achieving of the intended effect.

It was this way of understanding the matter that led Bellarmine to insist that the necessity of belonging to the church means that one has to belong to it at least *in voto*. It was likewise the basis of Suarez's idea that the lack of explicit Christian faith must be supplied by implicit faith in Christ, or, what seems equivalent, the desire of such faith. This meant that belief in Christ was not merely a matter of law, but that it entered into the process of salvation, since all salvation came through Christ. Perrone, on the other hand, saw these things as merely matters of the "gospel law"; they did not bind those to whom the law had not been adequately promulgated.

At the same time, however, he did insist on one absolutely indispensable means of salvation: this was the supernatural virtue of faith, which had to be faith in God on the basis of divine revelation. (A Spanish Jesuit of the seventeenth century, Juan de Ripalda, had taught that people invincibly ignorant of divine revelation could be saved with a faith that was based on knowledge of God obtained through the use of reason, but this opinion had been condemned by Pope Innocent XI in 1679.)[14] Holding that faith in God on the basis of divine revelation was absolutely necessary for salvation, Perrone agreed with his predecessors at the Roman College in holding that such faith was available to everyone. Even those who had no chance to hear the gospel preached would be provided the means by which they could arrive at an act of supernatural faith in God. Here is how he put it.

It belongs to divine providence to offer sufficient means for salvation to all men. In virtue of the fact that God wills that all should be saved, and that no one can be saved without faith, God bestows on all who do not put an obstacle in the way—and sometimes even to those who do, for this grace is not merited— out of his mercy, and in view of the merits of Christ, either an internal supernatural illumination or revelation, or he brings it about that they receive instruction from others about faith: and in this way they can be justified and saved. Furthermore, this way of God's acting is not to be reckoned as miraculous, be- cause it belongs to God's ordinary supernatural providence.[15]

We have seen above that, in Perrone's view, it was only those who died in a culpable state of heresy or unbelief who would be excluded from salvation by reason of their being outside the church. By "unbelief" here he evidently refers to a lack of faith in Christ, since a lack of belief in God would clearly exclude one, and in his view would always be culpable. From Perrone's premises, it ought logically to follow that he would agree with his predecessor, De Lugo, that Jews and Moslems could be saved through their faith in God, provided that their lack of belief in Christ was not culpable. On the other hand, a remark that Peronne made in the course of answering an objection suggests that he thought it unlikely that any Jews or Moslems would be saved.

The objection against the need of faith for salvation was based on the description of the last judgment in the gospel (Mt 25:31–46), from which the argument was drawn that people will be con- demned not for their lack of faith but for their failure to do works of charity for those in need. Perrone replies:

Failure to do works of charity is not the only reason why some are damned, nor will all who have done such works be saved. Otherwise, one could conclude that, provided that they had done some works of charity, adulterers, drunkards and thieves, and even Jews and Moslems and idolaters, would be saved. But that is absurd![16]

Evidently, Perrone did not doubt that Jews and Moslems might have done works of charity. Nor does it seem likely that he denied that they could have faith in God on the basis of divine revelation. If, in this remark, he was being consistent with his own theology, he must have presumed that their lack of belief in Christ was culpable. On the other hand, this remark may simply betray an ingrained and unexamined prejudice concerning Jews and Moslems, and not a judgment based on careful theological reasoning.

Whatever be the explanation of this offhand remark, the fact remains that Perrone's prestige as the leading theologian of the Roman College goes far to account for the fact that, by the middle of the nineteenth century, his view that only those guilty of culpable heresy, schism or unbelief were excluded from salvation by being "outside the church" had become the common opinion among Catholic theologians. In the year 1854, this opinion was confirmed by no less an authority than Pope Pius IX.

Pope Pius IX (Reigned 1846–1878)

In the year 1854 Pope Pius IX solemnly defined the immaculate conception of the Blessed Virgin Mary as a dogma of Catholic faith. He had invited the bishops of the whole Catholic Church to come to Rome for this extraordinary event, and a very large number of them accepted his invitation. While they were assembled, Pope Pius took the occasion to address to them an allocution in which he spoke of various problems facing the church at that time. Two of these had to do with the question of salvation "outside the church." One was the accusation of which we have already seen an example in the *Émile* of Rousseau: namely, that the God of Christian revelation must be an unjust God, if he condemns innocent people simply for not being Christians. The other was a reaction to this charge on the part of some Catholics who tended to abandon the doctrine about the need of belonging to the church, and to accept what was in fact another of Rousseau's ideas, that it did not matter what religion people professed, or what church they belonged to, as long as they lived good lives. This was known as "religious indifferentism." In his allocution, Pope Pius exhorted the bishops to warn their people against the error of indifferentism, by insisting on the necessity of belonging to the true church for salvation, while at the same time defending the truth that God is just and does not condemn the innocent. Here are the pope's words.

Not without sorrow have we known that another error, not less deadly, has taken possession of certain parts of the Catholic world, and has entered the minds of very many Catholics who think that they can well hope for the eternal salvation of all those who have in no way lived in the true Church of Christ. For that reason they are accustomed to inquire frequently what is going to be the fate and the condition of those who have never given themselves to the Catholic faith, and led on by most useless reasons, they expect an answer which will favor this depraved opinion. Far be it from Us to presume to establish limits to the divine mercy, which is infinite. Far be it from Us to wish to scrutinize the hidden counsels and judgments of God, which are "a great deep" and which human thought can never penetrate. In accordance with our apostolic duty We desire to stir up your episcopal solicitude and vigilance to drive out of the minds of men, to the extent to which you are able to use all your energies, that equally impious and deadly opinion, that the way of eternal salvation can be found in any religion. With all the skill and learning at your command, you should prove to the people committed to your care that the dogmas of the Catholic faith are in no way opposed to the divine mercy and justice. Certainly we must hold it as of faith that no one can be saved outside of the apostolic Roman Church, that this is the only ark of salvation, that the one who does not enter this is going to perish in the deluge. But nevertheless, we must likewise hold it as certain that those who labor in ignorance of the true religion, if that ignorance be invincible, will never be charged with any guilt on this account before the eyes of the Lord. Now who is there who would arrogate to himself the power to point out the extent of such ignorance according to the nature and variety of peoples, regions, talents, and so many other things?[17]

Evidently, Pope Pius was not satisfied that these errors had been eliminated from the minds of the Catholic faithful, when, nine years later, he addressed these same issues in an encyclical letter to all the bishops of Italy.

Here we must again mention and reprove a most serious error in which some Catholics have unhappily fallen, thinking that men living in errors and altogether apart from the true faith and Catholic unity can attain to eternal life. This indeed is completely opposed to Catholic doctrine. It is known to Us and to you that those who labor in invincible ignorance concerning our most holy religion and who, assiduously observing the natural law and its precepts which God has inscribed in the hearts of all, and being ready to obey God, live an honest and upright life can, through the working of the divine light and grace, attain eternal life, since God, who clearly sees, inspects and knows the mind, the intentions, the thoughts and habits of all, will, by reason of his supreme goodness and kindness, never allow anyone who has not the guilt of willful sin to be punished by eternal sufferings. But it is also a perfectly well known Catholic dogma that no one can be saved outside the Catholic Church, and that those who are contumacious against the authority and the definitions of that same Church, and who are pertinaciously divided from the unity of that Church and from Peter's successor, the Roman Pontiff, to whom the custody of the vineyard has been committed by the Savior, cannot obtain eternal salvation.[18]

Looking back on what we have quoted from these two papal documents, it is not immediately evident how we are to reconcile what seem to be contradictory tenets: that on the one hand, there is no salvation outside the Catholic Church, and, on the other, that those who are invincibly ignorant of their obligation to belong to this church can be saved. I suggest that the apparent contradiction can be solved, if we realize that Pope Pius has substantially affirmed the thesis of Giovanni Perrone: that *extra ecclesiam nulla salus* refers only to those who are *culpably* outside the church. It is true that the pope does not use the word "culpably," but he uses equivalent ones when he declares that those who are *contumacious* against the authority of the Catholic Church, or are *pertinaciously* divided from the unity of that church, cannot obtain eternal salvation. As the two terms which we have emphasized are used in Catholic moral theology and canon law, they always attribute culpability to those to whom they are applied. We must keep these terms in mind, therefore, as the key to interpreting the other passages in which the pope affirms the traditional axiom: "No salvation outside the church." For the first time in the history of the Catholic Church, we have papal authority for explaining that this axiom means: "No salvation for those who are *culpably* outside the church."

The addition of the word "culpably" also solves the problem

about the justice of God in excluding from eternal salvation those who die "outside the church." The implication, of course, is that if it is those who are culpably outside who are not saved, then it is possible for people who are outside, but not culpably so, to be saved. Again, for the first time in the history of the Catholic Church, we have an explicit statement of this truth by a Roman pontiff, in the words of Pius IX which we have quoted above:

> It is known to Us and to you that those who labor in invincible ignorance concerning our most holy religion and who, assiduously observing the natural law and its precepts which God has inscribed in the hearts of all, and being ready to obey God, live an honest and upright life can, through the working of the divine light and grace, attain eternal life.

Earlier in this book we have quoted statements equivalent to this from the works of Catholic theologians of the sixteenth and seventeenth centuries, but the influence of Jansenism had practically eliminated such ideas from Catholic theology by the end of the eighteenth century. It is all the more remarkable that such a statement was now made with papal authority. No pope in history had ever explicitly declared that people "ignorant of our most holy religion" could be saved. It is especially significant that the expression used by Pius IX would apply to non-Christians as well as to non-Catholic Christians.

It is important to note *how* Pope Pius said they can be saved, because he has sometimes been taken to mean that people can be saved by ignorance, or merely by keeping the natural law. If one reads his statement carefully, one sees that being "invincibly ignorant of our most holy religion" is a *condition* that must be fulfilled to avoid culpability, but is in no sense a *cause* of salvation. Neither is it correct to say that people are saved merely by keeping the natural law; this would be to fall into Pelagianism, of which Pius IX is surely not guilty. The operative words in his statement are: "through the working of the divine light and grace." It is this that effects salvation, provided, of course, that people freely cooperate with divine grace.

Leonard Feeney and his followers have interpreted Pius IX to mean that if those outside the Catholic Church are "ready to obey God," and are docile to the "working of the divine light and grace," they will be saved by joining the Catholic Church before they die. In other words, Fr. Feeney could not believe that Pius IX meant that some people could actually be saved outside the Catholic Church. No doubt Pope Pius hoped that by the working of the divine light and grace, many who were outside would indeed find their salvation in the Catholic Church. But his statement, in its context, cannot seriously be taken to mean that no one who did not die as a Roman Catholic could be saved.

I have expressed my opinion above that Pius IX has confirmed Perrone's interpretation of the axiom, "No salvation outside the church." I would further suggest that Perrone probably had a hand in preparing these documents for the pope. The resemblance between the following sentences, especially as seen in their original Latin, would otherwise be an altogether remarkable coincidence.[19]

Perrone	*Pius IX*
Dei enim bonitas et clementia non patitur quempiam aeternis cruciatibus addici qui voluntariae culpae reus non sit.	*Deus . . . pro summa sua bonitate et clementia minime patiatur, quempiam aeternis puniri suppliciis, qui voluntariae culpae reatum non habeat.*
Porro contumaces adversus ecclesiae definitiones, seu pertinaciter ab ecclesiae unitate divisos, salutem obtinere non posse . . .	*. . . contumaces adversus eiusdem Ecclesiae auctoritatem, definitiones, et ab ipsius Ecclesiae unitate . . . pertinaciter divisos aeternam non posse obtinere salutem . . .*

It is obvious that both content and expression of these sentences are practically identical. It is not at all unusual that a Roman professor would be asked to prepare a draft of an encyclical letter for the pope.

One last remark about this doctrine of Pius IX is that it can be understood, just as Perrone's can, to mean that the necessity of the church for salvation is merely a necessity of precept. In other words, the obligation to belong to the Catholic Church is based on a law which simply does not oblige those who are invincibly ignorant of that law. The positive side of this position is that it recognizes that people who are invincibly (= inculpably) ignorant of their obligation to belong to the Catholic Church can be saved. But its weakness lies in the fact that it could be understood to mean that the church has nothing to do with the salvation of those who are saved without actually belonging to the church. This would mean dropping the traditional idea that the church, like baptism, is necessary for salvation with a necessity not only of precept but also of means. This is why Bellarmine and Suarez had insisted that those inculpably outside the church must belong to it at least *in voto*, which means that the church would still have something to do with their salvation. It is understandable that the pope did not wish to enter into this aspect of the question in the documents we have cited. However, one would expect Perrone to have done so in his treatise on the matter if he had thought it important to maintain the teaching of his predecessors at the Roman College, who had held that the church was necessary for salvation not only with a necessity of precept but also of means.

A more satisfactory approach to this question was taken by the Tyrolese Jesuit, Johann B. Franzelin, who joined the faculty of theology at the Roman College in 1858, and taught there until 1876, when he was made a cardinal by Pope Pius IX.

Johann B. Franzelin (1816–1886)

Franzelin's treatise on the church was unfinished at his death and was published posthumously with the title *Theses de Ecclesia Christi.*[20] The twenty-fourth of his theses is entitled: "On union with the church as a necessary means for justification and salvation."[21] The supposition of this thesis is the doctrine already affirmed by Pope Pius IX that those outside the Catholic Church, whether Christians or not, who are invincibly ignorant about the truth of the Catholic faith and of their obligation to adhere to it can still arrive at justification and salvation. In his thesis 24, Franzelin supplies what is missing in the doctrine of Perrone and Pius IX, by showing how the Catholic Church is involved in the justification and salvation of those who are saved without being its visible members. His initial summary of the contents of the thesis is as follows.

Although, as was said in the previous thesis, some people can be justified and saved even though they are not recognized in the external forum as belonging to the visible church, nevertheless: 1) such people are not saved except *through the church*, to which the word of faith belongs, and in view of which saving graces are given; and they are not saved except *in the church*, insofar as they are united not only to her spirit but also to her visible elements by their will, which is accepted by God in lieu of the fact. Now these visible elements, by divine institution, are necessary for justification and salvation not only with necessity of precept but also with necessity of means; hence, in the time of the New Testament, justification is never brought about without a relationship to these elements and without at least a spiritual union of the person with them. Thus, in the eyes of God and the church triumphant, there is no justification without union with the church on earth.

We must now see how Franzelin develops his thesis, that non-Catholics can be saved, as he puts it, "by the merciful grace of Christ," but only "through the church and by virtue of their relationship with the church."[22]

(1) *Through the Church*. Franzelin bases his argument on the truth that there is no justification without supernatural faith. Now such faith comes either through the hearing of the message of revelation, or through an interior grace of illumination which God provides for those who have no other access to revealed truth. If faith comes through hearing, then no matter from whom one immediately hears the message, ultimately it has come through the church, as the community which received and has preserved and handed on the deposit of faith. If faith has come through an interior illumination, such a grace was also given through the church, not in this case as the dispenser of the grace, but as the proximate end in view of which it was given. Franzelin explains the ecclesial orientation of such illumination by pointing to the fact that it is given with a view to the person's ultimate salvation, which consists in participation in the eschatological church, with which the church on earth forms a single communion.

(2) *By a Relationship with the Church*. Franzelin explains that "No salvation outside the church" means that there is no salvation without a saving relationship with the visible church on earth. This

follows from the fact that the church is necessary not only with a necessity of precept, but also with a necessity of means. The necessary relationship with the church must be not only with its "soul" (that is, the spiritual elements of the church such as grace, charity, etc.), but also with its "body." The reason is that it is the very nature of the church on earth that it is composed of both visible and invisible elements. One cannot share in the grace of its "soul" without a positive relationship with its "body."

In the case of those invincibly ignorant of the necessity of belonging to the Catholic Church, but who are in the state of grace, their dispositions of faith and supernatural charity include an implicit desire of belonging to the true church (since objectively this is what God has established as the means of their salvation). This *votum ecclesiae*, which is implicit in their dispositions, establishes a saving relationship not only with the soul, but also with the body of the church, such that they can be said to belong to the church, in the sight of God, even though they are outside of it in the eyes of men.

It is important to note that while Franzelin holds that non-Catholics who are in the state of grace can be said to be "in the church" in the eyes of God, and to be in a state of spiritual union with the Catholic Church, he does not speak of such people as constituting an invisible church. He insists that there is but one church, composed of both visible and invisible elements. The fact that some people can be on the way to salvation by virtue of a spiritual relationship to the church, and that this relationship is visible only to God, does not make the church itself any the less visible.

We have now examined the contribution which two Roman theologians of the nineteenth century made to our question. As we shall now see, some of their ideas found a place also in the draft of a dogmatic statement on the church which was prepared for the First Vatican Council.

Vatican I (1869–1870)

It was the intention of Pope Pius IX and the bishops at the First Vatican Council to promulgate a dogmatic constitution on the church, which would include a treatment of the question of the necessity of belonging to the Catholic Church for salvation. A *schema de ecclesia,* or draft of a dogmatic constitution on the church, was prepared and distributed to the bishops for their comments. However, during the spring of 1870 it was decided to extract from this draft the section dealing with the authority of the pope, and to add to it a new section on papal infallibility. The council succeeded in discussing and approving only this part of the material on the church before adjourning in July 1870. As a consequence of the outbreak of the Franco-Prussian war that summer, and the end of papal temporal power over Rome in September, the council came to an abrupt end without finishing the work it had planned to do. Thus, the chapters of the *schema de ecclesia* which dealt with our question never received a full conciliar discussion or became the object of a conciliar vote. They are not without interest, however, since they indicate how the theologians of the drafting committee intended to treat the questions with which we are dealing in this book. Both Perrone and Franzelin were members of the committee, and we shall see that some of their ideas are reflected in the terms of the *schema.*

Two chapters of the *schema de ecclesia,* 6 and 7, dealt with our question. The following are the parts of those chapters of greatest interest for our purpose.

> *6. The church is a society that is altogether necessary for obtaining salvation.*
>
> We therefore teach that the church is not a free society, as though it made no difference for one's salvation whether one recognized it or ignored it, whether one entered it or left it. Rather, it is altogether necessary, and indeed with a necessity that is not merely of the Lord's precept, by which the Savior commanded all nations to enter it, but with a necessity of means, because in the divinely instituted order of saving providence, the communication of the Holy Spirit, and the sharing of truth and life is not obtained except in the church and through the church, of which Christ is the Head.
>
> *7. No one can be saved outside the church.*
>
> Moreover it is a dogma of faith, that no one can be saved outside the church. On the other hand, those who labor under invincible ignorance concerning Christ and his church are not to be damned to eternal punishment on account of such ignorance, since they incur no guilt for this in the eyes of the Lord, who

wishes all men to be saved and to come to the knowledge of the truth, and who does not deny grace to a person who is doing what lies in his power, so that such a one can obtain justification and eternal life. But no one obtains this who dies in a culpable state of separation from the unity of the faith or the communion of the church. Anyone who is not in this ark of salvation will perish in the prevailing flood.[23]

I expect that the reader will have immediately recognized the doctrine of Franzelin in chapter 6, and that of Perrone and Pius IX in chapter 7. The insistence on "necessity of means" and on the salvation of all "in the church and through the church" in chapter 6 clearly reflects Franzelin's ecclesiology. Chapter 7, on the other hand, while repeating the "dogma" that no one is saved outside the church, defends the justice of God, and his salvific will, as we have seen Pius IX and Perrone do, by insisting that it is only those who are culpably outside the church who will be condemned, while those who are invincibly ignorant of their obligation to belong to the true church can still be saved. As we have remarked before, this doctrine lacked the idea, which Franzelin supplied, that the church plays a necessary role in the salvation even of those who are inculpably "outside."

The commission which prepared the *schema de ecclesia* also provided the bishops of the council with a *relatio*, or "report," which explained some of the terms used in it. The *relatio* on chapter 7 gives us an insight into the discussion that went on in the commission, and seems worth quoting at least in part here.

In the section that speaks of "invincible ignorance," it is pointed out that it is possible that a person who does not belong to the visible and external communion of the church can still obtain justification and eternal life. . . . However, lest it seem to follow from this that someone can be saved outside the church, in another form of the *schema* it was said: If they do obtain [eternal life] they are not thus saved outside the church, for all who are justified belong to the church either *in re* (in fact) or *in voto* (in desire). However, since the formula "either *in re* or *in voto*" did not please a number of the consultors, it was decided that it would be sufficient to declare explicitly that no one could be saved who died separated from the church through his own fault, while it would be understood as implicitly meant, that whoever is saved could not be totally and *simpliciter*, as they say, outside the church. Some thought that this should be expressed more clearly, and suggested saying that no one obtained justification or eternal life who *in no way* belonged to the church. By this they meant one who belonged neither to the body of the church nor to its soul, and thus who do not belong to the church at all, either *in re* or *in voto*.[24]

In this *relatio* we see that a number of the consultors taking part in the preparation of the *schema de ecclesia* were reluctant to introduce into the conciliar document the distinction between belonging to the church in fact and belonging to it in desire. It is not clear why they were opposed to using this distinction in the text; possibly they thought it too technical a way of expressing the doctrine. It will be recalled that it was Robert Bellarmine who first used this distinction with reference to membership in the church, and that it had been used by Suarez and others after him. Another distinction which is mentioned in the *relatio*, but does not appear in the *schema*, also goes back to Bellarmine: that between belonging "to the body" and "to the soul" of the church. In Bellarmine's ecclesiology, "soul" and "body" were the invisible and the visible elements in the makeup of the church. It was Bellarmine's idea that people could be "of the soul" of the church (by sharing in faith and charity) without being "of its body" (if they were not joined to the church by the visible bonds of membership). He certainly did not mean that those who were visibly joined to the church constituted its "body," while those who were invisibly joined to it, by faith and charity, constituted its "soul." This misunderstanding of Bellarmine's distinction between the soul and body of the church led to what amounted to a distinction between a visible and an invisible church. In the period following Vatican I this became a rather popular way of solving the problem of the salvation of those "outside the church." If they did not belong to the "body" of the church, they could be saved by belonging to its "soul"; if they did not belong to the "visible church," they could be saved by belonging to the "invisible church." But the discussion of solutions like these, and of the more satisfactory ones that took their place in the twentieth century, belongs to the matter of our next chapter.

8 || The Twentieth Century Prior to Vatican II

The teaching of Pius IX in his encyclical *Quanto conficiamur moerore* of 1863 had authorized Catholic theologians to hold that people who are invincibly ignorant of the Christian religion, but who cooperate with divine grace, can arrive at justification and eternal salvation. On the other hand, in the same encyclical Pius IX had reaffirmed "the well-known Catholic dogma" that no one can be saved outside the Catholic Church.

Catholic theologians did not understand the pope to mean that non-Catholics are saved only if they arrive at actual membership in the Catholic Church before they die. They understood him to mean that non-Catholics can be saved even if they never become conscious of the obligation to become Roman Catholics. In other words, from the time of Pius IX it was common Catholic doctrine that there are people in the state of grace and on the way to salvation who will never be visibly joined to the Catholic Church.

On the other hand, if it was still "Catholic dogma" that no one can be saved outside the church, as the pope also said, such people must in some sense be in the church in order to be saved, even if they are not actual members of the Catholic Church.

This led Catholic theologians during the period following that encyclical to propose various answers to the question how people could be "in the church" without being its recognized members. We have already seen Cardinal Franzelin's answer to this question. Other solutions, in my opinion, were less sound than his, because they tended to require a distinction between two churches: one the visible Roman Catholic Church, and the other an invisible church embracing all who are actually in the state of grace and on the way to salvation. "No salvation outside the church" was thus understood to mean "outside the invisible church," which was also described as the "soul of the church" or the "mystical body." Let us look briefly at these other solutions.

The distinction between a "visible" and an "invisible" church is commonly associated with Lutheran ecclesiology. Luther and the Lutheran tradition distinguished between the church in an empirical sense, the church that includes all baptized Christians, both saints and sinners, and the church in a vision of faith, consisting only of "true believers." A modern Lutheran theologian assures us: "The intention was never to bifurcate the church, as if visible and invisible referred to two churches that existed side by side."[1] In the Lutheran sense, the "invisible church" is found only within the "visible church," since Lutherans would recognize as "true believers" only those members of the visible Christian church who are justified by sincere faith in God's mercy. In that sense, their "invisible church" is "hidden" within the visible church; it does not exist apart from it, and does not extend beyond it, at least as far as this world is concerned.

It was quite a different application of the distinction between an invisible and a visible church when some modern Catholic writers sought to reconcile the possibility of salvation for non-Catholics with the "dogma" that no one is saved outside the church by extending the frontiers of the church so as to have it include all those who are in the state of grace, whether they are baptized or not. This necessitated making a distinction between the visible boundaries of the church and its invisible boundaries, and thus between the visible Roman Catholic Church and the invisible church of all who are actually in the state of grace and on the way to salvation. Thus, for instance, A.D. Sertillanges distinguished between the visible church and the church which he described as "the universal society of souls united to God through Christ under the influence of grace."[2] No doubt it is true that no one can be justified and on the way to salvation who is not within that "universal society of souls united to God through Christ under the influence of grace." But such a "universal society" would in reality be an invisible church, since only God could know who belonged to it. Nor would it be "hidden within" the visible church, since its members would not necessarily belong to the visible church. And finally, to save the axiom "No salvation outside the church" by explaining it to mean "No salvation outside the universal society of souls united to God through Christ under the influence of grace" really amounts to no more than saying that no one is on the way to salvation who is not in the state of grace. This solution, then, is unsatisfactory on at least two counts. It contradicts the unity of the church by effectively dividing it into a visible and an invisible church. And the solution which it offers is in reality only an apparent one. It provides no answer to the real question, whether it is possible to be saved without having some relationship to the Catholic Church and receiving some salvific influence from it.

As we have seen above, the distinction between the "soul" and "body" of the church was used by Robert Bellarmine as a way of expressing the difference between the spiritual elements in the makeup of the church, such as faith, charity and grace, on the one hand, and the visible bonds by which people are linked to the church, such as the profession of the faith, reception of sacraments and communion with the pastors under the pope. While he insisted that these three visible bonds were necessary for actual membership in the church, he recognized the possibility that persons lacking one or another of these elements which constitute the "body" of the church might still partake of the church's "soul" by sharing in the spiritual elements of charity and grace. Such persons, while not members of the church *in re*, would, by reason of their interior dispositions which conformed them to the will of God, be members of the church *in voto*. In Bellarmine's language, they would be *de anima*, "of the soul," though not *de corpore*, "of the body" of the church. On the other hand, he certainly did not describe the total number of such persons as the "soul" of the church, as distinct from the visibly joined members who would be its "body."

Bellarmine's distinction has often been misused, when the "soul" of the church has been identified not with the internal, spiritual elements in the makeup of the church, but with all those people whom Bellarmine would describe as being "of the soul" without being "of the body" of the church. Used in this way, it really becomes a distinction between the visible church as "body" and an invisible church consisting of all the just, as "soul." Here we have a soul that extends far beyond the limits of the body, depending on how optimistic one is about the number of those who are not in the body of the church but are in the state of grace. Castelein, for instance, says:

> We have to distinguish between the soul of the church, which consists in the invisible society of all the souls that are actually in the state of grace and have a right to salvation, and the body of the church, which consists in the visible society of Christians under the authority of the Pope.[3]

In this solution, besides the division of the one church into a visible and an invisible church, there is the added incongruity of maintaining that while Catholics constitute the church's "body," non-Catholics in the state of grace constitute its "soul." It further involves the same tautology as the previous one, since it really amounts to saying that no one is on the way to salvation who is not in the state of grace.

It must be admitted that when Catholic writers explained that people who do not belong to the body of the church can be saved by belonging to its soul, it is often not clear whether they intended to use the terms "soul" and "body" in the way that Bellarmine used them, or in the way that Castelein and others used them. To my mind, this is true of the use which John Henry Newman made of this distinction in his famous *Letter to the Duke of Norfolk*. He was explaining his notion of the "legitimate minimizing" which he defended as appropriate in the interpretation of church dogmas. Here is how he applied this notion to the interpretation of the dogma "No salvation outside the church."

> One of the most remarkable instances of what I am insisting on is found in a dogma, which no Catholic can ever think of disputing, viz., that "Out of the Church, and out of the faith, is no salvation." . . . But it does not follow, because there is no Church but one which has the Evangelical gifts and privileges to bestow, that therefore no one can be saved without the intervention of that one Church. . . . The . . . doctrine in its Catholic form is the doctrine of invincible ignorance—or, that it is possible to belong to the soul of the Church without belonging to the body; and, at the end of 1,800 years, it has been formally and authoritatively put forward by the present Pope (the first Pope, I suppose, who has done so), on the very same occasion on

which he has repeated the fundamental principle of exclusive salvation itself.[4]

The first observation I would make is that while Pius IX did say that people invincibly ignorant of the true religion could be saved, he did not explain this by distinguishing between belonging to the soul and belonging to the body of the church. Newman's use of this distinction as a paraphrase of the pope's teaching indicates that Newman was aware that this explanation of how non-Catholics could be saved was one that a number of Catholic theologians of his day had adopted.[5]

My second observation is that Newman's reference to this distinction is too brief to provide a certain answer to the question as to how he understood it. Third, it is not evident to me exactly what he meant by saying that "it does not follow . . . that therefore no one can be saved without the intervention of that one Church." It is my understanding of the matter that "No salvation outside the church" does in fact mean that no one can be saved without the intervention of the church. But this supposes a specific interpretation of the term "intervention," which will be explained later on in this book. I suspect that Newman may have meant that people could be saved without experiencing the church's ministry of word and sacrament; and of course I would agree that people can be saved without that kind of intervention on the part of the church.

During the period between the First and the Second World Wars, the distinction between the "body" and "soul" of the church, as a way of explaining that all who are saved are in the church, since they are at least in its "soul," was largely abandoned in favor of the distinction between the "mystical body" and the "visible church." For many years, Catholic theologians had been accustomed to discussing the notion of the mystical body in their treatise on grace, whereas their ecclesiology dealt almost exclusively with the institutional church as a "perfect society." Membership in the mystical body was understood to depend on the degree to which one shared in the life of Christ by grace, whereas membership in the institutional church required professing Catholic faith, receiving the sacraments and being in communion with the Catholic bishops and with the pope. At the same time, it was also understood that the term "mystical body" was a traditional way of referring to the church.

Thus one could explain how no one is saved "outside the church," because people who are not members of the church as a visible society are, if they are in the state of grace, members of the mystical body.

One of the most important studies of the theology of the mystical body to be written during the period between the First and the Second World Wars was that by Émile Mersch, S.J., published in English translation with the title *The Theology of the Mystical Body.*[6] This work was widely acclaimed, and undoubtedly has great merit; however, in the following passage we see that Mersch distinguished between the church and the mystical body in a way that suggests the distinction between a visible and an invisible church.

In the ordinary language of the Church, "mystical body" connotes the entire multitude of those who live the life of Christ, with a life that admits of degrees (cf. St. Thomas, *Summa* III, 8, 3), whereas the word "Church" represents the society of the baptized faithful as organized under their lawful pastors.

The two realities are closely related, and the present chapter will show how the one necessarily involves the other. But the two are not absolutely identified on this earth. A person can be a member of the visible society of the Church without actually living the life of Christ as a perfect member of the mystical body; this is the case with a Catholic hardened in sin. Likewise, one can truly live the life of Christ without being actually attached to the visible society that is His Church; an example is a pagan who would have received grace and charity without being aware of the Church, or a fervent catechumen.

It is quite true that the Church visible alone, as established over the entire earth, fully represents what Jesus Christ desires. But it is also true that the visible Church is far from having achieved that position, and Jesus Christ foresaw this. Accordingly the great number of souls effectively living the life of Christ is one thing, and the visible Church is another; in a matter so delicate, dealing with such important objects, we shall find it useful to have two different words to designate two realities that differ *de facto*, however closely they may be related *de jure*.[7]

It is obvious how Mersch's theology of the mystical body lent itself to an apparently easy solution to the problem of reconciling the possibility of salvation for non-Catholics, with the axiom that no one is saved outside the church. While they would not be members of the visible society of the church, since this was identified with the Roman Catholic Church, still, if they were living the life of Christ by grace, they would be members of the mystical body, and in this sense they would not be "outside the church."

While this explanation attracted many adherents among Catholic writers during the period between the two world wars, not all found it satisfactory. Yves Congar, for instance, saw the danger that it would identify the mystical body with an invisible church, really distinct from the visible church. In his pioneer essay on the theology of ecumenism, *Chrétiens désunis*, he wrote:

> The Church as institution is the instrument of the Church as Mystical Body, and the two are organically united so as to be one single reality which is, purely and simply, the Church of Christ.[8]

While Congar refused to separate the church and the mystical body into two distinct realities, he did recognize the presence of "elements" of the mystical body outside the Catholic Church. It was through the efficacy of these "elements" of the mystical body (faith, grace, etc.) that non-Catholics living in the grace of Christ could be said to belong to the church "invisibly," and "incompletely," and yet "really." He explained it this way.

> They belong to the Church in so far as they belong to Christ, because what unites them to Christ is a fiber of his Mystical Body, a constituent element of his Church. The existence of this element apart from and outside the Church is indeed abnormal and untoward, for of its very nature it calls for integration in the one Body of Christ, at once visible and invisible, which is the Catholic Church. But if, by reason of their good faith, on which everything depends, that element of the Church preserves at any rate the essential of its efficacy, it produces its effect of incorporation into the people of the New Covenant: it effectively produces a spiritual incorporation (*voto*) in the Church,

and tends of its own weight toward an entire and visible (*re*) incorporation in the ecclesiastical Catholic body.[9]

Here we see that for Congar there are not two churches, one visible and the other invisible; but there is the one church, which is both visible and invisible. Neither are the mystical body and the church two different realities, although elements of the mystical body can exist abnormally outside the church. Where such elements exist effectively, i.e. where non-Catholics live by the grace of Christ, they belong to the church by desire, if not in fact.

Another well-known Catholic theologian who treated this question during the period between the two world wars was Henri de Lubac. Chapter 7 of his book *Catholicism* is entitled: "Salvation through the Church." De Lubac's approach differs from that of the theologians whom we have thus far considered, in that rather than focusing on the way that individual non-Catholics can be saved, he stresses the role of the church in the salvation of humanity as a whole. Referring to two of the solutions that we have discussed, he describes the "body-soul" solution as neither sufficient nor exact, and the "*re-voto*" solution as incomplete. He adds:

> These explanations take on again their true force and can be used without danger, once it is recognized, by interpreting them collectively, that, for humanity taken as a whole, there can be no salvation outside the church: that this is an absolute necessity, and a necessary means to which there can be no exception.[10]

> And so it is that God, desiring that all men should be saved, but not allowing in practice that all should be visibly in the Church, wills nevertheless that all those who answer his call should in the last resort be saved through his Church. *Sola Ecclesiae gratia, qua redimimur.*[11]

I have to admit that I am not certain in what sense de Lubac intends his statement that all salvation comes "through the church." His final Latin phrase suggests that since the only grace by which we are redeemed is the grace of Christ, it is also in some sense grace of the church. As God has established Christ as the one mediator of salvation for all of humanity, he has also established the church as the means through which salvation will come to all humanity. But, as de Lubac recognizes, it is not all of humanity, but those who "answer God's call" who will be saved, and they will be saved through the church. This suggests that by responding to God's call, i.e. by corresponding with his grace, an individual is brought into a saving relationship with the church. While de Lubac criticized the "re-voto" solution as incomplete, it seems to me that the relationship with the church which he proposed is substantially the same idea as being related to the church by desire. Speaking of a person who has had no direct contact with the church, he says that if that person is docile to the suggestions of grace, his soul already tends spontaneously to the church as to its natural home; he is already a Catholic "by anticipation"; he can be said to "aspire" to the fullness which the church would offer him, and in which he would be ready to "lose himself" once the obstacles that hide it from him were removed.[12] The language is different, but the concept seems pretty much what others have meant by being related to the church "by desire."

We have been looking at theories that were proposed by Catholic theologians in the period between the two world wars. In 1943, while the second of those wars was raging, Pope Pius XII issued an encyclical letter which marked a turning point in Catholic theology of the church, and gave an authoritative answer to the question about the salvation of those "outside the church."

Pius XII, Mystici corporis (1943)

It is not my intention to give a full account of the doctrine contained in this encyclical, but to focus on the contribution which it made to our question of salvation for those "outside the church." This contribution is premised on the fundamental thesis of the encyclical, namely, that the Roman Catholic Church, and it alone, is the mystical body of Christ. Since only Roman Catholics are really members of the church, only they are really members of the mystical body. In the pope's words:

> Among those who are really (reapse) members of the church, those only are to be numbered who have received baptism and profess the true faith, and have neither deplorably separated

themselves from the unity of the body nor been separated from it by legitimate authority for their most serious crimes. . . . Anyone who refuses to listen to the church is, by command of the Lord, to be treated as a pagan or a tax-collector. Wherefore, those who are divided from one another in faith or government cannot live in a body of this kind, nor by its one divine Spirit.[13]

This last phrase suggests that non-Catholics not only are not really members of the mystical body, but that they cannot have supernatural life, since they cannot "live by its one divine Spirit." However, it would seem reasonable to interpret this phrase in the light of the preceding reference to those who refuse to listen to the church and deserve to be treated as pagans and tax-collectors—in other words, to those who are culpably divided from the church. In any case, a later passage of the encyclical shows that Pius XII recognized the possibility of salvation for those inculpably outside the Catholic Church.

In section 100 of the encyclical, Pius XII urged Catholics to pray for "those who are not yet members of the church." He made it clear that he meant both Christians and non-Christians, by mentioning two groups: those who have not yet been enlightened by the gospel, and those separated from the Catholic Church by a breach of faith and unity. In section 101 he went on to say that he desired nothing more ardently than that those who do not belong to the visible structure of the Catholic Church should "have life and have it more abundantly." For this reason, he said:

We urge each and every one of them to be prompt to follow the interior movements of grace, and to seek earnestly to rescue themselves from a state in which they cannot be sure of their own salvation. For even though, by a certain unconscious desire and wish, they may be related to the Mystical Body of the Redeemer, they remain deprived of so many and so powerful gifts and helps from Heaven, which can be enjoyed only within the Catholic Church.

The passage just quoted was surely the most important papal statement about the salvation of those "outside the church" since the 1863 encyclical of Pope Pius IX, and deserves to be analyzed in detail. First of all, while it does not say in so many words that non-Catholics can be saved, neither does it say that they cannot; rather, they are in a state in which "they cannot be sure of their own salvation," and in which they are deprived of many helps to salvation. This clearly recognizes that salvation is possible, even though more problematic, for non-Catholics.

Secondly, the pope explains how the salvation of non-Catholics can be reconciled with the principle that there is no salvation outside the Catholic Church. While such people are not really (*reapse*) members of the Catholic Church, and therefore not really members of the mystical body, they can be related (*ordinantur*) to the mystical body "by a certain unconscious desire and wish" (*inscio quodam voto ac desiderio*). In this phrase, papal authority has been given to the solution which Bellarmine proposed back in the sixteenth century: those who are not actually members of the church can be saved by the desire of belonging to it. Furthermore, the pope has confirmed the teaching of Suarez that even an implicit desire can suffice.

The language used by the pope was carefully chosen. Given the strict identification between the Catholic Church and the mystical body which was the theme of the encyclical, he did not say that non-Catholics could be saved by being *members* of the mystical body; rather, they could be *related* to it, and thus to the Catholic Church, by wish and desire. He admitted that such a desire could be "unconscious" (*inscio*); thus he excluded an interpretation which would have limited the possibility of salvation through "desire" to those who had an explicit desire of joining the Catholic Church. Presumably he recognized the fact that most non-Catholics would have no such explicit desire, and yet he did not exclude the possibility of their salvation.

While the statement of Pius XII undoubtedly made a positive contribution to Catholic thinking on the question of salvation for those "outside the church," it came in for a good deal of criticism. Some objected to the notion of an "unconscious wish," asking how it was possible to have a wish of which one was not conscious, and how one could attribute a desire to join the Catholic Church to people who insisted they had no such desire. The answer, which the pope did not give, but which he no doubt expected Catholic theologians to supply, was that such a desire was implicit in the person's dispositions. Those who sincerely wished to do the will of

God implicitly desired what God required of them, even if they did not know what that was. Speaking more accurately, it was not the desire as such, but a specific object of the desire, of which they were not conscious.

The most common criticism of this part of the encyclical was that it made no distinction between Christians and non-Christians when it said that they could be related to the mystical body of Christ by an unconscious desire. It was objected that this ignored the fact that by virtue of their baptism, Christians are sacramentally incorporated into Christ, and must belong to his mystical body in a way that the unbaptized do not. Among criticisms raised by Catholic commentators on the encyclical, this was the one most often voiced by those open to the ecumenical movement. It must be admitted that they had grounds for their criticism; the clarification they desired would be made at the Second Vatican Council.

The question of the necessity of belonging to the church for salvation came up briefly again in Pius XII's encyclical *Humani generis* of 1950. Here the pope complained that some Catholic theologians were "reducing to a meaningless formula the necessity of belonging to the true church in order to gain eternal salvation."[14] There was no further explanation given of what such a "meaningless formula" might be. I would hazard a surmise that the pope was referring to one or another of the explanations which we have already described as amounting to no more than saying that in order to be on the way to salvation one must be in the state of grace. Such would be, for instance, that it is sufficient to belong to the "invisible church," or to the "soul" of the church, or to the "mystical body," when each of these terms means simply the "entire multitude of all those in the state of grace."

Much of the criticism of the doctrine of Pope Pius XII's encyclical *Mystici corporis* came from those who would have preferred a more ecumenical approach to the question of salvation outside the Catholic Church, especially with reference to non-Catholic Christians. However, there were some Catholics who would have preferred it if Pope Pius had simply reaffirmed the ancient doctrine that there was no salvation outside the Catholic Church and left it at that. The most vociferous of these were Fr. Leonard Feeney and his followers at St. Benedict Center in Cambridge, Massachusetts. We have mentioned this group already at the beginning of this book.

Coming back to them now, after following the development which had taken place in Catholic thinking since the sixteenth century, we shall have a better idea of how utterly out of harmony their position was with the thinking of the Catholic Church in the middle of the twentieth century.

Leonard Feeney and St. Benedict Center

The doctrine which this group was propagating during the late 1940s in the archdiocese of Boston can be summed up in the following propositions. "No salvation outside the Roman Catholic Church" is a defined dogma of faith, and anyone who denies it, or waters it down, is guilty of heresy. This dogma means that no one is saved who does not live and die as a Roman Catholic. The only exception to actual membership is had in the case of a baptized person who explicitly desires and is preparing to enter the Catholic Church, and who dies unexpectedly before being admitted. The statements of Popes Pius IX and Pius XII must be understood to mean that if non-Catholics correspond to divine grace, they can be saved by entering the Catholic Church before they die. It is absurd to think that Protestants and Jews have an unconscious desire of belonging to the Catholic Church, or that they could be saved by having such a desire. The idea that they can be saved outside the Catholic Church is not only false but pernicious, since it kills the zeal which Catholics ought to have to seek to draw their non-Catholic friends and neighbors into the Catholic Church. It eliminates a strong motive which they ought to be able to use, namely, that it is only by actual membership in the Catholic Church that anyone can be saved.[15]

Fr. Feeney and his followers based their first proposition— that *Extra ecclesiam nulla salus* is a defined dogma of faith—on the statements of the medieval popes and councils which we cited in Chapter 1. As we have seen, the *Decree for the Jacobites* of the Council of Florence shows that medieval Christians really believed that anyone who died outside the Catholic Church would be condemned to the eternal torments of hell. At the same time, it is equally certain that they believed that God is just, and that he does not condemn the innocent to eternal torment. The unspoken element in the medieval understanding of the dogma has to be: those who die outside the Catholic Church must be guilty of grave and unrepented sin, of heresy, schism, or unbelief, for which God will justly condemn them.

We have every reason to believe that Fr. Feeney and his followers also believed that God is just, and that he does not condemn the innocent to the torments of hell. I do not know how they could return to the medieval understanding of *Extra ecclesiam nulla salus*, unless they also returned to the unspoken premise of that understanding: namely, that all those who die outside the Catholic Church must be guilty of the sin of heresy, schism, or unbelief. It is possible to understand how medieval Christians could have made such a judgment, given their limited knowledge of the world outside Christendom, and their apparent inability to imagine how Jews or Moslems could be without guilt in their refusal to become Christians. But it is indeed hard to understand how Fr. Leonard Feeney, a man of the twentieth century, could make such a judgment about all the millions of people in the world who were not Roman Catholics. But if he did not judge them all guilty, the only alternative is that he must have believed that God condemns the innocent to the torments of hell, and that would be a more grievous error than the first.

After Fr. Feeney had publicly accused the archbishop of Boston of heresy for allowing that non-Catholics could be saved, an appeal was made to Rome for an authoritative interpretation of the axiom *Extra ecclesiam nulla salus*. The response came in the form of a letter of the holy office, the bureau of the holy see responsible for doctrine, addressed to Archbishop Cushing. As has so often been the case, the controversy had the beneficial effect of bringing forth a clearer and more detailed presentation of the church's teaching than had previously been made. The document is important enough for our subject to justify a fairly lengthy quotation.[16]

Letter of the Holy Office to Archbishop Cushing (1949)

The infallible dictum which teaches us that outside the Church there is no salvation, is among the truths that the Church has always taught and will always teach. But this dogma is to be understood as the Church itself understands it. For the Saviour did not leave it to private judgment to explain what is contained in the deposit of faith, but to the doctrinal authority of the Church.

The Church teaches, first of all, that there is question here of a very strict command of Jesus Christ. In unmistakable words He gave His apostles the command to teach all nations to keep whatever He had commanded (cf. Mt 28:19). Not least among Christ's commands is the one which orders us to be incorporated by baptism into the mystical Body of Christ, which is the Church, and to be united to Christ and to His vicar, through whom He Himself governs the Church on earth in a visible way. Therefore, no one who knows that the Church has been divinely established by Christ and, nevertheless, refuses to be a subject of the Church or refuses to obey the Roman Pontiff, the vicar of Christ on earth, will be saved.

The Saviour did not make it merely a necessity of precept for all nations to enter the Church. He also established the Church as a means of salvation without which no one can enter the kingdom of heavenly glory.

As regards the helps to salvation which are ordered to the last end only by divine decree, not by intrinsic necessity, God, in His infinite mercy, willed that their effects which are necessary to salvation can, in certain circumstances, be obtained when the helps are used only in desire or longing. We see this clearly stated in the Council of Trent about the sacrament of regeneration and about the sacrament of penance.[17] The same, in due proportion, should be said of the Church in so far as it is a general help to salvation. To gain eternal salvation it is not always required that a person be incorporated in reality (*reapse*) as a member of the Church, but it is required that he belong to it at least in desire and longing (*voto et desiderio*). It is not always necessary that this desire be explicit, as it is with catechumens. When a man is invincibly ignorant, God also accepts an implicit desire, so called because it is contained in the good dispositions of soul by which a man wants his will to be conformed to God's will.

This is clearly taught by the Sovereign Pontiff Pope Pius XII in his doctrinal letter on the mystical Body of Christ. . . . Toward the end of the encyclical, when with all his heart he invites to union those who do not pertain to the body of the Catholic Church, the Pope mentions those "who are ordained to the mystical Body of the Redeemer by some kind of unconscious desire or longing." He by no means excludes these men from eternal salvation, but, on the other hand, he does point out that they are in a condition "in which they cannot be secure about their salvation . . . since they lack many great gifts and helps from God which they can enjoy only in the Catholic Church."

With these prudent words the Pope censures those who exclude from eternal salvation all men who adhere to the Church only with an implicit desire; and he also censures those who falsely maintain that men can be saved equally well in any religion.

It must not be imagined that any desire whatsoever of entering the Church is sufficient for a man to be saved. It is necessary that the desire by which a man is related to the Church be informed with perfect charity. And an implicit desire cannot have its effect unless a man has supernatural faith.

Since this letter of the holy office was issued during the pontificate of Pius XII, and was undoubtedly approved by him, we can be sure that it offers an explanation of the doctrine of *Mystici corporis* which is faithful to the intention of the pope. At the same time, it spells out the doctrine of the encyclical in more technical terms and in more detail than would have been appropriate in a papal letter addressed to the whole church. The key idea in the letter of the holy office is the distinction between two kinds of necessity of means for salvation. It might be appropriate to explain this a bit further here.

The necessity of belonging to the Catholic Church for salvation is a necessity both of divine precept and of means. There are two kinds of necessity of means. Some means are intrinsically necessary for salvation: such are faith in God and repentance for personal sin. For such means as these, in the case of adults, there is no possible substitute. Other things, however, have been established as means necessary for salvation by a positive divine decree. This is not the same as simple necessity of precept, since what has been established by divine decree *as a necessary means* must always, in some sense, enter into the obtaining of the intended effect. This is not true of what is necessary *simply* because it has been commanded by God.

It is the understanding of this matter in Catholic theology that when it is physically or morally impossible to make actual use of means that have been made necessary by a positive divine decree, such means must still enter into the obtaining of the effect, which they do if the person has the desire of using them. Such a desire need not in every case be explicit. People who are invincibly ignorant of the fact that God has established the church as a means necessary for their salvation can have a saving relation to the church by a desire which is implicit in their interior dispositions which signify the conformity of their wills to the will of God in their regard.

It is not difficult to see that in this explanation of the necessity of belonging to the Catholic Church for salvation, the holy office has given authoritative approval to an interpretation of *Extra ecclesiam nulla salus* which began with Bellarmine and Suarez in the sixteenth century, and in modern times was most fully developed by Franzelin. The holy office has given official sanction to the *in re–in voto* solution, to which, we recall, a number of the consultors of the drafting committee at Vatican I were opposed. This solution, however, has good credentials. It was adopted by the Council of Trent in its decree on the necessity of the sacrament of baptism. It is true that Trent did not specify that an implicit desire of baptism could suffice; but even on this point one could appeal to the authority of St. Thomas Aquinas, who had admitted this possibility. While it is true that neither Trent nor St. Thomas had applied the *in voto* solution to the necessity of belonging to the church, it is a logical corollary, given the fact that it is by baptism that one enters the church. Important elements of this solution, then, were to be found in the *Summa theologiae* and in the decrees of Trent, but it was only in the middle of the twentieth century that it was officially proposed as the Catholic Church's understanding of *Extra ecclesiam nulla salus*.

Needless to say, the letter of the holy office did not satisfy Fr. Feeney and his followers at St. Benedict Center, who remained adamant in their literal interpretation of "No salvation outside the Catholic Church." On one important point the letter of the holy office failed to satisfy ecumenically-minded Catholics as well; as was the case in *Mystici corporis*, the letter made no distinction between Christians and non-Christians as far as their relation to the mystical body is concerned. In either case, they could be related to it by desire; no reference is made to the fact that by their baptism Christians have a sacramental relationship to the church which non-Christians do not have.

I have suggested that this was a defect which needed to be remedied, and that the remedy would be supplied by Vatican II. It is time now to see what contribution that council has made to the development of Christian thought about the salvation of those "outside the church."

9 || The Second Vatican Council

After Pope John XXIII had announced the convocation of the Second Vatican Council, a preparatory theological commission was formed in 1960, with Cardinal Ottaviani, prefect of the holy office as its head, and Fr. Sebastian Tromp, S.J., chief collaborator with Pius XII in the writing of *Mystici corporis*, as its secretary. From the texts produced by this commission, one can safely judge that its expectation was that the council would in no case depart from what was already official Catholic doctrine. It is no surprise, then, that on the question of salvation for those outside the Catholic Church, it echoed the teaching of Pius XII and the further explanation given by the holy office in its letter of 1949 to Archbishop Cushing.

This commission prepared a draft of a constitution on the church, which was discussed by the council for one week during its opening period in 1962. Its first chapter, "On the Nature of the Church Militant," repeated the fundamental theme of *Mystici corporis*, that the Roman Catholic Church is the mystical body of Christ, and expressed this identification even more strongly by declaring: "Only the Roman Catholic Church has the right to the name 'church.'" [1] The question of the necessity of belonging to the Catholic Church for salvation was taken up in chapter 2, whose first section reads as follows:

> The holy council teaches, as the holy church of God has always taught, that the church is necessary for salvation, and that no one can be saved who, knowing that the Catholic Church was established by God through Jesus Christ, would refuse to enter or remain in it. Moreover, just as no one can be saved except by

141

receiving the sacrament of baptism, by which one who puts no obstacle in the way of incorporation becomes a member of the church, so also no one can obtain salvation unless one is a member of the church, or is related to it by desire. However, in order that a person reach salvation, it is not enough to be a member of the church or to be related to it by desire; it is further required that a person die in the state of grace, united with God by faith, hope and charity.[2]

The following section further explains who can be related to the church by desire.

It is not only catechumens, who, moved by the Holy Spirit, aspire to enter the church with a conscious and explicit intention, who are related to the church by desire; but others also who do not know that the Catholic Church is the only true Church of Christ, can, through the grace of God, obtain a similar effect through an implicit and unconscious desire. This is the case whether they sincerely wish what Christ himself wishes, or, not knowing Christ, they sincerely desire to fulfill the will of God their Creator. For the gifts of heavenly grace are by no means lacking to those who, with a sincere heart, wish and seek to be renewed by divine light.[3]

In the course of the one week (December 1–7, 1962) during which this preparatory draft of the Constitution on the Church was discussed, it received such strong criticism from the bishops that, at the end of the first period of the council, it was withdrawn without having been put to a vote. During the spring and summer of 1963 a new draft was prepared, which incorporated a good deal of material from the preparatory one, but differed substantially from it in tone and general approach. This new draft was presented to the council at the opening of the 1963 period, and was discussed for the whole month of October. It followed the previous text in asserting that the one and only church of Christ is the Roman Catholic Church, but it added the significant admission that "many elements of sanctification can be found outside its total structure," and that these are "things properly belonging to the church of Christ."[4]

The necessity of belonging to the Catholic Church for salvation was treated in the new draft in the following terms.

The holy council teaches, with Holy Scripture and Tradition, that the church is an institution necessary for salvation, and that therefore those cannot be saved who, knowing that the Catholic Church has been established by God through Jesus Christ as necessary, refuse to enter it or to remain in it. For what revelation affirms about the necessity of baptism (cf. Mk 16:16; Jn 3:5) undoubtedly applies also to the church, which one enters through baptism as by a door.[5]

It is normal that a conciliar text would not use the theological terms "necessity of precept" and "necessity of means." However, it was understood that the sacrament of baptism is necessary as a means of salvation, and not merely by virtue of a divine precept. Hence, the analogy between the necessity of baptism and that of the church suggests that the latter is also to be understood as the necessity of means.

The new draft also followed the previous one in insisting that only Roman Catholics are really (*reapse*) members of the church. It then explained that those who are not really members can be related to the church by desire.

Catechumens who, moved by the Holy Spirit, knowingly and explicitly seek to be incorporated in the church, are joined to her by desire [*voto*], and Mother Church already embraces them as her own with her love and care. In its own way the same is true [*Suo modo idem valet*] of those who, not knowing that the Catholic Church is the one true church of Christ, sincerely, with the help of grace, seek with interior faith, hope and charity to do the will of Christ, or, if they lack distinct knowledge of Christ, to do the will of God the Creator, who wishes all to be saved.[6]

The phrase "In its own way the same is true" clearly means that those who are ignorant of their obligation to join the Catholic Church can have a saving relationship with it *voto:* by desire. This will be "in its own way" however; they will not have an explicit desire as catechumens do, but one that is implicit in their sincere intention to do the will of Christ, if they are Christians, or the will of God the creator, if they are not. The new draft, therefore, continued to apply Pius XII's solution to the question of the salvation of those outside the Catholic Church, again without making any distinction between Christians and non-Christians as far as their relationship to the church is concerned. However, at this point it introduced a paragraph which supplied something that was lacking in the previous texts, namely the recognition of the many ways in which the Catholic Church is joined with other Christians in the common sharing of the goods of salvation. Among such goods are mentioned faith in Christ, baptism and other sacraments, faith with regard to the eucharist, sharing in prayer and other spiritual benefits, and a certain communion in the Holy Spirit, who works with his sanctifying power not only within the Catholic Church but also among other Christians.[7]

The following section of this draft has the title: "Concerning non-Christians as people to be drawn to the church." The main theme of this section, as the title indicates, is the missionary task of the church to evangelize the non-Christian world. However, it includes a positive statement about the values to be found in other religions, which are described as a "preparation for the Gospel and light given by God." After this we find the following statement about the possibility of salvation for non-Christians.

> Those who, without blame, do not know Christ or his church, but with a sincere heart seek God and his will, as it is known to them through the dictates of their conscience, and who, with the help of grace, try to fulfill God's will in their actions, can hope for eternal salvation. . . .[8]

This is what Pius IX said in 1863, with one exception: he said that under these same conditions, they *can* be saved, while the conciliar draft says only that they can *hope* for salvation. But perhaps the difference is not all that significant, since, during this mortal life, salvation must always remain an object of hope and not of certitude. In any case, we can presume that the dispositions which are mentioned here as justifying the non-Christian's hope for salvation are those in which the same draft would recognize the presence of an implicit desire of belonging to the Catholic Church.

This 1963 draft of the conciliar text on the church met with general approval, but received a very great number of proposals for emendation. During the interval before the next period of the council, a considerable revision was made in the light of those proposals. When the bishops gathered in the fall of 1964 they were working with a large volume entitled *Schema Constitutionis de Ecclesia*, which contained the 1963 draft and the revised text, along with the reports [*relationes*] of the theological commission, explaining the reasons for each change that had been made in the text. During the 1964 period the council voted its final approval of the revised text, with the result that on November 21, Pope Paul VI was able to promulgate the Dogmatic Constitution on the Church known as *Lumen gentium*. On the same date, Paul VI also promulgated the conciliar Decree on Ecumenism, *Unitatis redintegratio*. With the promulgation of those two conciliar texts, an extraordinary change took place in official Catholic doctrine about the salvation of non-Catholic Christians. Up until the 1963 draft, as we have seen, the official doctrine was that since there is only one church of Christ, which is exclusively identified with the Roman Catholic Church, it follows that the Catholic Church is the only ecclesial means of salvation, and that, therefore, salvation for other Christians must also come through the Catholic Church, by virtue of their implicit desire to belong to it. The recognition, both in *Lumen gentium* and in the Decree on Ecumenism, of the ecclesial value of the other Christian churches and communities introduced a profound change in our understanding of the way that other Christians reach salvation. This change is so significant that in my opinion "No salvation outside the church" is no longer a problem for Catholic theology as far as the members of the other Christian churches are concerned. In the light of Vatican II, we can now recognize their own churches as the ecclesial means by which non-Catholic Christians are being saved.

I shall first present the evidence which I believe warrants my interpretation of the teaching of Vatican II with regard to the salvation of other Christians. Then I shall take up what now has to be seen as a distinct question: that of the role of the church in the salvation of non-Christians.

Vatican II on the Salvation of Other Christians

First we shall consider the new elements that were introduced into the draft of the Constitution on the Church between 1963 and

1964, and which remain in the text of *Lumen gentium*. Then we shall look at what the Decree on Ecumenism says about our question.[9]

The first momentous change was the dropping of the claim of exclusive identity between the church of Christ and the Roman Catholic Church. The 1963 text had said: "The Church of Christ *is* the Roman Catholic Church." The final text, in LG 8, says: "The Church of Christ *subsists in* the Roman Catholic Church." There would have been no point in making this change if "subsists in" had the same exclusive sense as the flat assertion that the one *is* the other. Now what is affirmed is that the church which Christ founded and entrusted to St. Peter and the other apostles continues to exist, under the leadership of the successors of Peter and the apostles, in the Catholic Church. This is a positive statement about the Catholic Church, but it does not say or imply that the church of Christ exists nowhere else than in the Catholic Church. It leaves that question open, in a way that official Catholic doctrine had never done before. Hence, practically all commentators have seen in this change of wording a significant opening toward the recognition of ecclesial reality in the other Christian churches and communities.[10]

The second momentous change was the dropping of the statement that only Roman Catholics are really (*reapse*) members of Christ's church. Now, instead of saying that only Catholics are *really* members of the church, the text of LG 14 says that *only those* Catholics are *fully* incorporated in the church who are living in the state of grace. This change signifies a break with the idea that belonging to the church is an "either-or," "all-or-nothing" proposition. It introduces the idea of different degrees of fullness of incorporation in the church, applying this in the first instance to Catholics themselves. But if some Catholics are more fully incorporated than others, it would seem logical to acknowledge degrees of incorporation in the church on the part of other Christians as well, since baptism has always been seen as the sacrament by which one becomes a member of the church.

This line of reasoning led to another important change in the text. We have seen that the 1963 draft still maintained that non-Catholics could be saved by virtue of an implicit desire of belonging to the Catholic Church. We have seen how long a history lay behind this *in voto* solution to the problem of the salvation of those outside the Catholic Church. In the final revision of *Lumen gentium* the only persons who are said to belong to the church "by desire" are catechumens. The idea that in order for non-Catholics to be saved, they must have an implicit desire to belong to the Catholic Church, disappeared from the text of *Lumen gentium* and is found nowhere else in the documents of Vatican II. The explanation given by the theological commission for dropping the phrase "In its own way the same is true" reads as follows:

> The words of the previous text: *Suo modo idem valet*, are not retained by the Commission. The idea is now better expressed below, in no. 15. In any case, non-Catholic Christians do not have the desire of baptism (*votum baptismi*), but baptism itself. Hence they are not to be put in the same category with the non-baptized. Many of the Council Fathers spoke to this point.[11]

The final sentence undoubtedly reflects the dissatisfaction of many bishops with the fact that previously no distinction had been made between Christians and non-Christians as far as their relationship to the church was concerned; of both it was said that they could be related to it by desire. Now official recognition is given to the fact that by their baptism, other Christians are *really*, even if not *fully*, incorporated in the church of Christ.

Section 15 of *Lumen gentium*, to which the theological commission refers here, is the final version of that part of the 1963 text which described the many goods of salvation which Catholics share with other Christians. Here another emendation was made which has an important bearing on the question of the salvation of other Christians. The previous text had said of them that they receive baptism and other sacraments. The final text makes an extremely significant change by adding the phrase "in their own churches and ecclesial communities." Here we have a concrete application of the decision no longer to identify the church of Christ exclusively with the Roman Catholic Church. If other Christian bodies are rightly called "churches and ecclesial communities," they also must participate, in varying degrees, in the reality of Christ's church. Furthermore, they participate in the saving function of Christ's church inasmuch as it is in these churches and communities that people are brought to Christian faith and receive the sacraments of salvation. Christians are not saved in spite of, or independently of, the churches to which they belong, but rather through the ministry of word and sacrament which their own churches provide for them.

The positive approach taken by *Lumen gentium* in regard to the significance of the other Christian churches and communities was further developed in the Decree on Ecumenism. The idea of varying degrees of fullness, which in *Lumen gentium* had been applied to the notion of incorporation in the church, was here applied to the communion which already exists among the Christian churches, and to the reality of church itself, which the decree recognized as more fully present in those bodies which it called "churches" than in those which it called "ecclesial communities." This distinction is based on the principle that there is not the full reality of church where, "because of the lack of the sacrament of orders" (UR 22), there is not the full reality of the eucharist. However, even here the council insisted that it was using the term "ecclesial" correctly. The commission responsible for the Decree on Ecumenism defended its use of this term in the following way.

> It must not be overlooked that the communities that have their origin in the separation that took place in the West are not merely a sum or collection of individual Christians. On the contrary, they are constituted by social ecclesiastical elements which they have preserved from our common patrimony, and which confer on them a truly ecclesial character. In these communities the one sole Church of Christ is present, albeit imperfectly, in a way that is somewhat like its presence in particular churches, and by means of their ecclesiastical elements the Church of Christ is in some way operative in them.[12]

The final phrase here could well have been completed by adding the words: "for the salvation of those who in good faith belong to them." In other words, in this official explanation of the conciliar text, we have a clear recognition of the saving function of the other Christian churches and communities, in which the one church of Christ is really, if imperfectly, present and operative.

The Decree on Ecumenism spells out the saving function of these churches and communities even more explicitly in the following passage of its chapter entitled: "Catholic Principles of Ecumenism."

The brethren divided from us also carry out many of the sacred actions of the Christian religion. Undoubtedly, in ways that vary according to the condition of each church or community, these actions can truly engender a life of grace, and can be rightly described as capable of providing access to the community of salvation.

It follows that these separated churches and communities, though we believe they suffer from defects already mentioned, have by no means been deprived of significance and importance in the mystery of salvation. For the Spirit of Christ has not refrained from using them as means of salvation which derive their efficacy from the very fullness of grace and truth entrusted to the Catholic Church (UR 3).

It is the doctrine of Vatican II that it is only in the Catholic Church that the fullness of the means of salvation is to be found. Whatever "elements of sanctification and of truth" are present and operative in other Christian churches historically are derived from the one church of Christ which "subsists in" the Catholic Church. In some way, which the council does not further specify, their efficacy as means of salvation is also derived from that fullness which is found in the Catholic Church. But this does not conflict with the basic assertion of the text: that the Catholic Church now recognizes that other Christian churches and communities are used by God as instruments of salvation for those who belong to them in good faith. The necessary role of the church in their salvation is explained by the role which their own churches play in their salvation. In those churches, the one Church of Christ is effectively present and salvifically operative, even if it does not "subsist" there with the same unity and the same fullness of the means of grace with which it subsists in the Catholic Church. The conclusion which I draw from this, as I have said above, is that "No salvation outside the church" is no longer a problem for Catholic theology as far as the salvation of other Christians is concerned.

However, we must now test this conclusion in the light of the passage of *Lumen gentium* which speaks explicitly about the necessity of belonging to the Catholic Church, and explains for whom there is no salvation outside of it. Here is the conciliar text.

> Basing itself upon sacred Scripture and tradition, [this sacred synod] teaches that the Church, now sojourning on earth as an exile, is necessary for salvation. For Christ, made present to us in His Body, which is the Church, is the one Mediator and the unique Way of salvation. In explicit terms, He Himself affirmed the necessity of faith and baptism, and thereby affirmed also the necessity of the Church, for through baptism as through a door men enter the Church. Whosoever, therefore, knowing that the Catholic Church was made necessary by God through Jesus Christ, would refuse to enter her or to remain in her, could not be saved (LG 14).

We have seen above that at the First Vatican Council, the draft of the Constitution on the Church contained a paragraph on the necessity of the church, which specified that this was a necessity not only of precept but of means.[13] At Vatican II, several of the bishops requested that the text of LG 14 be amended to include explicit reference to the necessity of means. The theological commission replied that such necessity was sufficiently indicated by the analogy with the necessity of Christ as mediator and the necessity of baptism.[14]

The necessity of Christ as the one mediator of salvation, and the necessity of Christian faith and baptism, explain the necessity of joining the church for the salvation of those who lack Christian faith and baptism. On the other hand, the last sentence of the text we have cited would apply to non-Catholic Christians as well, if they became personally convinced of their obligation to join the Catholic Church. In their case, such an obligation would obviously not be based on the necessity of Christian faith and baptism, for they have those in their own churches. For them, would it then be merely a necessity of precept when they came to know that it was the will of God in their regard that they become Roman Catholics? Or would it be a relative necessity of means, in the sense of the necessity of belonging to the church in which the fullness of such means was to be found? Whichever answer is given, it is clear that it is only those who are culpably outside the Catholic Church who would thereby be excluded from salvation. The terms "knowing . . . would refuse" used in the conciliar text clearly indicate a sinful decision not to fulfill a known grave obligation.

The Second Vatican Council thus reaffirmed what had been

official Catholic doctrine since the time of Pius IX: that it is only those who are *culpably* outside the Catholic Church who are thereby excluded from salvation. In this book I have given my reasons for believing that the culpability of those "outside" has always been at least an unspoken assumption, when statements were made excluding them from salvation. The profound difference between the medieval view and the doctrine of Vatican II on the salvation of non-Catholics is that instead of a presumption of guilt, the attitude expressed by the council involves a presumption of innocence. This presumption was actually expressed by the theological commission in its note explaining the final sentence of the passage of LG 14 cited above. Referring to the words "knowing . . . would refuse to enter her or remain in her," the commission remarked that this would be an almost unreal hypothesis.[15] In other words, Vatican II presumes the absence of the culpability that would mean exclusion from salvation for those "outside" the Catholic Church. But if we presume that those outside are inculpable, then we must conclude that they can be saved. And this applies to the majority of the world's people who have neither Christian faith nor baptism. The question now is not whether, but how they can be saved. For an ecclesiologist, that means: whether the church is involved in their salvation, and, if so, how. These are the questions that we shall now try to answer.

Vatican II on the Role of the Church in the Salvation of Non-Christians

We have seen above that the intention of the theological commission in *Lumen gentium* 14 was to indicate that belonging to the church was necessary for salvation with necessity of means. From this it should logically follow that no one could be saved without at least the desire of belonging to the church. This was the official Catholic position under Pope Pius XII and in the early drafts of the Constitution on the Church at Vatican II. However, following the revision of the text that took place between 1963 and 1964, there is no mention in *Lumen gentium*, or anywhere else in the documents of Vatican II, of the necessity of such a *votum* of belonging to the church on the part of those who are not Catholics. Does this mean that Vatican II intended to abandon the *in voto* solution to the problem of the salvation of those "outside the church"? As far as other Christians are concerned, I believe the answer is yes. But I do not believe that this was the council's intention with regard to non-Christians. Given the doctrine of Trent that at least the desire to be baptized is required for justification, and since it is by baptism that one enters the church, it seems logical to say that for non-Christians to be saved, they must be related to the church by implicit desire. This, as we have seen, was the language used by Pope Pius XII. Vatican II chose not to use it, even though it is fully consonant with its intention to present the necessity of the church as necessity of means, on the analogy of the necessity of baptism. Where Pius XII had said that non-Christians were related to the church by an unconscious desire, Vatican II says merely that they are related to her "in various ways" (LG 16). Two questions present themselves: How does Vatican II explain these "various ways" by which non-Christians are related to the church, and what does this relatedness have to do with their salvation? It is to these questions that we must now turn.

The conciliar teaching is found in no. 16 of *Lumen gentium*, which begins by saying: "Finally, those who have not yet received the gospel are related in various ways to the People of God." As the word "finally" suggests, this article is the last of three articles (14, 15, 16), which develop the theme which was announced in the last paragraph of no. 13. That paragraph reads:

> All men are called to be part of this catholic unity of the People of God, a unity which is harbinger of the universal peace it promotes. And there belong to it, or are related to it in various ways, the Catholic faithful as well as all who believe in Christ, and indeed the whole of mankind. For all men are called to salvation by the grace of God (LG 13).

Both the first and the last sentence of this paragraph speak of a universal call. Since the term "the people of God" in the documents of Vatican II is synonymous with "the church," the first sentence means that all are called to belong to the church. The last sentence is an expression of belief in the universal salvific will of God, by whose grace all are called to salvation. There is a difference between these two calls: the "call to the church" obviously does not make it possible for every individual actually to enter the church by baptism, whereas the grace through which the call to salvation is given does make it possible for everyone to be saved.

The second sentence of this paragraph distinguishes two ways in which people stand in relation to the church: they either "belong" to it or are "related" to it. Those who "belong" to it are the Catholic faithful and all who believe in Christ; those who are "related" to it are the rest of mankind. It would seem clear that the reason why only Christians are said to "belong" is that it is by baptism that one becomes a member of the church. All others are said to be "related" to the church "in various ways." It is this "varied relatedness" that is explained in LG 16, which reads as follows.

> Finally, those who have not yet received the gospel are related in various ways to the People of God. In the first place there is the people to whom the covenants and the promises were given and from whom Christ was born according to the flesh (cf. Rom 9:4–5). On account of their fathers, this people remains most dear to God, for God does not repent of the gifts He makes nor of the calls He issues (cf. Rom 11:28–29).

> But the plan of salvation also includes those who acknowledge the Creator. In the first place among these there are the Moslems, who, professing to hold the faith of Abraham, along with us adore the one and merciful God, who on the last day will judge mankind. Nor is God Himself far distant from those who in shadows and images seek the unknown God, for it is He who gives to all men life and breath and every other gift (cf. Acts 17:25–28), and who as Savior wills that all men be saved (cf. 1 Tim 2:4).

> Those also can attain to everlasting salvation who through no fault of their own do not know the gospel of Christ or His Church, yet sincerely seek God and, moved by grace, strive by their deeds to do His will as it is known to them through the dictates of conscience. Nor does divine Providence deny the help necessary for salvation to those who, without blame on their part, have not yet arrived at an explicit knowledge of God, but who strive to live a good life, thanks to His grace. Whatever goodness or truth is found among them is looked upon by the Church as a preparation for the gospel. She regards such quali-

ties as given by Him who enlightens all men so that they may finally have life.

But rather often men, deceived by the Evil One, have become caught up in futile reasoning and have exchanged the truth of God for a lie, serving the creature rather than the Creator (cf. Rom 1:21, 25). Or some there are who, living and dying in a world without God, are subject to utter hopelessness. Consequently, to promote the glory of God and procure the salvation of all such men, and mindful of the command of the Lord, "Preach the gospel to every creature," the Church painstakingly fosters her missionary work (LG 16).

In this long article, five groups of people are distinguished on the basis of the source and kind of knowledge of God that is characteristic of each group. They are listed in a descending order, from those whose knowledge of God is closest to Christian faith, to those who have not yet arrived at an explicit knowledge of God.

First to be mentioned are the Jewish people, whose knowledge of God is based on divine revelation. Being still "God's dear people," they are uniquely related to the people of the new covenant, being, as St. Paul put it, the good olive tree onto which the Gentiles, as branches of a wild olive, were grafted (cf. Rom 11:17–21). The next group are the Moslems, who are mentioned first among those who "acknowledge the Creator" and who adore God as a merciful judge. After the Moslems come "those who in shadows and images seek the unknown God." Presumably the council is here referring to those who belong to other non-Christian religions, such as Hinduism and Buddhism, although no religions are mentioned by name.[16]

The following paragraph seems best understood as referring to people who do not practice any specific religion. Some are described as those "who sincerely seek God"; others as "those who, without blame on their part, have not yet arrived at an explicit knowledge of God." Of both groups it is said that they strive, with the help of grace, to live a good life according to the dictates of their conscience.

The question remains as to the sense in which these various groups of people are said to be "related to the church." There is no problem on this score with regard to the Jewish people, who are in a unique relationship to Christ and to his church. But the only factor that is common to all the other groups is that they are all included in God's plan of salvation, and that they all receive the offer of his grace. We do not know what proportion of those who receive this offer will respond to it in such a way as to arrive at salvation. Nor do we know how many of them will arrive at actual membership in the church before they die. And yet all, whether they will be saved or not, whether they will become Christians or not, continue to receive the offer of grace which directs them toward salvation.[17] It seems reasonable to conclude that it is because they are all recipients of God's offer of saving grace that they are also said to be "related to the church." This idea is not expressed in the text of LG 16, but we have good reason to believe that it was in the minds of those who drafted the text, for we find the following statement in the *relatio* of the theological commission on LG 16: "All grace has a certain communitarian quality, and looks toward the church."[18]

There are several reasons for saying that just as every offer of grace directs the recipient toward salvation, so also every offer of grace directs the recipient toward the church. One reason is that the ultimate goal of all such grace is that the person might be numbered among all those who "from Abel, the just one, to the last of the elect, will be gathered together with the Father in the universal Church" (LG 2). Grace whose goal is participation in the "universal church" of the eschatological kingdom of God must also be intrinsically ordered toward the church in its earthly state. Second, the grace that brings a person to supernatural justice must make possible an act of saving faith. Such faith, no matter how imperfect it may be in conceptual content, is intrinsically directed toward the full profession of faith in divine revelation, which is had only in the church. Third, the grace of salvation includes the gift of supernatural love of God and neighbor, and this is intrinsically ordered toward the communion in charity which is the inner life of the church. If I am not mistaken, it was for reasons such as these that the theological commission said: "All grace has a communitarian quality and looks toward the church." In other words, there is an ecclesial character, an orientation toward the church, in every offer of grace. And since the offer of grace is made to all, all are, by that fact, "related to the church."

Before the Second Vatican Council, Yves Congar had expressed the idea which we have just been discussing, in the following way:

> The Catholic Church remains the only institution (*sacramentum*) divinely instituted and mandated for salvation, and whatever grace exists in the world is related to her by finality, if not by efficaciousness. [19]

The question I now wish to raise is whether Vatican II gives us reason to believe that all grace for salvation is related to the church not only by finality, but also, in some sense, by efficaciousness. I believe that the basis for such an opinion can be found in the council's description of the church as the "universal sacrament of salvation."[20]

Vatican II on the Church as "Universal Sacrament of Salvation"

The following are the principal passages in the documents of the council which express this idea.

> By her relationship with Christ, the church is a kind of sacrament, that is, sign and instrument of intimate union with God and of the unity of all mankind (LG 1).

> God has gathered together as one all those who in faith look upon Jesus as the author of salvation and the source of unity and peace, and has established them as the church, that for each and all she may be the visible sacrament of this saving unity (LG 9).

> Rising from the dead, Christ sent his life-giving Spirit upon his disciples and through this Spirit has established his body, the church, as the universal sacrament of salvation (LG 48).

> Every benefit which the people of God during its earthly pilgrimage can offer to the human family stems from the fact that the church is the universal sacrament of salvation, manifesting and exercising the mystery of God's love for men (GS 45).

> The church has been sent by God to all nations that she might
> be the universal sacrament of salvation (AG 1).

A sacrament is an efficacious sign of grace. If the church is the universal sacrament of salvation, it must stand forth as a sign of the total work of salvation that God is accomplishing in the world, and somehow be involved as God's instrument in that work. The first question to be asked is: In what sense is the church the sign of that total work of salvation that God is accomplishing in the world? Using the language of St. Paul, we can describe God's work as "reconciling the world to himself" (2 Cor 5:18).

The first sense in which the church is a "sign" of God's work is that the church is entrusted with the message of reconciliation. It is the church's role to proclaim to the whole world that God is offering his peace and mercy to sinful humanity, and that he wants all men and women to be reconciled with him and with one another. But "actions speak louder than words." For the church to be a sign of salvation, it must show to the world a concrete example of what it means to be a people at peace with God and with one another. In other words, it must be a holy people. While the church on earth will always be imperfectly holy, still its holiness is an attribute which it cannot lose, and which will therefore always sustain its role as a "sign of salvation" to the world.

At this point the question might well be raised: How can the church be a "universal sign of salvation" if there are many people who have no knowledge of the church, and indeed if there are regions of the world in which the church is not allowed to be present? We are told that even there, "the Holy Spirit, in a manner known only to God, offers to every man the possibility of being associated with the paschal mystery" (GS 22). Here we can invoke the fact that the church has been established by God as the one, public, social sign of his saving work for all humanity. A sacrament is a visible sign of invisible grace. The church is the visible sign of that work of grace that the Holy Spirit is doing in human hearts "in a manner known only to God."

For the church to be the universal sacrament of salvation, it is not enough that it be a sign; it must also serve as an instrument of salvation. It must in some way be actively involved in the accomplishment of God's plan to reconcile the world to himself. Vatican

II suggests such an instrumental role for the church in God's universal plan of salvation when it says: "Established by God as a fellowship of life, charity and truth, it [the church] is also used by him as an instrument for the redemption of all" (LG 9).

It is not difficult to recognize such an instrumental role of the church in the salvation of those who are reached by her ministry. The question is whether the church can be said to have an instrumental or mediating role in the salvation of the great many people whom it does not reach with its word and sacraments.

One reason for giving an affirmative answer to this question can be drawn from the analogy which *Lumen gentium* proposes between the mystery of the church and the mystery of the incarnate Word. "Just as the assumed nature inseparably united to the divine Word serves Him as a living instrument of salvation, so, in a similar way, does the communal structure of the church serve Christ's Spirit who vivifies it, by way of building up the body" (LG 8). This means that as the humanity of Christ is the instrument of the divine Word in the total work of salvation, so also the church can be seen as the instrument of the Holy Spirit in the total work of bringing Christ's grace to every human person.

We still have to ask in what way the church can be said to exercise an instrumental or mediatory role in the salvation of all those people who apparently have no contact with the church. I propose that the answer to this question can be found in the role of the church as "priestly people." The following passage of *Lumen gentium* describes this aspect of the nature of the church.

> The baptized, by regeneration and the anointing of the Holy Spirit, are consecrated into a spiritual house and a holy priesthood. Thus through all those works befitting Christian men they can offer spiritual sacrifices and proclaim the power of Him who has called them out of darkness into His marvelous light. . . .
>
> The ministerial priest, by the sacred power he enjoys, molds and rules the priestly people. Acting in the person of Christ, he brings about the Eucharistic Sacrifice, and offers it to God in the name of all the people. For their part, the faithful join in the offering of the Eucharist by virtue of their royal priesthood. They likewise exercise that priesthood by receiving the sacra-

ments, by prayer and thanksgiving, by the witness of a holy life, and by self-denial and active charity.

Pope Pius XII, in his encyclical *Mystici corporis*, speaking of how the savior "wishes to be helped by the members of his Mystical Body in carrying out the work of redemption," said:

> Dying on the cross He left to his Church the immense treasury of the redemption; toward this she contributed nothing. But when these graces are to be distributed, not only does He share this work of sanctification with his spouse, but He wishes that it be due in a way to her activity. A truly awe-inspiring mystery this, and one unceasingly to be pondered: that the salvation of many depends on the prayers and voluntary penances which the members of the Mystical Body of Jesus Christ offer for this intention.[21]

Given the truth expressed by Pius XII that the "salvation of many" depends on the prayers and penances which are an exercise of the priesthood of the faithful, we have all the more reason to attribute to the offering of the eucharist a mediating role in the salvation of humanity. For what is made present in the celebration of the eucharist is the unique sacrifice which obtained the grace of redemption for the whole world. The eucharist is the principal channel through which that grace is now mediated to each succeeding generation. In its Constitution on the Liturgy, Vatican II has declared: "It is through the liturgy, especially the divine eucharistic sacrifice, that the work of our redemption is exercised" (SC 1). Later on in the same document, we read: "From the liturgy, and especially from the Eucharist, as from a fountain, grace is channeled into us, and the sanctification of men in Christ and the glorification of God . . . are most powerfully achieved" (SC 10).

The new eucharistic prayers, which are the fruit of the liturgical renewal mandated by the council, and reflect the doctrine of Vatican II, make it clear that the eucharist is offered not only for the Christian faithful, but for the salvation of all the world. In the third eucharistic prayer we find the following expressions of this universality: first in the prayer for the living and then in the prayer for the dead. "Lord, may this sacrifice, which has made our peace with you, advance the peace and salvation of all the world." "Welcome into your kingdom our departed brothers and sisters, and all who have left this world in your friendship." Here the "departed brothers and sisters" are those who have been members of the Christian family of faith; "all who have departed this world in your friendship" would include those who, without Christian faith and baptism, have died in the friendship of God.

The fourth eucharistic prayer likewise expresses the idea that the eucharist is offered for the salvation of the whole world. "We offer you his body and blood, the acceptable sacrifice which brings salvation to the whole world." "Remember those who take part in this offering, those here present, and all your people, and all who seek you with a sincere heart." Here the "people" and the "seekers" are undoubtedly the Christians and the non-Christians, for both of whom the eucharist is being offered. Finally: "Remember those who have died in the peace of Christ, and all the dead whose faith is known to you alone." These last are the ones who never had the opportunity to profess their faith with the Christian community, and yet who arrived at saving faith through the grace which the Holy Spirit offered to them "in a manner known only to God." It is not inconsistent with these prayers, or with the doctrine of Vatican II which they reflect, to believe that through the church's unique role as priestly people, offering the eucharistic sacrifice to the Father along with her divine head, the church plays an instrumental role in the hidden work of the Holy Spirit for the salvation of those "whose faith is known to God alone."

We thus come to the end of our chapter on the doctrine of the Second Vatican Council. It can hardly be denied that this council has marked a decisive change in Catholic thinking about the salvation of those "outside." Its opening to the ecumenical movement has introduced an altogether new understanding of the ecclesial status of the other Christian communities, and of their role in the salvation of those who belong to them in good faith. Perhaps even more striking is the optimism which characterizes the approach of Vatican II to the question of salvation for the great majority of the people in the world who have neither Christian faith nor baptism. We have tried to show that this optimism does not mean that the church has no role to play in the salvation of those who will never be her members on earth. Not only are they related to the church by the grace which the Holy Spirit offers to them, but the church is also the sign and instrument of their salvation. The necessity of the church for the salvation of humanity, which the axiom "No salvation outside the church" expressed in so negative and misleading a way, is the same truth that has received positive and profound theological expression in Vatican II's presentation of the church as the "universal sacrament of salvation."

10 ‖ "Anonymous Christians"

The development in Catholic thinking about salvation for those "outside the church," since Vatican II, is centered on the question of the means by which non-Christians can arrive at salvation. There is no doubt about the conciliar teaching that people who never arrive at Christian faith and baptism can be saved. Indeed, as we have seen, the doctrine of Vatican II on this point is characterized by an optimism which Karl Rahner has described as a more momentous change in Catholic thinking than even the acceptance of the notion of episcopal collegiality.[1]

The post-conciliar discussion of the question of the means by which non-Christians can be saved is analogous to the discussion that took place during the council with regard to the salvific role of the other Christian churches. There the question was solved by the recognition that the Holy Spirit makes use of the other Christian churches and ecclesial communities as means of salvation for those who belong to them. The question since the council has been whether we can recognize a salvific role for the non-Christian religions: in other words, whether they also can be seen as means of salvation for those who belong to them. A further question concerns the salvation of people who belong to no religion at all. Here again, the question is not whether they can be saved—Vatican II clearly affirms that they can—but how salvation is mediated to them.

We shall first see what light the texts of the council throw on these questions. Then we shall look briefly at two very contrasting answers which have been given by non-Catholic theologians. The rest of the chapter will be a presentation of the thought of Karl

Rahner as the Catholic theologian who has been most prominent in the discussion of these questions since the council. We shall also consider the objections which some leading Catholic theologians have raised against Rahner's theories.

Vatican II on "Salvation in Ways Known Only to God"

The first point I would note in the teaching of the council is that, in some texts in which it speaks of the way in which the grace of salvation comes to those who are not reached by the church's direct ministry, it seems to describe this offer of grace as though it were a work of God alone. Thus, in its Decree on the Missionary Activity of the Church (*Ad gentes*), the council says:

> Though God in ways known to Himself can lead those inculpably ignorant of the gospel to that faith without which it is impossible to please Him (Heb 11:6), yet a necessity lies upon the Church and at the same time a sacred duty, to preach the gospel (AG 7).

Similarly, in *Gaudium et spes*, having described Christians as being "linked with the paschal mystery" and thus "hastening toward resurrection in the strength which comes from hope," the council goes on to say:

> All this holds true not only for Christians, but for all men of good will in whose hearts grace works in an unseen way. For, since Christ died for all men, and since the ultimate vocation of man is in fact one, and divine, we must believe that the Holy Spirit in a manner known only to God offers to every man the possibility of being associated with this paschal mystery (GS 22).

The impression one might get from the texts we have cited is that where the church's ministry of word and sacrament is not available, it is God (the Holy Spirit) alone who accomplishes the work of bringing Christ's saving grace to people. There is no hint in these texts that in dealing with people who have no contact with the church, the Spirit might make use of other means, such as might be found in their own religions, as created helps toward salvation. It is also significant that both of these texts describe this work of the Spirit as taking place in ways that are known only to God. This suggests a reluctance on the part of the council to specify other means which might be used when the church's preaching and sacraments are not available.

However, another text of *Gaudium et spes* suggests a relationship between the activity of the Holy Spirit in the hearts of all people and the role of religion in their lives.

> She [the church] knows that man is constantly worked upon by God's Spirit, and hence can never be altogether indifferent to the problems of religion. The experience of past ages proves this, as do numerous indications in our own times. For man will always yearn to know, at least in an obscure way, what is the meaning of his life, of his activity, of his death (GS 41).

The reference to "the experience of past ages" suggests that in the religions of the world one can find a manifestation of this "constant working of the Spirit," since it is in their religions that people have sought the response to their yearning to know the meaning of their life, activity and death.

This raises the question whether there are elements in non-Christian religions that can be attributed to the presence and activity of the Holy Spirit. The Second Vatican Council has spoken more positively about non-Christian religions than any official document of the Catholic Church had ever done before. We must now look at the conciliar texts to see whether they offer any support for the idea that the Holy Spirit is at work in non-Christian religions and is the source of positive elements that are found in them.

Vatican II on the Positive Elements in Non-Christian Religions

As is well known, the Second Vatican Council devoted one of its documents to the consideration of the relations between the church and the non-Christian religions (*Nostra aetate*). We shall have to look closely at that document, but first we shall take note of the references to the non-Christian religions, which are found in several other documents of the council.

Lumen gentium, when describing the missionary activity of the church, refers to the "good that is found sown" not only in the hearts and minds of people, but also in their "rites and customs." The term "rites" undoubtedly refers to non-Christian religious practices. The text goes on to say that through the missionary work of the church, the good that is found in such rites and customs "not only is saved from destruction, but is purified, heightened, and perfected" (LG 17).

The Decree on the Church's Missionary Activity contains several references to the non-Christian religions. The first of these seems to reflect the view that such religions represent purely human endeavors to reach out to God. However, even such human initiatives fall under the sway of divine providence, and can serve as "preparation for the gospel."

> This universal design of God for the salvation of the human race is not carried out exclusively in a person's soul, with a kind of secrecy. Nor is it achieved merely through those multiple endeavors, including religious ones, by which people search for God, groping for Him that they may by chance find Him (though He is not far from any one of us) (cf. Acts 17:27). For these initiatives need to be enlightened and purified, even though, through the kindly workings of Divine Providence, they may sometimes serve as pedagogy toward the true God, or as a preparation for the gospel (AG 3).

Other passages of this decree, however, suggest that there are elements in the non-Christian religions which are not the fruit of merely human initiative, but have been sown there by the Holy Spirit. Thus, "whatever elements of truth and grace are to be found among the nations" are described as "a sort of secret presence of God" (AG 9). Again, missionaries are exhorted to make themselves "familiar with the national and religious traditions" of those to whom they are sent, "and gladly and respectfully to uncover the seeds of the Word which lie hidden in those traditions" (AG 11). The term "seeds of the Word" is drawn from the writings of St. Justin Martyr, whose ideas about the presence of the *Logos* or Word of God among the Gentiles have been mentioned earlier in this book.[2] In another passage of *Ad gentes* we are told that it is the Holy Spirit who "calls all men to Christ through the seeds of the Word

and by the preaching of the gospel" (AG 15). This suggests a pre-
liminary working of the Spirit, who has already sown "the seeds of
the Word," presumably in the non-Christian religious traditions,
before the missionaries arrive to preach the gospel.

In these passages it is clear that the council intends to recognize
the presence, in non-Christian religions, not only of human values,
but of divine gifts. It is important to note that these are described
not only as manifestations of goodness or holiness in non-Christians
as persons, but as objective elements in their religious traditions and
rites. There is a brief reference to such elements also in the Pastoral
Constitution on the Church in the Modern World, which encour-
ages Catholics to engage in dialogue with people of other religions,
who "preserve in their traditions precious elements of religion and
humanity" (GS 92).

Finally, we come to the conciliar document which treats explicitly of the non-Christian religions: *Nostra aetate*. Here we must
begin by making a distinction between the two religions which, in
different degrees, are based on biblical revelation, namely Judaism
and Islam, and all the other religions. At this point we are asking to
what extent Vatican II has recognized the presence of elements of
divine origin in other religions. It is obvious that it recognized such
elements in Judaism and Islam. Hence we shall focus our attention
on what it says about the other non-Christian religions.

Nostra aetate contains the most fully elaborated statement
which Vatican II has made with regard to the positive elements to
be found in the non-biblical religions. It singles out Hinduism and
Buddhism for special mention, as religions which have instilled the
lives of people with a profound religious sense. Then it goes on to
say:

> Likewise, other religions to be found everywhere strive vari-
> ously to answer the restless searchings of the human heart by
> proposing "ways" which consist of teachings, rules of life and
> sacred ceremonies.

> The Catholic Church rejects nothing which is true and holy in
> these religions. She looks with sincere respect upon those ways
> of conduct and life, those rules and teachings which, though
> differing in many particulars from what she holds and sets

forth, nevertheless often reflect a ray of that Truth which enlightens all men. . . .

The Church therefore has this exhortation for her sons: pru-
dently and lovingly, through dialogue and collaboration with
the followers of other religions, and in witness of Christian faith
and life, acknowledge, preserve, and promote the spiritual and
moral goods found among these men, as well as the values in
their society and culture (NA 2).

It is time to sum up what we have seen in the references to the
non-Christian religions in the documents of Vatican II. One extremely important affirmation here is that "the universal design of
God for the salvation of the human race is not carried out exclusively in people's souls, with a kind of secrecy" (AG 3). In other
words, we can expect that there will be some kind of visible, tangible mediations involved, which will be used by God in carrying out
the divine plan of salvation. Secondly, there is clear recognition of
the presence in the non-Christian religions, of "seeds of the Word"
and "a ray of that Truth which enlightens all men." In other words,
the Council does not hesitate to acknowledge the divine origin of
some elements in those religions. It likewise recognizes that such
elements can serve as "pedagogy toward the true God." But it also
insists that such elements have to be purified and further enlightened by the Christian message.

The key idea seems to be that the positive elements in the non-
Christian religions can be recognized as "preparation for the gospel."
Along with its positive attitude toward the possibility of salvation for
non-Christians, the council continues to insist on the necessity of
preaching the gospel to those who have not yet heard it.[3] Vatican II
provides no support for the idea that, given the presence of positive
elements in the non-Christian religions, there is no further urgency
about Christian missionary endeavor.

At the same time, there is an unavoidable question here, given
the fact that after almost two thousand years of missionary effort,
less than a third of the world's people are Christians. Of the other
two-thirds, the great majority belong to one of the non-Christian
religions. We cannot realistically expect that a great proportion of
them will become Christians during their lifetime. And yet we

must believe that the universal salvific will of God embraces every one of those millions of men and women who will live and die as adherents of a non-Christian religion. Vatican II has assured us that the design of God for their salvation will not be carried out exclusively in their souls, with a kind of secrecy. It has also recognized the presence of a number of positive elements in the religions which these people practice. While the council has not said so explicitly, it would seem reasonable to conclude that the positive elements in non-Christian religions must enter into God's plan of salvation for the people who adhere to those religions. The question which the council did not answer, and which has been the subject of intense discussion since then, is whether it is right to go beyond acknowledging the presence of some positive elements in non-Christian religions, and to recognize those religions themselves as mediating salvation to those who belong to them.

Can Non-Christian Religions Serve as "Mediations of Salvation"?

In the previous chapter we have seen that the council described the church as the "universal sacrament of salvation." Our understanding of this is that the church is both sign and instrument of salvation wherever and however it takes place. As "universal sacrament," the church has a unique role: it is the one divinely instituted, public, social sign of the entire work of salvation which God is accomplishing in the world. Furthermore, we have proposed that, as priestly people, the church also has a universal role of mediation in the divine offer of saving grace, especially through its celebration of the eucharist.

On the other hand, to identify the offering of the eucharist as fulfilling a universal role of mediation of salvation by no means excludes other ways in which the church mediates the grace of salvation. She does this, in the first place, by her work of evangelization, and then by her ongoing ministry of the Word of God and the sacraments. However, such mediation is not universal, since there are so many people whom the church does not reach with her direct ministry. Now if the church's universal mediation as priestly people does not exclude other ways in which the church mediates salvation, neither does it *a priori* exclude the possibility that the Holy

Spirit might make use of other, non-ecclesial realities as mediations of salvation. In other words, to ascribe to the church a *universal* role of mediation does not necessarily mean ascribing to it an *exclusive* role of mediation. The question is left open whether it would be consistent with Christian faith to recognize non-Christian religions as also having a role of mediation in the salvation of those who belong to them.

An adequate discussion of the various answers that have been given to this question would require another book. As I have indicated above, it is my intention to present the answer which Karl Rahner has given, and to discuss it in the light of the criticisms which other Catholic theologians have expressed regarding his views. Thus I shall mainly be concerned with the intra-Catholic debate on this issue. But first I shall very briefly indicate how this question has been answered by some non-Catholic theologians.

Two Contrasting Points of View

At one end of the spectrum, we find the negative view which has been expressed by Hendrik Kraemer in his writings on the Christian mission.[4] Following the lead of Karl Barth, Kraemer sees all religions as fundamentally wrong ways of approaching God.

> In the light of Christ who "of God was made wisdom, righteousness, sanctification and redemption" (1 Cor 1:30) one may say that when we probe more deeply into the religions in one way or another they are shown to be religions of self-redemption, self-justification and self-sanctification and so to be in their ultimate and essential meaning and significance, *erroneous.*[5]

For Barth and Kraemer, the non-Christian religions are human strivings to achieve salvation, and are doomed to failure. Salvation, on the contrary, is a gift of divine grace which comes only through Jesus Christ. Salvation, therefore, can be had exclusively through faith in God's revelation in Jesus Christ. This view, it must be noted, is shared by many fundamentalist Christians, and serves as a strong motive for their missionary work.

At the other end of the spectrum we find the view whose most vigorous exponent in recent years is John Hick.[6] He advocates a "copernican revolution" whereby Christianity, instead of being the center of the religious universe, would, like the other religions, be centered rather on God. In other words, he advocates a "theocentric pluralism" in which salvation can be found in any of the various religions that make up the religious universe. As is obvious, such a theory involves rejecting what has always been understood to be the central affirmation of Christian faith: that Jesus Christ is the unique Son of God and Savior of the whole world. What Hick denies is not merely the universal role of the church, but the universal role of Christ, in the divine plan of salvation. For Hick, Jesus Christ is but one of several agents of God's plan, and consequently the Christian religion is but one of several equally valid ways of salvation.

As must be obvious, Hick's theory is incompatible with Christian belief that Jesus Christ is the incarnate Word of God. What he calls "the myth of Christian uniqueness" depends on what he calls "the myth of God incarnate." For Hick, neither of these Christian beliefs is any longer tenable.[7] It is evident that the fundamental question here is whether Jesus Christ is truly the unique Son of God, or merely the human founder of one of the many religions through which God intends to work out his plan of salvation.

It is simply not possible, within the scope of the present book, to enter into the discussion of what is no longer merely a question of the role of the church, but the more fundamental question of the role of Christ in the divine plan for the salvation of the world. Others have done so, and no doubt much will still be written on it.[8] I will say only that I do not see how a Catholic could espouse the kind of religious pluralism that John Hick and others are advocating.[9] But since it would take me well beyond the limits of the present book to give an adequate treatment of that question, I feel justified in restricting myself to a discussion of the views of Catholics who accept the teaching of Vatican II about the possibility of salvation for non-Christians, and about the presence of positive elements in their religions, but at the same time insist that Jesus Christ is the unique savior of the world, and that the church of Christ is the universal sacrament of salvation. Catholics who remain within these parameters still differ on the question whether non-Christian religions can be described as ways of salvation for those who belong to them. We shall now consider the answer which Karl Rahner has given to this question.

Karl Rahner on the "Anonymous Christians"[10]

We begin with those elements of Rahner's theology which show how utterly opposed he is to the kind of religious pluralism advocated by John Hick and others today. For Rahner, there is no grace for salvation but the grace of Christ, of which the church of Christ is the tangible, historical presence in the world. Hence, Christianity is the absolute religion destined for all of humanity, after the coming of which all other religions are objectively abrogated. The salvation of the individual requires that the person respond to divine revelation with an act of supernatural faith, and in some real sense this faith must be ultimately directed to Christ as the mediator of salvation.[11]

At first sight, these conditions would seem to make salvation impossible for non-Christians. And yet Rahner insists that the salvific will of God embraces every human person without exception (even though he admits that we are left in ignorance as to how this is realized for those who die unbaptized before reaching the age of reason).[12] Since God's salvific will is universal, he must offer his saving grace to everyone, and since there is no salvation without faith, which has to be a personal response to divine revelation, Rahner concludes that the universal offer of grace must include the revelation necessary to ground a response of faith. This involves his notion of grace as God's self-communication to the human spirit. This divine self-communication, as offered to human freedom, and prior to being accepted, already effects a change in the recipients' unreflexive consciousness, and gives them a supernatural capacity of responding to the divine offer. At this point they may have no explicit concept of God, and know nothing about Christ; and yet God is revealing himself to them in the very offer of his grace, and their free positive response to God revealing himself has the nature of an act of faith.

This positive response to the divine self-communication takes place in their fundamental option to accept a demand of their conscience as absolutely binding, since in doing so they implicitly direct themselves toward God as the source of such an absolute demand, and as the ultimate reason for submitting to it. The demand of their conscience will require them to transcend their egoism and to love others as themselves, and the love of neighbor is ultimately love of God.[13] Thus, their graced response to the divine self-communication will involve acts of faith and charity, and hence the gift of supernatural friendship with God. Such persons may still know nothing about Christ, but since Christ is the source of the grace they have received, their faith and love are objectively directed toward him also, even though they may never have the opportunity to arrive at explicit Christian faith or membership in the church.

To describe such persons who are living by the grace of Christ without knowing him, Rahner has coined the term "anonymous Christians." They are not members of the church, since they lack explicit Christian faith and baptism, but they are in spiritual communion with the church, which is the sacramental sign of the life of Christ's grace which they share without knowing its source.

Rahner on the Salvific Role of Non-Christian Religions[14]

Rahner insists that the anonymous Christian's response to God's self-communication cannot be understood as a purely inward, private affair. He fully endorses the statement of Vatican II that God's saving design is not carried out exclusively in people's souls, with a kind of secrecy. The essentially social nature of human existence calls for some kind of communal expression of people's response to God. Normally, this will take the form of the religion which is part of their culture. Rahner concludes that, when Christianity is not a viable option, it must be within the providential design of God that people express their worship of God in the religion which is available to them. In other words, even though the non-Christian religions are objectively abrogated by the advent of Christianity, they continue to be legitimate religions for people who are inculpably ignorant of any obligation on their part to abandon the religion of their culture and to embrace Christianity.

Rahner insists that this means that until non-Christians become so convinced of their obligation to accept Christianity that it would be a mortal sin for them not to do so, their own religion continues to be the way in which God must intend that they express their relationship with him and arrive at their salvation. Needless to say, he agrees with Vatican II in presuming that those who have heard the Christian message and have not yet accepted it are in good faith, and are not guilty of sin in remaining in their own religion. From this it follows that the non-Christian religions must remain, under God's providence, legitimate ways of salvation for the majority of the world's people.

They are provisional ways, to be sure, objectively rendered obsolete by the advent of Christianity. They are not to be thought of as ways of salvation independent of Christ, who is the unique source of the grace by which their adherents are saved. But Rahner insists that because of the role which the non-Christian religions play in the divine plan of salvation for a great part of the world's people, we can reasonably expect to find supernatural elements in them, which make them apt to serve as mediations of divine grace. He further insists that a salvific role cannot be denied to the non-Christian religions on the grounds of the limitations and aberrations that may be found in them. He points out that even in the Hebrew religion certain elements needed to be corrected and purified as time went on, and that this did not contradict its being the way of salvation for the Hebrew people.[15]

It is time now to consider some of the objections that have been raised against Rahner's theories regarding the "anonymous Christian" and the salvific role of the non-Christian religions.

The Question of the Church's Missionary Task

The objection which Rahner seems to have taken most seriously, and to which he devoted the most space in his writings, was that his theory would effectively deprive the church's missionary task of its necessary motivation. In other words, if people are already "anonymous Christians," and if they can find salvation in their own religions, there would seem to be no point in trying to convert them to Christianity.[16]

The first point in Rahner's answer to this objection is that, in the light of the clear teaching of Vatican II, we can no longer base missionary effort on the motive that no one can be saved without explicit Christian faith, baptism, and membership in the church. Any Catholic who wishes to justify the work of evangelization must reckon with the optimism which is now the Catholic Church's official attitude regarding the salvation of people who will never become Christians.

Secondly, this optimism about ultimate salvation for non-Christians must include the recognition that many of them must already be living in the state of supernatural grace. But it is sound Catholic doctrine to attribute all such grace to Christ, whose cross and resurrection are the source of salvation for all of humanity. Vatican II clearly teaches this when it says: "We must believe that the Holy Spirit offers to everyone the possibility of being associated with the paschal mystery" (GS 22). From this it follows that if we are optimistic about the salvation of non-Christians, we must believe that many of them, without explicit Christian faith, are nonetheless living in the grace of Christ. And this is precisely what Rahner intends to say, when he describes such people as "anonymous Christians." Furthermore, he insists that the very success of missionary effort depends on the presence of such people among those to whom the gospel is being preached, on the grounds that it is those who are already positively responding to God's self-communication in grace who will be the best disposed to respond to the message of the gospel.

There is still the objection, however, that if people are already being saved as "anonymous Christians," and if their own religions are ways of salvation for them, then it would seem better to leave them in good faith in their own religion than to try to convert them to Christianity. To this objection, Rahner offers a twofold response. The first is based on the nature of the church as the social, incarnational presence of the grace of Christ in the world. The very nature of the church demands that it strive to become visibly present in every culture, and in every historical context. Just as the grace of Christ, which was at work in the world from the beginning of the human race, had to become incarnate in the historical Jesus, so also this grace must express its incarnational nature in the visible presence of the church, which demands the ongoing effort to plant the church wherever there is no vital Christian community.

His second reply concerns the reason for making the effort to evangelize people who can find salvation in their own religions. Here his answer is based on the fullness of the life of grace which only membership in the church can provide. Being a member of the church does not guarantee a person's salvation, nor make it "easier," but it does provide the opportunity to realize a greater fullness of life in Christ than would be available to "anonymous Christians."

Objections Raised by Catholic Theologians

We shall now consider the objections which have been raised against Rahner's theory by four prominent Catholic theologians: Henri de Lubac, Hans Urs von Balthasar, Hans Küng and Max Seckler.[17]

Henri de Lubac's criticism is directed principally against Rahner's use of the term "anonymous Christianity."[18] While he admits that there is theological justification for speaking of individuals as "anonymous Christians," he objects to the term "anonymous Christianity" on the grounds that this would suggest that the non-Christian religions would constitute an "anonymous Christianity." As de Lubac sees it, this would mean that the Christian revelation would simply make explicit what was already present in the non-Christian religions "anonymously." This would be to ignore the startling newness of the revelation brought by Christ, and to reduce the significance of explicit Christianity to merely putting a label on a jar that already contained the substance of all that Christianity has to offer.[19] Needless to say, this is not what Rahner meant by speaking of "anonymous Christianity." For him it meant the "being-Christian" of those who are living in the grace of Christ without explicit Christian faith. However, he acknowledged that the term Christianity could also be understood as de Lubac was taking it, and because of this ambiguity he said he had no objection if others preferred not to speak of "anonymous Christianity."[20]

De Lubac also objected to the description of non-Christian religions as "ways of salvation." He argued that this would mean being led to believe that various religious systems which might contradict one another in essential matters would nonetheless be bearers of salvation, positively willed and given by God. On the contrary, he insisted that we must hold that there is but one divinely willed way of salvation, namely through the gospel of Christ.[21]

De Lubac's objection does not seem to give adequate consideration to the fact that Rahner insists that objectively all other religions have been abrogated by the advent of Christianity. The "legitimacy" which he attributes to other religions as "ways of salvation" is provisional, and relative to the situation of those who in good faith fail to recognize Christianity as the religion which they must embrace in order to be saved.

In the original edition of his book *Cordula oder der Ernstfall*,[22] Hans Urs von Balthasar severely criticized Rahner's theory of the "anonymous Christian," claiming that it relativized the role of Christ in the mystery of salvation by making everything depend simply on the salvific will of God and on the human love of neighbor. This, he contended, would mean a radical devaluation of the theology of the cross, and of Christian life based on the personal love of Christ and readiness to follow him in the "decisive test" of self-sacrifice.[23]

However, when the French edition of his book was being prepared, von Balthasar added a postscript in which he substantially moderated his criticism, directing it now at those who were popularizing Rahner's ideas and drawing extreme conclusions from them, more than at Rahner himself.[24] Von Balthasar now expressed himself in agreement with Henri de Lubac, admitting the soundness of the theology underlying the term "anonymous Christians," but still rejecting the notion of an "anonymous Christianity." We have already seen that Rahner took this objection seriously, and agreed that the term was open to misunderstanding, unless one took it, as he did, simply to mean the "being-Christian-without-the-name" of those who were living in the grace of Christ without explicit Christian faith.

Hans Küng did not make the distinction which these two theologians had made, but summarily dismissed the notion of the "anonymous Christian" as a "theological fabrication" by which the formula "no salvation outside the church" is saved by "an elegant gesture which sweeps the whole of good-willed humanity into the back door of the holy Roman church."[25] In my view, this is a caricature of Rahner's theory, and I do not know that he ever dignified it with a published reply. He did, however, reply to a further objection which Küng and others have made: namely, that "it is impossible to find anywhere in the world a sincere Jew, Muslim or atheist, who would not regard the assertion that he is an 'anonymous Christian' as presumptuous."[26] Rahner's reply is that this term is intended to express a specifically Christian understanding of how non-Christians can be saved. He admits that it may not be an appropriate term for use in inter-religious dialogue. He is also aware of the ambiguity involved in describing as "anonymous Christians" people who have no conscious wish to be Christians. But he points out the presence of ambiguity in other terms which are commonly used in Christian discourse, such as the use of the term "sin" in "original sin." In any case, he declared himself ready to substitute another term, if one can be proposed which expresses equally well the truth which his term is intended to express.[27]

Max Seckler has criticized Rahner's description of non-Christian religions as "ways of salvation" on the grounds that it is not discriminating enough; it attributes a salvific function to other religions in a "wholesale" manner, without giving sufficient attention to the possibility that some of their beliefs and practices would be more likely to hinder than to help people on the way to salvation.[28] Seckler notes that Rahner makes the salvation of "anonymous Christians" depend on their fundamental option to love their neighbor, since this involves the implicit love of God. The question, therefore, whether a religion is a "way of salvation" should depend on whether its beliefs and practices are conducive to making the fundamental option of loving one's neighbor. Seckler's objection to Rahner's theory is that it attributes a saving function to the practice of whatever happens to be the religion of a particular culture, independently of the specific nature of its beliefs and practices, which might hinder as well as help people toward salvation.

While Rahner did not refer explicitly to Seckler's critique in the context, the following passage of his work *Foundations of Christian Faith* does provide the needed qualification of his assertion that non-Christian religions can be seen as "ways of salvation."[29]

> When a non-Christian attains salvation through faith, hope and love, non-Christian religions cannot be understood in such a way that they do not play a role, or play only a negative role in the attainment of justification and salvation. This proposition is not concerned about making a very definite Christian interpretation and judgment about a concrete non-Christian religion. Nor is there any question of making such a religion equal to Christian faith in its salvific significance, nor of denying its depravity or its provisional character in the history of salvation, nor of denying that such a concrete religion can also have negative effects on the event of salvation in a particular non-Christian.
>
> But presupposing all of this, we still have to say, if a non-Christian religion could not or may not have any positive influ-

ence at all on the supernatural event of salvation in an individual person who is a non-Christian, then we would be understanding this event of salvation in this person in a completely ahistorical and asocial way. But this contradicts in a fundamental way the historical and social nature of Christianity itself, that is, its ecclesial nature.

We conclude our presentation of Rahner's thought with a brief account of the way in which he treats the question of the salvation of people who profess no religion at all.

Rahner on the Salvation of Atheists[30]

He first observes that Vatican II, in its treatment of atheism in *Gaudium et spes* 19–21, made no mention of what had been the common judgment in Catholic moral theology, that no one could remain an atheist for long without committing grave sin. The council does say: "Undeniably, those who willfully shut out God from their hearts and try to dodge religious questions are not following the dictates of their consciences. Hence they are not free of blame" (GS 19). On the other hand, the council does not attribute such a sinful attitude to all those who profess to be atheists in the world today. This is clear from its statement: "Divine Providence does not deny the help necessary for salvation to those who, without blame on their part, have not yet arrived at an explicit knowledge of God, but who strive to live a good life, thanks to His grace" (LG 16). The "optimism" of Vatican II with regard to the universal possibility of salvation undoubtedly includes atheists as well as members of non-Christian religions.

The problem, then, is to explain how people who never arrive at explicit faith in God can be saved, since it is a Catholic dogma that no one can be justified without faith.[31] Rahner's solution for atheists is substantially the same one that he used for the members of non-Christian religions. The self-communication which is involved in the continual offer of grace which God makes to everyone, including atheists, can be understood as revelation, to which a person's graced response can be understood as an act of faith. As we have seen above, this positive response need not involve a conceptualized affirmation of God; it can remain at an unreflexive level of consciousness. To put it in Rahner's words:

> The person who accepts a moral demand from his conscience as *absolutely* valid for him and embraces it as such in a free act of affirmation—no matter how unreflected—asserts the absolute being of God, whether he knows or conceptualises it or not, as the very reason why there can be such a thing as an *absolute moral demand at all*.[32]

The key point in Rahner's theory here is that the atheist's free decision to accept a moral demand of conscience as absolutely binding is really an act of implicit faith in God, since it is the person's response to God's revelation of himself in the offer of grace which makes this response possible. As long as such an act of implicit faith remains at the unreflexive level of consciousness, it can coexist with an explicit denial of the existence of God on the part of the same person. Nor is it certain that all professed atheists who persevere in the fundamental choice to love their neighbor will inevitably be led to explicit faith or explicit love of God. However, their love of neighbor is ultimately directed to God, even though they are not consciously aware of this. It is likewise directed toward Christ, whose paschal mystery is the unique source of the grace by which they can arrive at their salvation. Rahner insists that everyone who has a saving faith must have a relationship with Jesus Christ in such faith. He describes this as a "christological quest"; they are "seeking Christ" in their faith and love, even though they do not know this.[33]

Secular Mediations of Grace and Salvation

As we have seen above, Rahner insists that to deny to non-Christian religions a role in the salvation of those who belong to them would be to deny the social character of the economy of salvation. The question then is: What provides this social character of the economy of salvation in the case of atheists? In other words, what are the created mediations of saving grace for them?

Rahner's answer is that while such created mediations of grace are always necessary, they are not in every case of the specifically religious kind. Secular reality can also provide the material for the decision in which a person effectively responds to the self-communication of God which we call grace.

> The transcendent reference of man to God is mediated through categorial objects (at least in cases other than genuine mystical experiences). But this object does not necessarily have to be a religious concept. The transcendent reference to God can be found in the mediations of ordinary, secular material, as long as man by means of this material freely comes to a position of complete responsibility and self-determination.[34]

> This mediating, categorial objectivity . . . does not have to be an explicitly religious act. It can be formed by a particular moral decision in which a man is responsible for himself and accepts (or rejects) himself.[35]

Other Catholic theologians have described, more explicitly than Rahner has done here, the things that can serve as secular mediations of grace and salvation for people who profess no religion, and consider themselves atheists. Yves Congar, for instance, has observed that among such people one finds those who unselfishly devote their lives to such transcendent values as Duty, Peace, Justice, Fraternity, Humanity. He describes such absolute values, which are worthy of unconditional love, as capable of serving as *incognitos* of God for those inculpably lacking any explicit religion. But of all such mediations of grace, he insists that the preeminent one is the "mystery of the neighbor." It is the other person who is most worthy of self-sacrificing love, and through whom the atheist who offers such love reaches out to the God whom he does not know.[36]

Gustave Thils has developed the thesis that some kind of mediation of grace is available to everyone, describing various examples of "individual" and "collective" mediations, through which, with or without any practice of religion, people can arrive at the attitudes of faith and love which are essential for their salvation. As examples of individual mediations he mentions the law written in hearts, the "seeds of the Word," interior illumination, and conscience; as collective mediations he names the covenants of God with humanity, the divine "dispositions," general revelation, and non-biblical wisdom and prophetism. His thesis is that there is no one for whom God does not provide some such mediation, whether of a religious or a secular nature, whereby the person can respond to God in such a way as to reach salvation.[37]

These reflections of Congar and Thils should make it obvious that Karl Rahner is not the only Catholic theologian who recognizes that both non-Christian religions and secular realities can serve as mediations of grace and salvation for people who do not share Christian faith. It occurs to me that, by presenting only Rahner's thought in this chapter, and mentioning the criticisms which some Catholic theologians have made of his theories, I may have left the reader with the impression that Rahner represents an isolated, or at least a minority, position on these questions among Catholic theologians. The fact is that, apart from questions of terminology such as "anonymous Christianity," and with differences of emphasis and detail, Rahner's position that both non-Christian religions and secular realities must be recognized as serving as mediations of salvation for non-Christians is undoubtedly the position of "mainstream" Catholic theology today. In its favor one can cite such representative Catholic theologians as Wolfgang Beinert,[38] Yves Congar,[39] Jacques Dupuis,[40] Johannes Feiner,[41] Piet Fransen,[42] Heinrich Fries,[43] Walter Kasper,[44] Hans Küng,[45] Joseph Ratzinger,[46] Otto Semmelroth,[47] Bernard Sesboüé,[48] Gustave Thils,[49] and Hans Waldenfels.[50]

Earlier in this chapter we mentioned the severe criticism which Hans Urs von Balthasar had directed at Rahner's theory of the "anonymous Christian" in the original edition of his work *Cordula*, which appeared in 1966. It seems a fitting conclusion to this chapter to note that twenty years later, von Balthasar wrote a book which has been published in English with the title *Dare We Hope That All Men Be Saved?*[51] The thesis of this book is that there is nothing in Christian revelation which obliges us to believe that any human person has been or will be condemned to hell, and that on the contrary there are good grounds for *hoping* that all will be saved. One could hardly think of a more eloquent expression of the "salvation optimism" which Karl Rahner has described as one of the most extraordinary developments in Catholic thinking in modern times.

11 ‖ Papal Teaching After Vatican II

It seems appropriate that we should conclude our history of Christian thought on the question of salvation for those "outside the church" by examining the principal statements which Popes Paul VI and John Paul II have made on this issue. In this chapter, as in the previous one, we shall focus our attention on the question of the salvation of non-Christians, with particular attention to the question of the role which the non-Christian religions play in their salvation. After presenting the principal statements of each of the two popes, we shall ask whether their teaching manifests any further development of this question beyond the position reached by the Second Vatican Council. We shall also try to assess the impact which post-conciliar Catholic theology of religions has had on papal teaching. We shall begin with that of Pope Paul VI.

Pope Paul VI

Paul VI was elected pope on June 21, 1963, during the interval between the first and second periods of Vatican II. About a year later, during the interval between the second and third periods, he did two things that are relevant to our question: on May 19, 1964 he established the Secretariat for Non-Christians, and on August 6, 1964 he published his first encyclical letter, *Ecclesiam Suam*. In both of these he manifested his desire that the Catholic Church engage in dialogue with the other religions of the world.

The promotion of such dialogue was always the primary aim of the Secretariat for Non-Christians; this has been made explicit in its new title: "Pontifical Council for Inter-religious Dialogue."[1] Dialogue between the Catholic Church and the rest of the world was also the key theme of Paul VI's first encyclical. He described the partner of this dialogue as consisting of a series of concentric circles, one of which is made up of "those who adore the one supreme God whom we also adore." He described this circle in the following terms.

> We refer to the children, worthy of our affection and respect, of the Hebrew people, faithful to the religion which we call that of the Old Testament. Then to the adorers of God according to the conception of monotheism, the Moslem religion especially, deserving of our admiration for all that is true and good in their worship of God. And also to the followers of the great Afro-Asiatic religions. Obviously we cannot share in these various forms of religion nor can We remain indifferent to the fact that each of them, in its own way, should regard itself as being the equal of any other and should authorize its followers not to seek to discover whether God has revealed the perfect and definitive form, free from all error, in which He wishes to be known, loved and served. Indeed, honesty compels Us to declare openly our conviction that there is but one true religion, the religion of Christianity. It is Our hope that all who seek God and adore Him may come to acknowledge its truth.

> But We do, nevertheless, recognize and respect the moral and spiritual values of the various non-Christian religions, and We desire to join with them in promoting and defending common ideals of religious liberty, human brotherhood, good culture, social welfare and civil order. For Our part, We are ready to enter into discussion on these common ideals, and will not fail to take the initiative where Our offer of discussion in genuine, mutual respect, would be well received.[2]

At the time when this encyclical was issued, the Second Vatican Council was already considering a "Declaration Concerning the Jews," but there was as yet no conciliar *schema* concerning the non-Christian religions in general. It was only during the third period of the council, on November 20, 1964, that the "Declaration on the Relationship of the Church to Non-Christian Religions" was first presented for discussion. Thus, the positive statements of Paul VI in *Ecclesiam suam* expressing admiration for "all that is true and good in [Moslem] worship of God," and respect for "the moral and spiritual values of the various non-Christian religions" are rather an anticipation than a consequence of the doctrine of Vatican II.

It was during this same period of the council that Paul VI visited India on the occasion of the Eucharistic Congress held at Bombay, December 2–5, 1964. His address to members of the non-Christian religions of India contains the following expression of his deep respect for their religious culture:

> Yours is a land of ancient culture, the cradle of great religions, the home of a nation that has sought God with a relentless desire, in deep meditation and silence, and in hymns of fervent prayer. Rarely has this longing for God been expressed with words so full of the spirit of Advent as in the words written in your sacred books many centuries before Christ: "From the unreal lead me to the real; from darkness lead me to light; from death lead me to immortality."[3]

Pope Paul VI's admiration for the spiritual values to be found in other religions was not limited to those of ancient culture such as he met in India. On October 29, 1967, he published a document addressed to all the peoples of Africa, in which he spoke admiringly of the "spiritual sense of life which is fundamental to the traditions of Africa." He went on to say that the deepest element of this "spiritual sense" is a "notion of God as the first and ultimate cause of all things: a notion that is more truly perceived than described in words, more truly put into practice in life than comprehended in thought."[4]

There can be no doubt of the sincerity of the admiration for the spiritual values in the non-Christian religions which Paul VI expressed here and on other occasions. However, there was another aspect of his thought concerning the non-Christian religions which is of no less importance for an understanding of his mind concerning the possible significance of those religions in the divine economy of salvation. It is the contrast which he emphasized between those religions and the one true religion which is Christianity. One brief but emphatic expression of this contrast is found in the exhortation which he gave to the faithful in Rome on the fourth Sunday of Lent, 1966.

It is religion that determines our relationship with God, and the Catholic religion is the one that fully establishes that relationship: one that is genuine, true, unique; this is the religion that makes God our communion and our salvation. And the other religions? They are attempts, efforts, endeavors; they are arms raised toward Heaven to which they seek to arrive, but they are not a response to the gesture by which God has come to meet man. This gesture is Christianity, Catholic life.[5]

These two facets of his thought—esteem for the spiritual values to be found in non-Christian religions, and at the same time a sharp contrast between them and Christianity—characterize the most important statement which Paul VI made on this issue, which is found in his apostolic exhortation on Evangelization in the Modern World, *Evangelii nuntiandi*.[6] It seems important enough to be quoted in full.

This first proclamation [of the Gospel] is also addressed to the immense sections of mankind who practice non-Christian religions. The Church respects and esteems these non-Christian religions because they are the living expression of the soul of vast groups of people. They carry within them the echo of thousands of years of searching for God, a quest which is incomplete but often made with great sincerity and righteousness of heart. They possess an impressive patrimony of deeply religious texts. They have taught generations of people how to pray. They are all impregnated with innumerable "seeds of the Word" and can constitute a true "preparation for the Gospel," to quote a felicitous term used by the Second Vatican Council and borrowed from Eusebius of Caesarea.

Such a situation certainly raises complex and delicate questions that must be studied in the light of Christian Tradition and the Church's Magisterium, in order to offer to the missionaries of today and of tomorrow new horizons in their contacts with non-Christian religions. We wish to point out, above all today, that neither respect and esteem for these religions nor the complexity of the questions raised is an invitation to the Church to withhold from these non-Christians the proclamation of Jesus Christ. On the contrary the Church holds that these multitudes have the right to know the riches of the mystery of Christ—

riches in which we believe that the whole of humanity can find, in unsuspected fullness, everything that it is gropingly searching for concerning God, man and his destiny, life and death, and truth. Even in the face of natural religious expressions most worthy of esteem, the Church finds support in the fact that the religion of Jesus, which she proclaims through evangelization, objectively places man in relation with the plan of God, with his living presence and with his action; she thus causes an encounter with the mystery of divine paternity that bends over towards humanity. In other words, our religion effectively establishes with God an authentic and living relationship which the other religions do not succeed in doing, even though they have, as it were, their arms stretched towards heaven.[7]

If one compares this passage of *Evangelii nuntiandi* with the sentences we have quoted above from a sermon given by Paul VI in Rome in 1966,[8] it is obvious that the encyclical expresses a judgment concerning the non-Christian religions which Paul VI had formed at least eight years earlier. While *Evangelii nuntiandi* was the fruit of the synod of bishops of 1974, whose theme was evangelization, on this point it seems rather to express the personal thought of Paul VI than to represent the views which the bishops had expressed at the synod. At least some of the bishops, especially those from Asia, had expressed a much more positive judgment about the non-Christian religions than one finds in the papal document. Jacques Dupuis, a theologian who was particularly well acquainted with the contribution which the bishops from India and Asia had made to the synod, made the following comment.

> At the Synod the Indian and Asian bishops had advocated an open theology of non-Christian religions which would look upon these religions not merely as expressions of men's aspirations towards God but as embodying for their followers a first though incomplete approach of God towards men. The Document [*Evangelii nuntiandi*] refuses to follow this line of thought. . . .[9]

It is evident, from the passage we have quoted from the sermon which Paul VI gave in Rome in 1966, that at that time he had already formed the judgment which he later spelled out in greater detail in *Evangelii nuntiandi*. Naturally the question arises as to what might have influenced his thinking about the significance of the non-Christian religions. I shall venture the guess that it was an article by the noted French theologian, Jean Daniélou, which appeared in *Etudes* in 1964.[10] It is well known that Paul VI followed the writings of certain French Catholic theologians with special attention. His esteem for Jean Daniélou is evidenced by the fact that in 1969 he named him a cardinal. There is a striking similarity, not to say identity, between the judgment expressed by Paul VI both in his 1966 sermon and in *Evangelii nuntiandi*, and the following excerpts from the 1964 article by Daniélou.

> The religions are a gesture of man towards God; revelation is the witness of a gesture of God towards man. . . . The religions are creations of human genius; they witness to the value of exalted religious personalities, such as Buddha, Zoroaster, Orpheus. But they also have the defects of what is human. Revelation is the work of God alone. . . . Religion expresses man's desire for God. Revelation witnesses that God has responded to that desire. Religion does not save. Jesus Christ grants salvation.[11]

Besides this article of Daniélou, another factor that may have influenced Paul VI's treatment of the non-Christian religions in *Evangelii nuntiandi* was the fact that some Catholic theologians were describing the non-Christian religions as the "ordinary way of salvation," and Christianity as the "extraordinary way."[12] Toward the end of *Evangelii nuntiandi*, Paul VI speaks of various "excuses" which people were using to justify giving up the work of evangelization. Here I believe we can see one of the motives for his negative attitude toward recognizing a salvific role for the non-Christian religions.

> The most insidious of these excuses are certainly the ones for which people claim to find support in such and such a teaching of the Council. . . . Why proclaim the Gospel when the whole world is saved by uprightness of heart? We know that the world and history are filled with "seeds of the Word"; is it not therefore an illusion to claim to bring the Gospel where it already exists in the seeds that the Lord himself has sown? Anyone who takes the trouble to study in the Council's documents the ques-

tions upon which these excuses draw too superficially will find quite a different view. . . .

God can accomplish this salvation in whomsoever he wishes by ways which he alone knows. And yet, if his Son came, it was precisely in order to reveal to us, by his word and by his life, the ordinary paths of salvation. And he has commanded us to transmit this revelation to others with his own authority.[13]

It can hardly be doubted that Paul VI's insistence that Christ has revealed to us the "ordinary paths of salvation" manifests his disapproval of the idea put forward by H.R. Schlette and others that the non-Christian religions constitute the "ordinary way of salvation." There is good reason to believe that Paul VI shared the fears expressed by some missionaries, that to attribute a positive role to the non-Christian religions in the economy of salvation would have a negative effect on the work of evangelization. Hence I suggest that his description of those religions as human strivings toward God which never succeed in establishing an authentic relationship with him was influenced both by Daniélou's theology of religions and by a pastoral concern lest a more positive appreciation of their role would lead to a loss of missionary zeal in the Catholic Church.

At the beginning of this chapter I said that I would be comparing the papal teaching on salvation for non-Christians with the doctrine of Vatican II and with post-conciliar Catholic theology. How, then, does the teaching of Paul VI compare with that of Vatican II? Looking first at the expressions of respect and esteem for the values to be found in the non-Christian religions, and comparing them with what was said by Vatican II, we can say that Paul VI has been even more positive than the council was in its description of such values. For instance, the council did not say that those religions "possess an impressive patrimony of deeply religious texts." It did not say that "they have taught generations of people how to pray." It spoke of the presence in them of "seeds of the Word," but it did not say that they are *all* impregnated with *innumerable* "seeds of the Word." So we can say that Paul VI was more generous than Vatican II had been, in his description of the positive elements to be found in those religions.

On the other hand, we do not find in the documents of Vatican II anything quite so negative in its assessment of the non-Christian religions as we also find in statements by Paul VI. They are "natural religious expressions," while it is only the religion of Jesus that objectively places man in the living presence of God. Although non-Christian religions "have their arms stretched out towards heaven," they do not succeed in bringing people into an authentic and living relationship with God. The non-Christian religions are human strivings toward God but they never reach him. It is only in Christianity that an authentic encounter with God takes place, because it is only here that the divine Father himself bends down to humanity.

That raises the question: How did Paul VI understand these two aspects of his thought to be consistent with one another? If the non-Christian religions are "all impregnated with innumerable seeds of the Word," how can they be merely natural expressions of religious striving toward God? Would not the presence in them of such "seeds of the Word" mean that the Holy Spirit had sown these seeds, as Vatican II suggested (AG 15)? Would not the elements of "truth and grace" to be found among them manifest a "sort of secret presence of God," as Vatican II also said they would (AG 9)? It is not clear to me how Paul VI resolved the tension between these two aspects of his thought.

On the other hand, it is fairly clear which direction in post-conciliar theology Pope Paul preferred to follow: it is that taken by Jean Daniélou and Henri de Lubac, and not that taken by Karl Rahner and many other respected Catholic theologians. I do not know of any statement of Paul VI in which he has explicitly rejected the notion that the non-Christian religions can be understood as "mediations of salvation" for those who belong to them in good faith. But neither have I found any statement of his that would favor such an understanding of their role in the economy of salvation. On the contrary, his description of the other religions as "natural religious expressions" which "do not succeed in establishing an authentic and living relationship with God" would suggest that he had little sympathy for the development of Catholic thinking about the salvific role of non-Christian religions which we have followed in our previous chapter. We must now see what Pope John Paul II has said on this issue.

Pope John Paul II

On March 4, 1979, during the first year of his pontificate, Pope John Paul II issued his first encyclical, entitled *Redemptor Hominis*, in which he expressed the desire of the Catholic Church to engage in dialogue with members of the other religions of the world. It is significant that in this first encyclical, John Paul already stressed the aspect of his thought about the non-Christians that would become the key element of his teaching in their regard. This is: respect for the presence and activity of the Holy Spirit in non-Christians and in their religions—a presence and activity which is seen above all in their practice of virtue, their spirituality and their prayer. We see this in the following passages of his encyclical.

> What we have just said must be applied—although in another way and with the due differences—to activity for coming closer together with the representatives of the non-Christian religions, an activity expressed through dialogue, contacts, prayer in common, investigation of the treasures of human spirituality, in which, as we know well, the members of these religions also are not lacking. Does it not sometimes happen that the firm belief of the followers of the non-Christian religions—a belief that is also an effect of the Spirit of truth operating outside the visible confines of the mystical body—can make Christians ashamed of being often themselves so disposed to doubt concerning the truths revealed by God . . .[14]

> The missionary attitude always begins with a feeling of deep esteem for "what is in man," for what man has himself worked out in the depths of his spirit concerning the most profound and important problems. It is a question of respecting everything that has been brought about in him by the Spirit, which "blows where it wills."[15]

Two years later, during his first visit as pope to Asia, John Paul addressed a radio message to the people of that continent in which he said:

> I have come to Asia to be a witness to the Spirit who is active in the history of peoples and of nations. . . . Coming to the peoples of Asia . . . I encounter . . . the local heritage and the

ancient cultures that contain praiseworthy elements of spiritual growth, indicating the paths of life and conduct that are often so near to those found in the Gospel of Christ. . . . The Catholic Church accepts the truth and goodness found in these religions, and she sees reflections there of the truth of Christ. . . .

What seems to bring together and unite, in a particular way, Christians and the believers of other religions is an acknowledge-ment of the need for prayer as an expression of man's spiritual-ity directed towards the Absolute. Even when, for some, he is the Great Unknown, he nevertheless remains always in reality the same living God. We trust that whenever the human spirit opens itself in prayer to this Unknown God, an echo will be heard of the same Spirit who, knowing the limits and weakness of the human person, himself prays in us and on our behalf, "expressing our plea in a way that could never be put into words" (Rom 8:26). The intercession of the Spirit of God who prays in us and for us is the fruit of the mystery of the Redemp-tion of Christ, in which the all-embracing love of the Father has been shown to the world.[16]

In his visits to countries with a significant non-Christian popu-lation, Pope John Paul invariably addressed the leaders of their religions. A typical example of his expression of esteem for their spirituality is seen in the following passage of the address which he gave in Madras to the leaders of the religions of India.

The Catholic Church recognizes the truths that are contained in the religious traditions of India. This recognition makes true dialogue possible. Here today the Church wishes to voice again her true appreciation of the great heritage of the religious spirit that is manifested in your cultural tradition. The Church's ap-proach to other religions is one of genuine respect; with them she seeks mutual collaboration. This respect is twofold: respect for man in his quest for answers to the deepest questions of his life, and respect for the action of the Spirit in man.[17]

Pope John Paul's visit to India took place in February 1986. During that same year he issued his encyclical letter on the Holy Spirit, *Dominum et Vivificantem*, in which he developed the theme of the universal action of the Holy Spirit.

We cannot limit ourselves to the 2,000 years which have passed since the birth of Christ. We need to go further back, to embrace the whole of the action of the Holy Spirit even before Christ—from the beginning, throughout the world and especially in the economy of the old covenant. For this action has been exercised in every place and at every time, indeed, in every individual, according to the eternal plan of salvation whereby this action was to be closely linked with the mystery of the incarnation and redemption, which in its turn exercised its influence on those who believed in the future coming of Christ. . . . But we need to look further and go further afield, knowing that "the wind blows where it wills," according to the image used by Jesus in his conversation with Nicodemus. The Second Vatican Council, centered primarily on the theme of the church, reminds us of the Holy Spirit's activity also "outside the visible body of the church." The council speaks precisely of "all people of good will in whose hearts grace works in an unseen way. For, since Christ died for all, and since the ultimate vocation of man is in fact one, and divine, we ought to believe that the Holy Spirit in a manner known only to God offers to every man the possibility of being associated with this paschal mystery."[18]

During that same year, 1986, at the invitation of Pope John Paul II, there took place at Assisi an event that was surely unique in the history of the world: a Day of Prayer for Peace in which representatives of the major Christian confessions and the major non-Christian religions of the world took part. The clearest explanation of the pope's intention in initiating this Day of Prayer, and his understanding of its significance, is found in his Christmas address to the members of the Roman curia on December 22, 1986. In this he said:

At Assisi, in an extraordinary way, there was the discovery of the unique value that prayer has for peace; indeed, it was seen that it is impossible to have peace without prayer, the prayer of all, each one in his own identity and in search of the truth. In keeping with what we have said, one must see in this another wonderful manifestation of that unity which binds us together, beyond the differences and divisions which are known to all. Every authentic prayer is under the influence of the Spirit "who intercedes insistently for us . . . because we do not even know how to pray as we ought," but he prays in us "with unutterable groanings" and "the One who searches hearts knows what are the desires of the Spirit" (cf. Rom 8:26–27). We can indeed maintain that every authentic prayer is called forth by the Holy Spirit, who is mysteriously present in the heart of every person.[19]

His most recent encyclical, *Redemptoris Missio*, "On the Permanent Validity of the Church's Missionary Mandate," has given Pope John Paul the opportunity to develop, in a more systematic way, his thoughts on the significance of the non-Christian religions. His first reference to them comes in the form of an objection: "Is it not possible to attain salvation in any religion? Why then should there be missionary activity?"[20] In his reply, Pope John Paul insists that the recognition of spiritual gifts in other religions in no way diminishes the unique role of Christ as the "one mediator between God and mankind."

> In the process of discovering and appreciating the manifold gifts—especially the spiritual treasures—that God has bestowed on every people, we cannot separate those gifts from Jesus Christ, who is at the center of God's plan of salvation. Just as "by his incarnation the Son of God united himself in some sense with every human being," so too "we are obliged to hold that the Holy Spirit offers everyone the possibility of sharing in the Paschal mystery in a manner known to God" (GS 22). God's plan is "to unite all things in Christ, things in heaven and things on earth" (Eph 1:10).[21]

John Paul insists that while salvation is offered to all, it is always salvation in Christ.

> The universality of salvation means that it is granted not only to those who explicitly believe in Christ and have entered the Church. Since salvation is offered to all, it must be made concretely available to all. But it is clear that today, as in the past, many people do not have an opportunity to come to know or accept the Gospel revelation or to enter the Church. The social and cultural conditions in which they live do not permit this, and frequently they have been brought up in other religious traditions. For such people salvation in Christ is accessible by

virtue of a grace which, while having a mysterious relationship to the Church, does not make them formally part of the Church but enlightens them in a way which is accommodated to their spiritual and material situation. This grace comes from Christ; it is the result of his Sacrifice and is communicated by the Holy Spirit. It enables each person to attain salvation through his or her free cooperation.[22]

Here we find an extremely important statement concerning the way in which non-Christians are saved: for "those who are brought up in other religious traditions," the grace which comes from Christ "enlightens them in a way which is accommodated to their spiritual" condition. Since their spiritual condition can be expected normally to reflect the religious traditions in which they have been brought up, it would logically follow that the grace they receive will also be accommodated to those religious traditions. Can we conclude that their religious traditions can serve in some way as "mediations" of such grace? John Paul II does not draw this conclusion. But he does say that the unique mediation of Christ does not exclude participated forms of mediation. Here are his words:

Although participated forms of mediation of different kinds and degrees are not excluded, they acquire meaning and value *only* from Christ's own mediation, and they cannot be understood as parallel or complementary to his.[23]

While we do not know whether John Paul II would think of including the non-Christian religions, or at least elements of their spirituality, among such "participated forms of mediation," which he recognizes to be of different kinds and degrees, at least it is clear that he acknowledges the existence and saving function of such other mediations, provided that they are not understood as parallel or complementary to the unique mediation of Christ. This is certainly a fundamental principle in the theory we have described in the previous chapter, even though the pope has not spelled out its application in the way that Rahner and others have done.

In any case, the encyclical on the missions gave John Paul the opportunity to develop further a theme which, as we have seen, characterizes his approach to non-Christians: namely, his appreciation of the evidence of the action of the Holy Spirit both in individuals and in their religions.

> It is the Spirit who sows the "seeds of the Word" present in various customs and cultures, preparing them for full maturity in Christ. Thus the Spirit, who "blows where he wills" (cf. Jn 3:8), who "was already in the world before Christ was glorified" (AG 4), and who "has filled the world . . . holds all things together [and] knows what is said" (Wis 1:7), leads us to broaden our vision in order to ponder his activity in every time and place. I have repeatedly called this fact to mind, and it has guided me in my meetings with a wide variety of peoples. The Church's relationship with other religions is dictated by a twofold respect: "Respect for man in his quest for answers to the deepest questions of his life, and respect for the action of the Spirit in man." Excluding any mistaken interpretation, the inter-religious meeting held in Assisi was meant to confirm my conviction that "every authentic prayer is prompted by the Holy Spirit, who is mysteriously present in every human heart."[24]

It is not surprising that John Paul II, who personally engages in dialogue with members of other religions during his many "pilgrimages," should have described inter-religious dialogue as part of the Church's evangelizing mission. He has explained the reason for this in the following way.

> Understood as a method and means of mutual knowledge and enrichment, dialogue is not in opposition to the mission *ad gentes:* indeed it has special links with that mission and is one of its expressions. This mission, in fact, is addressed to those who do not know Christ and his Gospel, and who belong for the most part to other religions. In Christ, God calls all peoples to himself and he wishes to share with them the fullness of his revelation and love. He does not fail to make himself present in many ways, not only to individuals but also to entire peoples through their spiritual riches, of which their religions are the main and essential expression, even when they contain "gaps, insufficiencies and errors."[25]

> Dialogue does not originate from tactical concerns or self-interest, but is an activity with its own guiding principles, re-

quirements and dignity. It is demanded by deep respect for everything that has been brought about in human beings by the Spirit who blows where he wills. Through dialogue, the Church seeks to uncover the "seeds of the Word," a "ray of that truth which enlightens all men"; these are found in individuals and in the religious traditions of mankind. Dialogue is based on hope and love, and will bear fruit in the Spirit. Other religions constitute a positive challenge for the Church; they stimulate her both to discover and acknowledge the signs of Christ's presence and of the working of the Spirit, as well as to examine more deeply her own identity and to bear witness to the fullness of Revelation which she has received for the good of all.[26]

We have now followed the thought of Pope John Paul II with regard to non-Christians, from his first encyclical to his latest one. It is time now to see whether, and in what respect, he has gone beyond the teaching of Vatican II, and how his teaching compares with the developments that have taken place in Catholic theology since the council, especially on the question of the significance of the non-Christian religions.

There is good reason to say that the text of Vatican II which has been foundational in John Paul II's approach to this question is the one which says that grace works in an unseen way in the heart of every person of good will, and that we must believe that the Holy Spirit offers to every person the possibility of being associated with the paschal mystery of Christ (GS 22). The difference is that in the documents of Vatican II this reference to the universal presence and activity of the Holy Spirit, offering grace to every human person, is a rare occurrence, and receives no significant development. On the contrary, in the writings and addresses of John Paul II it has become a principal theme in every context in which he has spoken about the non-Christian world. Furthermore, while this conciliar text spoke only of the working of the Spirit in individuals, Pope John Paul has consistently recognized the fruits of the activity of the Spirit also in non-Christian religions. It is here that we must recognize the contribution which he has made to official Catholic teaching on this question. He has spoken more positively about the evidence of the presence and working of the Holy Spirit in the non-Christian religions than either Vatican II or Paul VI had done. And more eloquent than any discourse was his invitation to the leaders of the major non-Christian religions to join him at Assisi for the Day of Prayer for Peace. Here he gave dramatic proof of his conviction that "every authentic prayer is prompted by the Holy Spirit, who is mysteriously present in every human heart."[27]

What about his attitude regarding the post-conciliar developments in Catholic theology on this question? First of all, it is obvious that he emphatically rejects any theory that would displace Christ from the center of the divine plan of salvation. He likewise insists that, as the "universal sacrament of salvation," the church retains a necessary role in the salvation of the world, which, in the case of non-Christians, means that the grace by which salvation is accessible to them has a "mysterious relationship to the Church."[28] As did Paul VI, he indicated his disapproval of the suggestion that the non-Christian religions constitute the "ordinary way" of salvation, by insisting that "the Church is the ordinary means of salvation, and she alone possesses the fullness of the means of salvation."[29]

Does John Paul II recognize the non-Christian religions as "extraordinary means of salvation"? As far as I know, he has not used any such term in speaking of them. In fact, I have not found any passage in which he explicitly takes up the question of their significance for the *salvation* of their adherents. He certainly recognizes the role of those religions in inculcating faith in God, habits of prayer, and other virtuous dispositions that surely have something to do with people's relationship with God, and hence with their salvation. But I have not found any explicit reference to the question whether non-Christian religions can be understood as "mediations" of salvation for their adherents.

The statement of John Paul II which seems to me to have the most significant bearing on this question is one I have quoted above, in which, after speaking of Christ's universal mediation, he went on to say: "Although participated forms of mediation of different kinds and degrees are not excluded, they acquire meaning and value only from Christ's own mediation, and they cannot be understood as parallel or complementary to his."[30] One can only conjecture whether he would recognize the non-Christian religions as such "participated forms of mediation" for the salvation of their adherents. As we have seen in the previous chapter, the recognition of such a role of mediation for the non-Christian religions in the divine plan of salvation is a key element in the thinking of many

Catholic theologians since Vatican II. Pope John Paul has not explicitly endorsed the conclusions to which they have come, but neither have I found anything in his writings or addresses that would signify a repudiation of their views.

Finally, I would suggest that John Paul II sees the question whether it would be consistent with Christian faith to attribute to the non-Christian religions a role of "participated mediation" in the salvation of their followers as a matter that needs much further study before the official magisterium can take a position on it. That this is his view is suggested by what he said to the members of the Secretariat for Non-Christians at the conclusion of their plenary assembly in 1987.

> There remain many questions which we have to develop and articulate more clearly. How does God work in the lives of people of different religions? How does his saving activity in Jesus Christ effectively extend to those who have not professed faith in him? In the coming years, these questions and related ones will become more and more important for the Church in a pluralistic world, and pastors, with the collaboration of experienced theologians, must direct their studious attention to them.[31]

I cannot think of any more appropriate note on which to conclude this chapter on papal teaching since Vatican II than the one sounded by John Paul II in this address to the body which he subsequently renamed Pontifical Council for Inter-Religious Dialogue. What it tells us is that, while the official magisterium of the Catholic Church has come far on this issue, it is still open to further development, and it looks to "experienced theologians," as we have seen it do in the past, to lead the way.

Conclusion

As we come to the end of our history of Christian thought about salvation for those outside the church, it seems appropriate to reflect on what we have learned about the way in which the teaching of the church can develop and change in the course of the centuries. We begin our reflections by recalling the key statement made by Pope John XXIII in his opening address to the bishops at the Second Vatican Council: "The substance of the ancient doctrine of the deposit of the faith is one thing, and the way in which it is presented is another."[1]

About ten years later, the Congregation for the Doctrine of the Faith in its declaration *Mysterium Ecclesiae* spelled out some of the reasons why, in the course of the centuries, there have been changes in the way the church's teaching has been presented. For the first time an official document of the Catholic Church explicitly recognized the "historical conditioning" which inevitably affects the way in which her faith has been expressed. It acknowledged the fact that at an earlier period a dogmatic truth might be expressed incompletely or imperfectly, and only later, when considered in a broader context of faith or human knowledge, receive a fuller and more perfect expression.[2]

Pope John distinguished the "substance" of the church's doctrine from the way it has been expressed. As I see it, the "substance" of the doctrine whose history we have been following is that God has assigned to the church a necessary role in the divine economy of salvation. As Christ is the one mediator, so his body, the church, has a subordinate but necessary role of mediation in the salvation of mankind.

199

However, during most of the church's history, this truth has been expressed in a negative way by the formula: "No salvation outside the church." This formulation of the doctrine frequently led to the naming of categories of people who, being "outside the church," were thought to be excluded from salvation and destined for eternal damnation.

The Congregation for the Doctrine of the Faith has encouraged us to look for the historical factors that have influenced the way in which the church has expressed her faith. It would seem useful, as a conclusion of our study, to recall the factors that have historically conditioned the formulation of the doctrine of the church's necessity for salvation down through the centuries.

Our study has shown that during the first three centuries of church history, the saying: "No salvation outside the church" was used exclusively as a warning to Christians who had separated themselves from the *catholica* through adherence to an heretical or schismatic sect. Those who coined or used this formula were, with few exceptions, bishops entrusted with pastoral care of the Christian community, and responsible for maintaining its unity. Identifying *communio* with *caritas*, they looked upon heresy and schism as sins against charity, infecting not only the founders of the sects, but all who followed them. Convinced as they were that dissident Christians were guilty of grave sin in their adherence to an heretical or schismatic sect, it is understandable that their pastoral concern would lead them to express the doctrine of the necessity of the church in the form of a warning to dissident Christians that there was no salvation for them if they remained outside the *catholica*.

As long as Christianity was a forbidden and persecuted religion, we have found no instance of such a warning being addressed to the pagans who were still the majority in the Roman empire. But from the end of the fourth century, when Christianity had become the official religion of the empire, we begin to find the fathers of the church addressing a similar warning to pagans and Jews. Here their argument was that by now the gospel had been preached everywhere in the world, all had had ample opportunity to hear and respond to it, and there was no excuse for those who persisted in their refusal to accept it. Now, not only Christian heretics and schismatics, but pagans and Jews as well, were judged guilty of grave sin for refusing to join the Christian community. And so, in the sixth century, we find Fulgentius, bishop of Ruspe, formulating the doctrine of the necessity of belonging to the church in terms of the belief that all pagans, Jews, heretics and schismatics would be condemned to hell. That this remained the standard expression of the doctrine for almost a thousand years is shown by the fact that the Council of Florence, in 1442, incorporated Fulgentius' formula into its Decree for the Jacobites.

What are the historical factors that conditioned medieval Christians to express the doctrine of the necessity of the church in so negative a fashion? First of all, there was the fact that their world was practically identical with Christian Europe. They were aware of the Moslem world, of course, but that was the world of the infidel, the enemy against whom the crusades were fought. If they were vaguely aware of a world beyond the limits of Christendom, it did not seem to enter into their theological speculation. When they spoke of the possibility that someone might never have heard the gospel preached, they imagined the case of a child brought up in the wilderness. The limits of their geographical horizon led them to the conviction that everyone had had ample opportunity to hear and respond to the gospel.

At the same time, the limits of their grasp of human psychology led them to the conviction that all those who had heard the message of the gospel and did not accept it must be guilty of sinning against the truth which surely was evident to them. The medieval Christian does not seem to have been capable of understanding how Jews, for instance, living in the midst of Christendom, could fail to recognize the truth of the Christian religion, or how their persistence in their own religion could be anything else than a sin of obduracy.

These limits of the geographical and psychological horizons of medieval Christians are historical factors which profoundly conditioned their expression of the doctrine of the necessity of the church for salvation. The atrocious formulation of this doctrine, which the Council of Florence incorporated into its Decree for the Jacobites, can be understood only if one takes into consideration the cultural factors which conditioned medieval Christians to think that all those outside the church must be guilty of grave sin, and hence that God would justly condemn them all to hell.

The limits of this geographical horizon were to be drastically expanded just fifty years after the Council of Florence, when Columbus discovered America. Awareness that there were whole continents inhabited by people who had never before had the opportunity to believe in Christ led Catholic theologians to express the doctrine of the necessity of the church for salvation in terms consistent with belief in God's salvific will in regard to all those generations prior to the arrival of the missionaries. Interestingly enough, the necessity of rethinking the medieval solution to this question stimulated some of those theologians to question the assumption that all who had heard the gospel but had not accepted it must be guilty of sin in rejecting the salvation that was offered to them.

It would take several centuries more for the limits of the psychological horizon to expand sufficiently so that the presumption of guilt, which was characteristic of the medieval judgment concerning all those outside the church, would gradually change, first into a recognition that some of them might be in good faith, and then into the general presumption of innocence which is now the official attitude of the Catholic Church.

Our final question, then, is: What factors have contributed to forming the positive attitude concerning the salvation of those outside the church, which is so striking a characteristic of the Second Vatican Council? In the first place, I would mention a development that exemplifies what Vatican II called "remembering that in Catholic teaching there exists an order or 'hierarchy' of truths" (UR 11). This involves recognizing the primary importance of the truth that God wills the salvation of every human being. To attribute to the universal salvific will of God the first place in a hierarchy of truths means giving a subordinate place to the necessity of such means of salvation as baptism and membership in the church. Such secondary truths, then, have to be understood and formulated in such a way as to confirm, rather than conflict with, the primary truth.

Besides this theological development, other factors have also played an important part in bringing about the positive attitude of the modern Catholic Church concerning the salvation of those "outside." Perhaps the best way to describe these factors is to speak of a "broadening of horizons." In place of a "ghetto mentality" that was rather typical of Catholicism in the past, Catholics are now open to the values present in the world "outside the church." In the first place, through the impact of the ecumenical movement, which came to them at first from the Protestant and Anglican churches, Catholics have come to recognize other Christians as brothers and sisters in Christ. Then, more gradually, there has been the opening of the minds of Catholics to the people who do not share Christian faith, and to the values to be found in their religions. It is obvious that when people are no longer seen as strangers and adversaries, but are accepted as partners in dialogue, they are much less likely to be judged guilty of sin for remaining faithful to their own religious traditions.

The conclusion we come to is that cultural factors have had a decisive influence on the way that the dogmatic truth about the necessity of the church for salvation has been expressed by the Catholic Church in the past, and on the way that it is being expressed now. The limited horizons of the medieval Christian mentality, on the one hand, and the expansion of those horizons that began with the discovery of the new world just five hundred years ago, are elements of the "historical conditioning" which the Congregation for the Doctrine of the Faith has told us we must take into account in interpreting church teaching. Indeed, without taking this into account, it would be hardly possible to explain the difference between what the Catholic Church said in 1442 and what it is saying today about the possibility of salvation for all those people who are "outside the church."

To conclude this book where we began, let us return in our mind's eye to Still River, Massachusetts, and to the gravestone with the epitaph: EXTRA ECCLESIAM NULLA SALUS. I have often heard fellow Jesuits remark on the irony of the situation in which Leonard Feeney found himself for many years: that a man who was so deeply convinced that there was no salvation outside the Catholic Church should himself be "outside" by virtue of a sentence of excommunication. I have no doubt that in his own mind he was not outside at all, being convinced that no one could be validly excommunicated for defending a dogma of Catholic faith. It is important to keep in mind that Leonard Feeney was not condemned for heresy. What got him eventually excommunicated was the fact that he accused the Congregation for the Doctrine of the Faith of heresy, and then refused to go to Rome to discuss the matter.

Is his epitaph, then, a heresy, or a dogma of Catholic faith? It is not a heresy, of course. What we have tried to show in this book is that it is only one way, and a very imperfect way at that, in which Christians have expressed their belief that God has given to his church a necessary part to play in his plan to save the world. We cannot be too grateful for the fact that in our day the Catholic Church has found a much better way than this to speak of its own role in the divine economy of salvation.

Notes

1. "Extra Ecclesiam Nulla Salus"

1. As reported in the Newark *Advocate* for October 31, 1974; see Thomas Mary Sennott, *They Fought the Good Fight*, Monrovia, 1987, pp. 259f.

2. My assurance that this choice was made not by Fr. Feeney himself but by some of his "extra-zealous followers" is based on the testimony of Mother Mary Clare Vincent, Superior of St. Scholastica Priory in Petersham, Massachusetts. She is one of the members of Fr. Feeney's community who, after their reconciliation with the Catholic Church, became Benedictine nuns.

3. *The Church and I*, Garden City, 1974, p. 166.

4. DS 792.

5. DS 802.

6. DS 870.

7. DS 875.

8. DS 1351.

9. DS 1870.

10. DS 2865.

11. DS 2867.

12. LG 15.

13. UR 3.

14. LG 16.

15. GS 22.

16. "Observations on the Problem of the Anonymous Christian," in *Th. Inv.* 14, p. 284.

17. DS 3020. The final sentence is from Vincent of Lerins, *Commonitorium primum* 23; PL 50:668.

18. DS 3541.

19. AAS 54 (1962) 792.

20. AAS 65 (1973) 402–03.

2. The Fathers Prior to St. Augustine

1. *Dialogue with Trypho* 45, tr. Thomas B. Falls, FC 6:215.

2. *First Apology* 46, tr. Falls, FC 6:83–84.

3. *Adversus haereses* 4:22,2; PG 7:1047 A–B.

4. *Stromata* 7:2; PG 9:409–10.

5. *Contra Celsum* 4:7; PG 11:1035–38.

6. *In Ioannem hom.* 8; PG 59:67–68.

7. *Letter to Philadelphians* 3:3; tr. K. Lake, *The Apostolic Fathers* (Cambridge, 1965), vol. 2, pp. 242–43.

8. *Adversus haereses*, 3:24,1; PG 7:966–67.

9. *Homiliae in Jesu Nave* 3:5; PG 12:841–42.

10. *Epist.* 4,4; CSEL 3,2:476–77; tr. R.B. Donna, FC 51:13.

11. *Epist.* 52:1; CSEL 3,2:617; FC 51:128.

12. *Epist.* 73:21; CSEL, 3,2:795; FC 51:282.

13. *The Unity of the Catholic Church*, 14; tr. M. Bévenot, ACW 25:56.

14. *The Unity of the Catholic Church* 6; ACW 25:48–49.

15. Quoted from M. Bévenot, "*Salus extra ecclesiam non est* (St. Cyprian)" in *Fides Sacramenti, Sacramentum Fidei*, ed. H.J. Auf der Maur, Assen, 1981, p. 105.

16. *In Psalm. 118 Sermo* 8:57; PL 15:1318.

17. *Oratio catechetica* 30; PG 45:76–77.

18. *In Epist. ad Rom. hom.* 26:3–4; PG 60:641–42.

19. *In 1 Tim 2 hom.* 7:2; PG 62:537.

20. *Discourses Against Judaizing Christians*, 3:6; tr. Paul W. Harkins, FC 68:66.

3. St. Augustine and His Followers

1. *Epist.* 102:8; CSEL 34,2:551–52.

2. *Epist.* 102:11–15; CSEL 34,2:553–58.

3. *Sermo* 341:9,11; PL 39:1499–1500.

4. See Y. Congar, "Ecclesia ab Abel" in H. Elfers, F. Hofmann (eds.), *Abhandlungen über Theologie und Kirche*, Düsseldorf, 1952, pp. 79–108.

5. *Enarr. in Ps.* 61:6; CCL 39:777.

6. *Epist.* 141:5; CSEL 44:238.

7. *De Baptismo* 3:16,2; CSEL 51:212.

8. *Epist.* 185:50; CSEL 57:44.

9. *De Baptismo* 3:10,13; CSEL 51:205.

10. *Sermo ad Caesariensis ecclesiae plebem*, 6; CSEL 53:174–75.

11. *De Baptismo* 4:17,24; CSEL 51:250.

12. *De Baptismo* 1:5,6; CSEL 51:152.

13. *Epist.* 43:1; CSEL 34,2:85.

14. *Epist.* 43:3,6; CSEL 34,2:88–89.

15. *Epist.* 43:9,27; CSEL 34,2:108–09.

16. *De Baptismo* 5:27,38; CSEL 51:295.

17. *Enarr. in Ps.* 106:14; CCL 40:1581.

18. *De spiritu et littera* 33:58; PL 44:238.

19. *Adversus judaeos* 10:15; PL 42:63–64.

20. *Epist.* 199:12,46; CSEL 57:284.

21. *Epist.* 197:4; CSEL 57:233–34.

22. *Enchiridion ad Laurentium de fide et spe et caritate*, 23:93; CCL 46:99.

23. *De natura et gratia* 4–5; PL 44:249–50.

24. *De correptione et gratia* 7:11–12; PL 44:923.

25. *Contra Julianum* 4:8,44–45; PL 44:760–61.

26. DS 377.

27. *De vocatione omnium gentium*, PL 51:647–722: tr. P. De Letter, ACW 14.

28. *De vocatione* 2:21; PL 51:707; ACW 14:127.

29. *De vocatione* 2:16; PL 51:702–03; ACW 14:118–19.

30. *De vocatione* 2:17; PL 51:704; ACW 14:121.

31. *De vocatione* 2:18–19; PL 51:706; ACW 14:125.

32. *De veritate praedestinationis* 3:16–18; PL 65:660–61.

33. *De fide, ad Petrum* 38 (79); PL 65:704.

4. Medieval Councils, Popes and Theologians

1. *De praedestinatione Dei et libero arbitrio, dissertatio posterior*, PL 125:66–474.

2. DS 623–24; cf. PL 125:211.

3. *De fide orthodoxa*, 2:29; PG 94:968–69.

4. DS 780.

5. This was one of the "Errors of the Synod of Pistoia," which were censured by Pope Pius VI in 1794; see DS 2626.

6. For the identification of the places where St. Thomas used this axiom, I am indebted to the work of George Sabra, *Thomas Aquinas' Vision of the Church*, Mainz, 1987, pp. 158–69.

7. *In I Decret.* ed. Parma, 16:305.

8. *In IV Sent.* d.9, q.1, a.5, sol.4, ad 2; ed. Parma 7:616.

9. *In Ioan.* 6:7, ed. Parma 10:419.

10. *In Symbolum* art. 9, ed. Parma 16:147.

11. *Summa theologiae* III, q.73, a.3.

12. II–II, q.1, a.7.

13. II–II, q.2, a.8, ad 1.

14. I–II, q.106, a.1, ad 3.

15. II–II, q.2, a.7, ad 3.

16. II–II, q.10, a.4, ad 3.

17. II–II, q.2, a.7.

18. *In III Sent.* d.25, q.2, a.1, sol.1, ad 1; ed. Parma 7:272.

19. *De veritate*, q.14, a.11, ad 1; ed. Parma 9:246.

20. *Contra Gentiles*, 3:159; ed. Parma 5:287.

21. III, q.67, a.3.

22. *In III Sent.* d.25, q.2, a.1, sol.1, ad 1; ed. Parma 7:272.

23. *De veritate*, q.14, a.11, ad 1; ed Parma 9:246.

24. *In Rom*, c.10, lect.3, ed. Parma 13:107–08.

25. II–II, q.2, a.5, ad 1.

26. J. de Guibert, "Quelle a été la pensée définitive de S. Thomas sur le salut des infidèles?" *Bull. Lit. Eccl.* 1913, 337–355.

27. See note 21. In the context, St. Thomas was referring to the easy availability of baptism, but the principle he enunciated should also apply to the availability of what was required for an act of faith.

28. *In Psalm*, 48:1, ed. Parma 14:335.

29. Humbert composed the letter of Pope Gregory X to Emperor Michael Paleologus: Mansi 24:115–116.

30. I–II, q.106, a.4, ad 4.

31. II–II, q.10, a.1.

32. II–II, q.10, a.5.

33. II–II, q.10, a.6.
34. II–II, q.10, a.3, ad 2.
35. III, q.68, a.1.
36. III, q.68, a.2.
37. III, q.69, a.4, ad 2.
38. III, q.73, a.3.
39. III, q.73, a.3.
40. I–II, q.89, a.6.

5. Before and After the Discovery of the New World

1. DS 870.
2. DS 872.
3. DS 873. The Latin word which we have translated by "establish" is *instituere*, which could also mean "instruct."
4. DS 875.
5. *Contra errores graecorum*, pars 2, cap. 32 (ed. Parma 15:257), where Thomas is proving the necessity of being in communion with the Roman pontiff as the supreme pastor of Christ's flock. It can hardly be doubted that his sentence "Ostenditur etiam, quod subesse Romano Pontifici sit de necessitate salutis" is the source of Boniface's "Porro subesse Romano Pontifici omni humanae creaturae declaramus, dicimus, diffinimus omnino esse de necessitate salutis."
6. For one recent example of this explanation, one can consult C. Journet, *L'Eglise du Verbe Incarné*, vol. 2 (Paris, 1962) 1093–96.
7. George Tavard, "The Bull *Unam sanctam* of Boniface VIII," in *Papal Primacy and the Universal Church* (Lutherans and Catholics in Dialogue, V), Minneapolis: Augsburg, 1974, pp. 105–119.
8. DS 1351.
9. See above, p. 42.
10. *De fide, ad Petrum*, c. 39, n. 80, PL 65:704 b.
11. *De Indis et de Iure Belli Relectiones*, ed. E. Nys, tr. J.P. Bates (*The Classics of International Law*), Washington, 1917, p. 142.
12. *De Indis*, p. 140.
13. *De Indis*, pp. 142–43.
14. *De Indis*, p. 143.
15. *De Indis*, p. 144.

16. *Opera*, ed. Cologne, 1678, pp. 753ff.

17. *De natura et gratia*, lib. 2, cap. 12, Paris, 1549, pp. 148–49.

18. *Institutes of the Christian Religion*, III, 21, 5; tr. Henry Beveridge, Grand Rapids, 1962, vol. 2, p. 206.

19. *Institutes*, III, 21, 7; tr. Beveridge, vol 2, pp. 210–11.

20. *Institutes*, III, 24, 12; tr. Beveridge, vol. 2, p. 251.

21. *De libero hominis arbitrio et divina gratia libri X*, Cologne, 1542.

22. *De libero hominis arbitrio*, lib. X, fol. 180 v–181 r.

23. *De libero hominis arbitrio*, lib. X, fol. 181 v.

24. *De libero hominis arbitrio*, lib. X, fol. 181 r–v.

6. The Jesuits and the Jansenists

1. *Large Catechism*, II, 45, 56; T.G. Tappert, ed., *The Book of Concord*, Philadelphia: Muhlenberg, 1959, pp. 416, 418.

2. DS 1529.

3. DS 1532.

4. DS 1524.

5. *Summa theologiae*, III, q.69, a.4, ad 2.

6. Georg Schurhammer, S.J., *Francis Xavier, His Life, His Times*, tr. M. Joseph Costelloe, S.J., vol I, Rome, 1973, p. 249.

7. Karl Rahner, for instance, has written: "St. Francis Xavier still told the Japanese whom he wished to convert that obviously all their ancestors were damned in hell." "What is heresy?" *Th. Inv.* 5, p. 474. And Walter Kasper has written: "It is well known that St. Francis Xavier, as he was detained along the coast of China, was tormented by the thought that all men who would not be brought to faith and baptism through his preaching would be lost forever in the fires of hell." "Are Non-Christian Religions Salvific?" in *Evangelization Dialogue and Development* (Documenta Missionalia 5), ed. M. Dhavamony, Rome, 1972, p. 157.

8. G. Schurhammer, *Francis Xavier*, tr. J. Costelloe, vol. 4, Rome, 1982, p. 235.

9. Schurhammer, tr. Costelloe, vol. 4, pp. 505–06.

10. Cf. Rom 2:15.

11. Schurhammer, *Francis Xavier*, tr. Costelloe, vol. 4, p. 222.

12. *De controversiis*, II, lib. 3, *De Ecclesia militante*, cap. 2 (ed. J. Giuliano, Naples 1857), vol. 2, p. 75.

13. *De Ecclesia militante*, cap. 3; ed, Giuliano, vol. 2, p. 76.

14. *De Ecclesia militante*, cap. 6; ed. Giuliano, vol. 2, p. 80.

15. *De gratia et libero arbitrio*, lib. 2, cap. 5, ed. Giuliano, vol. 4, p. 301.

16. *De gratia et libero arbitrio*, lib. 2, cap. 8, ed. Giuliano, vol. 4, p. 308.

17. *De fide theologica*, Disp. 12, sect. 4, n. 11; ed. Vives, Paris, 1858, vol. 12, pp. 353–54.

18. This would be the *ecclesia ab Abel*, to which belong all and only the just.

19. *De fide theologica*, disp. 12, sect. 4, n. 22; ed. Vives, vol. 12, p. 359. The reference to St. Thomas is to III, q.69, a.4, ad 2.

20. *De auxiliis gratiae*, lib. 4: *De auxilio sufficienti*, n. 17, ed. Vives, vol. 8, p. 318.

21. *De virtute fidei divinae*, disp. 12, n. 50–51, Lyon, 1646, vol. 3, p. 286.

22. *De virtute fidei divinae*, disp. 12, n. 104, p. 300.

23. *De virtute fidei divinae*, disp. 18, n. 25, p. 496.

24. *De virtute fidei divinae*, disp. 20, n. 149, pp. 566–67.

25. DS 1925.

26. DS 1968.

27. DS 2005.

28. DS 2006.

29. DS 2304.

30. DS 2305.

31. DS 2308.

32. DS 2311.

33. DS 2330.

34. *De la nécessité de la foi en Jésus Christ pour être sauvé*, in *Oeuvres d'Arnauld*, Paris, 1777, vol. 10, pp. 39–377.

35. *Oeuvres*, vol. 10, p. 270.

36. DS 2429.

7. The Nineteenth Century

1. A typical example of eighteenth century Jesuit teaching on this point is found in Heinrich Kilber's treatise on the virtue of

faith, which is part of a four-volume *summa* of dogmatic theology produced by the Jesuit faculty at the University of Würzburg between 1766 and 1771. Kilber insisted, against the Jansenists, on the universal salvific will of God, and on the sufficiency of faith in God for those inculpably ignorant of the Christian message. See *Theologia Wirceburgensis*, ed. 2a, Paris, 1852, vol. 4/2, n. 127–133, pp. 109–16.

2. This has been translated and published, with an introduction, by Arthur H. Beattie, in the series "Milestones of Thought," New York, F. Ungar Co., 2nd ed., 1957.

3. *The Creed of a Priest of Savoy*, p. 55.

4. *The Creed*, p. 68.

5. *The Creed*, pp. 68–69.

6. *The Creed*, p. 71.

7. *Censure de la Faculté de Théologie de Paris contre le livre intitulé Émile ou de l'Éducation*, in Migne, *Theologiae Cursus Completus*, vol. 2 (Paris 1838) 1111–1248.

8. Louis Capéran, *Le Problème du Salut des Infidèles, Essai Historique*, Toulouse, 1934, p. 400.

9. *Summa theologiae* II–II, q.10, a.1.

10. Migne, *Theologiae cursus completus*, vol. 2 (Paris 1838), 1179–1182.

11. Giovanni Perrone, *Praelectiones theologicae de virtutibus fidei, spei et caritatis*, Ratisbon: Pustet, 1865, *De fide*, nn. 325–28, pp. 116–17.

12. *De virtutibus fidei spei et caritatis*, *De fide*, nn. 378–79, p. 135.

13. *De vera religione*, pars II, prop. XI, n. 265, in *Praelectiones theologicae*, vol. 1, ed. 34 (Torino: Marietti 1900), p. 214.

14. DS 2123.

15. *De virtutibus fidei spei et caritatis; De fide*, n. 321, p. 115.

16. *De vera religione*, pars II, prop. XI, n. 284, p. 221.

17. *Singulari quadam*, Acta Pii IX, I/1, 626.

18. *Quanto conficiamur moerore*, Acta Pii IX, I/3, 613.

19. The second sentence, which I quote here from Perrone, is in the paragraph immediately following the one I have quoted above: n. 266, p. 215.

20. My references are to the second edition, Rome, 1907.

21. *Theses de Ecclesia Christi*, ed. 2, 1907, p. 413.

22. *Theses*, pp. 415ff.
23. Mansi 51, 541–42.
24. Mansi 51, 570–71.

8. The Twentieth Century Prior to Vatican II

1. Philip J. Hefner, *The Church*, in *Church Dogmatics*, ed. Carl E. Braaten and Robert J. Jenson, Philadelphia, Fortress Press, vol. 2, p. 198.

2. *L'Eglise*, Paris, 1917, vol. 2, p. 130. Similar ideas arc found in P. Lippert, *Die Kirche Christi*, Freiburg, 1956, pp. 258–73, and in O. Karrer, *Religions of Mankind*, tr. E.I. Watkin, London, 1936, pp. 250–78.

3. A. Castelein, *La rigorisme, le nombre des élus, et la doctrine du salut*, Brussels, 1898, p. 212. Similarly, for E.I. Watkin, the "soul of the church" is "the invisible church-body of all souls who share in the supernatural life," in *God and the Supernatural*, London, 1920, p. 178. P. Lippert identified the "soul of the church" with "all those who are called and really are children of God," in *Die Kirche Christi*, p. 262.

4. *A Letter Addressed to His Grace the Duke of Norfolk on the Occasion of Mr. Gladstone's Recent Expostulation*, New York, 1875, pp. 159f.

5. John J. King's research demonstrates that this indeed was the case. See his dissertation: *The Necessity of the Church for Salvation in Selected Theological Writings of the Past Century*, Washington, 1960, pp. 58–87.

6. Tr. C. Vollert, S.J., St. Louis, Herder, 1951.

7. *The Theology of the Mystical Body*, pp. 479–80. It should be noted that Mersch's final redaction of this part of his work was lost; the editors used a prior redaction dating from about the year 1935.

8. *Chrétiens désunis, Principes d'un "Oecuménisme" Catholique*, (Unam sanctam 1), Paris, 1937, p. 103.

9. *Chrétiens désunis*, p. 292.

10. *Catholicism, A Study of Dogma in Relation to the Corporate Destiny of Mankind*, New York, 1964, p. 126. This translation was made from the fourth French edition, of 1947; the first edition was published in 1938.

11. *Catholicism*, p. 125.

12. *Catholicism*, p. 127.

13. *Mystici corporis*, no. 21. (I am citing the encyclical using the numbers supplied in the edition of Sebastian Tromp, Rome, 1943.)

14. AAS 42, 571.

15. See Raymond Karam, "Reply to a Liberal," in *From the Housetops* 3, no. 3, Spring 1949. The "liberal" to whom Karam was replying was Philip J. Donnelly, S.J., professor of theology at Weston College, who had written a paper explaining the current teaching of the Catholic Church on salvation "outside the church." Fr. Donnelly's paper was being privately circulated at Boston College and in Cambridge. The holy office referred to this article of Raymond Karam in its critique of the doctrine of St. Benedict Center.

16. The full Latin text, with an English translation, was first published in AER 127 (1952) 308–15. The Latin text is also given in DS 3866–72. It is referred to by the opening words: *Suprema haec sacra*.

17. DS 1524, 1543.

9. The Second Vatican Council

1. AS I/4, p. 15.

2. AS I/4, p. 18.

3. AS I/4, p. 18.

4. AS II/1, p. 220.

5. AS II/1, p. 220.

6. AS II/1, pp. 220–21.

7. AS II/1, p. 221.

8. AS II/1, p. 221.

9. On this, see my article: "The Decree on Ecumenism: Presuppositions and Consequences," *One in Christ* 26 (1990) 7–19.

10. On this, see my article: "The Significance of Vatican II's Decision to say of the Church of Christ not that it 'is' but that it 'subsists in' the Roman Catholic Church," *One in Christ* 22 (1986) 115–23.

11. AS III/1, p. 203.

12. AS III/2, p. 335.

13. Mansi 51, 541.

14. AS III/1, p. 202.

15. As III/1, p. 202.

16. In Vatican II's "Declaration on the Relationship of the Church to Non-Christian Religions," specific mention is made of Hinduism and Buddhism as among religions which have endeavored to reply to human questions about the divinity "with more refined concepts and more highly developed language" (NA 2).

17. This point is brought out very effectively in the following sentence of the Pastoral Constitution *Gaudium et spes:* "Since Christ died for all men and since the ultimate vocation of man is in fact one, and divine, we must believe that the Holy Spirit, in a manner known only to God, offers to every man the possibility of being associated with the paschal mystery" (GS 22). "Being associated with the paschal mystery" obviously means sharing in its fruit: justification and eternal salvation.

18. AS III/1, p. 206. The Latin reads: "Omnis gratia quandam indolem communitariam induit et ad ecclesiam respicit."

19. "Hors de l'Église pas de salut," in *Sainte Église* (Unam Sanctam 41), Paris, 1963, pp. 431–32. As Congar explains in a note on p. 417, this is the original text of an article prepared in 1956, and first published in 1959 in the encyclopedia *Catholicisme*, 5:948–56.

20. On this, see chapter 6: "Universal Sacrament of Salvation," in my book: *The Church We Believe In: One, Holy, Catholic and Apostolic*, Mahwah, 1988, pp. 109–31.

21. AAS 35 (1943) 213.

10. "Anonymous Christians"

1. See chapter 1, note 16.

2. See above, p. 15.

3. This is clearly the main thrust of the council's Decree on the Church's Missionary Activity (*Ad gentes*), as well as of LG 17.

4. *The Christian Message in a Non-Christian World*, London, 1947; *Why Christianity of All Religions?* London, 1962.

5. *Why Christianity of All Religions?* p. 94.

6. Among his recent works are: *The Second Christianity*, London, 1983; *God Has Many Names: Britain's New Religious Pluralism*, London, 1980; *Problems of Religious Pluralism*, London, 1985.

7. John Hick (ed.), *The Myth of God Incarnate*, London, 1977; John Hick and Paul Knitter (eds.), *The Myth of Christian Uniqueness: Towards a Pluralistic Theology of Religions*, Maryknoll, 1987.

8. On this question I recommend Jacques Dupuis' *Jesus Christ at the Encounter of World Religions*, Maryknoll, 1991. One could also profitably consult the doctoral dissertation done by Gregory H. Carruthers under the direction of J. Dupuis at the Gregorian University: *The Uniqueness of Jesus Christ in the Theocentric Model of the Christian Theology of World Religions. An Elaboration and Evaluation of the Position of John Hick*, Rome, 1988.

9. One Catholic writer who shares Hick's view is Paul Knitter, co-editor with Hick of *The Myth of Christian Uniqueness*, and author of *No Other Name? A Critical Survey of Christian Attitudes toward the World Religions*, Maryknoll/London, 1985.

10. "Anonymous Christians," *Th. Inv.* 6, 390–98; "Observations on the Problem of the 'Anonymous Christians,' " *Th. Inv.* 14, 280–94.

11. "The One Christ and the Universality of Salvation," *Th. Inv.* 16, 199–224.

12. "The One Christ and the Universality of Salvation," *Th. Inv.* 16, 201.

13. "Reflections on the Unity of the Love of Neighbor and the Love of God," *Th. Inv.* 6, 231–49.

14. "Christianity and the Non-Christian Religions," *Th. Inv.* 5, 115–34; "Church, Churches and Religions," *Th. Inv.* 10, 30–49; "On the Importance of the Non-Christian Religions for Salvation," *Th. Inv.* 18, 288–95.

15. "Christianity and the Non-Christian Religions," *Th. Inv.* 5, 126–27.

16. "Anonymous Christianity and the Missionary Task of the Church," *Th. Inv.* 12, 161–78.

17. The objections raised by de Lubac and von Balthasar are discussed by Bernard Sesboüé in "Karl Rahner et les 'Chrétiens anonymes,' " *Etudes* 361 (1984) 521–536.

18. *Paradoxe et Mystère de l'Eglise*, Paris, 1967, pp. 152–63.

19. *Paradoxe et mystère de l'Eglise*, p. 156.

20. "Observations on the Problem of the 'Anonymous Christian,' " *Th. Inv.* 14, 281, 292.

21. De Lubac, *Paradoxe et Mystère de l'Eglise*, pp. 148–49.

22. Einsiedeln, 1966.

23. *Cordula ou l'épreuve décisive*, Paris, 1968, pp. 79–90.

24. *Cordula ou l'épreuve décisive*, pp. 117–22. As an example of such, von Balthasar refers to the work of H.R. Schlette, *Die Religionen als Thema der Theologie* (Quaestiones Disputatae 22), Herder, 1963. What von Balthasar probably had in mind was Schlette's description of the non-Christian religions as the "ordinary" way of salvation, while Christianity would be the "extraordinary" way.

25. *On Being a Christian*, tr. Edward Quinn, Glasgow, 1978, p. 98.

26. *Ibid.*

27. "Anonymous Christianity and the Missionary Task of the Church," *Th. Inv.* 12, 162–65.

28. Max Seckler, "Sind Religionen Heilswege?" *Stimmen der Zeit* 186 (1970) 187–94; "Theologie der Religionen mit Fragezeichen," *Theol. Quar.* 166 (1986) 164–84.

29. *Foundations of Christian Faith. An Introduction to the Idea of Christianity*, New York, 1978, p. 314.

30. "Atheism and Implicit Christianity," *Th. Inv.* 9, 145–64; "Anonymous and Explicit Faith," *Th. Inv.* 16, 52–59; "The Church and Atheism," *Th. Inv.* 21, 137–50.

31. Council of Trent, Decree on Justification, cap. 7, DS 1529.

32. "Atheism and Implicit Christianity," p. 153.

33. "The One Christ and the Universality of Salvation," *Th. Inv.* 16, 218–24.

34. "Anonymous and Explicit Faith," *Th. Inv.* 16, p. 55.

35. "Anonymous and Explicit Faith," *Th. Inv.* 16, p. 58.

36. Yves Congar, *Vaste monde ma paroisse*, Paris, 1966, pp. 142–43.

37. Gustave Thils, *Pour une théologie de structure planétaire*, Louvain-la-Neuve, 1983.

38. "Die alleinseligmachende Kirche. Oder: Wer kann gerettet werden?" *Stimmen der Zeit* 115 (1990), 75–85, 264–78.

39. In addition to the work already cited, also "Non-Christian Religions and Christianity," in *Evangelization, Dialogue and Development* (Documenta Missionalia 5) Rome, 1972, 133–45; "Les religions non bibliques sont-elles des médiations de salut?" in *Essais oecuméniques*, Paris, 1984, pp. 271–96.

40. "The Salvific Value of Non-Christian Religions," in *Documenta Missionalia* 5, pp. 169–93; *Jesus Christ at the Encounter of World Religions*, Maryknoll, 1991.

41. "Particular and universal saving history," in H. Vorgrimler (ed.), *One, Holy, Catholic and Apostolic*, London, 1968, pp. 163–206.

42. "How can non-Christians find salvation in their own religions?" in *Hermeneutics of the Councils and Other Studies*, Leuven, 1985, pp. 321–60.

43. "Das Heil in Christus," in *Heil in den Religionen und im Christentum*, St. Ottilien, 1982, pp. 212–42.

44. "Are Non-Christian Religions Salvific?" in *Documenta Missionalia* 5, pp. 157–68.

45. "The World Religions in God's Plan of Salvation," *Indian Ecclesiastical Studies* 4 (1965) 182–222; "The Challenge of the World Religions," in *On Being a Christian*, tr. E. Quinn, Glasgow, 1978, pp. 89–116.

46. "Christianity and the World Religions," in *One, Holy, Catholic and Apostolic*, pp. 207–36.

47. "No Salvation Outside the Church?" in *The Church and Christian Belief*, New York, 1966, pp. 103–32; "Révélation et salut hors de l'Eglise visible," *Spiritus* 10 (1969) 350–64.

48. "Karl Rahner et les 'Chrétiens anonymes,' " *Etudes* 361 (1984) 521–36.

49. Besides the work already cited, also "Quelli che non hanno ancora ricevuto il Vangelo," in G. Barauna (ed.), *La Chiesa del Vaticano II*, Firenze, 1965, pp. 668–78.

50. "Theologie der nichtchristlichen Religionen. Konsequenzen aus 'Nostra aetate,' " in E. Klinger (ed.), *Glaube im Prozess*, Freiburg, 1989, pp. 751–75.

51. San Francisco, 1988.

11. Papal Teaching After Vatican II

1. This title was given to the Secretariat by Pope John Paul II in his apostolic constitution *Pastor bonus* of June 28, 1988; AAS 80 (1988) 902.

2. AAS 56 (1964) 654–55.

3. AAS 57 (1965) 132.

4. AAS 59 (1967) 1077.

5. *L'Osservatore Romano*, March 23, 1966, p. 1.

6. December 8, 1975; AAS 68 (1976) 5–76, Eng. ed., Catholic Truth Society, London, 1976. In following citations, I shall give the number of the section, and the page of the CTS edition.

7. *Evangelii nuntiandi*, n. 53; CTS pp. 65–67.

8. See above, p. 185.

9. Jacques Dupuis, SJ, "Apostolic Exhortation *Evangelii nuntiandi* of Pope Paul VI," *Vidyajyoti* 40 (1976) 218–30; here 229–30.

10. "Christianisme et religions non-chrétiennes," *Etudes* 321 (1964) 323–36.

11. *Etudes* 321 (1964) 327.

12. One such was H.R. Schlette in his book *Towards a Theology of Religions*, New York, 1966.

13. *Evangelii nuntiandi*, n. 80, CTS pp. 115–17.

14. *Redemptor hominis*, 6; Eng. tr. in *Origins* vol. 8/40 (March 22, 1979), pp. 629–30. In subsequent citation of *RH*, I shall give the number of the section, and the page in *Origins*.

15. *Redemptor hominis* 12, *Origins*, p. 632.

16. AAS 73 (1981) 392f, *Bulletin* n. 46, vol. 16/1 (1981) 12–14.

17. AAS 78 (1986) 767; *Bulletin* n. 62, vol. 21/2 (1986) 139.

18. *Dominum et vivificantem* n. 53; *Origins* 16/4 (June 12, 1986) 94. The final quotation is from GS 22: a passage of the documents of Vatican II which appears again and again in the writings and addresses of Pope John Paul II.

19. AAS 79 (1987) 1089; *Bulletin* n. 64, vol. 22/1 (1987) 60–61.

20. *Redemptoris missio*, n. 4, Eng. tr. Libreria Editrice Vaticana, 1991, p. 9. For the following citations from *RM*, I shall give the number of the section of the encyclical and the page of the English edition.

21. *RM*, n. 6, p. 11.

22. *RM*, n. 8, p. 15.

23. *RM*, n. 5, p. 10.

24. *RM*, n. 28–29, p. 36.

25. *RM*, n. 55, p. 70. The final words are quoted from Paul VI's address at the opening of the second session of Vatican II, September 29, 1963, AAS 55 (1963) 858.

26. *RM*, n. 56, pp. 72–73.

27. *RM*, n. 29, p. 36.

28. *RM*, n. 10, p. 15.
29. *RM*, n. 55, p. 72.
30. *RM*, n. 5, p. 10.
31. *Bulletin*, n. 66, vol. 22/3 (1987) 225.

Conclusion

1. AAS 54 (1962) 792.
2. AAS 65 (1973) 402–03.

Index

Cushing, Richard, 1, 3, 136
Cyprian, St., 20–23

Damascene, St. John, 45
Daniélou, Jean, 187, 189
De Guibert, J., 54–55, 208
De Lubac, Henri, 130–31,
    175–76, 189, 216
Donatists, 29, 33
Donnelly, Philip, 214
Dupuis, Jacques, 181, 216, 219

ecclesia ab abel, 30, 211

Feeney, Leonard, 1, 3–5, 115–
    16, 134–36, 139, 203, 205
Feiner, Johannes, 181
Flanagan, Bernard, 4
Fransen, Piet, 181
Franzelin, Johannes B., 117–
    21, 123, 139
Fries, Heinrich, 181
Fulgentius of Ruspe, 42–43,
    67, 201

Gottschalk, 44
Gregorian University, 1, 84,
    216
Gregory X, Pope, 208
Gregory of Nyssa, 25

Hefner, Philip J., 213
hierarchy of truths, 202
Hick, John, 169–71, 216
Hincmar of Riems, 44–45
Hinduism, 154, 166
holy office, 136–39, 141
Humbert of Romans, 55, 208

Ignatius of Antioch, 18
Indifferentism, 112
Innocent III, Pope, 5, 46, 47
Innocent X, Pope, 100
Innocent XI, Pope, 110
Irenaeus, St., 16, 19

Jacobites, 6, 66–69, 135, 201
Jansen, Cornelius, 100
Jansenists, 46, 100–01, 103
Jesuits, 82–100, 103
Jews, 8, 14, 26, 28, 30, 35–36,
    66–69, 95–98, 104, 111–
    12, 154
John Paul II, Pope, 190–98,
    218
John XXIII, Pope, 10, 141, 199
Journet, Charles, 209
Justin, St., 14–16, 165

Karam, Raymond, 214
Karrer, O., 213
Kasper, Walter, 181, 210
Kilber, Heinrich, 211–12
King, John J., 213
Knitter, Paul, 216
Kraemer, Hendrik, 169
Küng, Hans, 176, 181

Lawlor, Francis X., 2
Legrand, M., 106
Limbo, 46
Lippert, P., 213
Lombard, Peter, 46, 48
Lugo, Juan de, 94–98
Luther, Martin, 82, 124

Marco Polo, 55
Mersch, Emile, 128–29, 213